LEWIS IN HISTO

THE EAST COAST

LEWIS IN HISTORY AND LEGEND

THE EAST COAST

BILL LAWSON

BIRLINN

First published in 2011 by
Birlinn Limited
West Newington House
10 Newington Road
Edinburgh
EH9 1QS

www.birlinn.co.uk

ISBN: 978 1 84158 369 3

British Library Cataloguing-in-Publication Data
A catalogue record for this book is available from the British Library

Typeset by Brinnoven, Livingston
Printed and bound by GraphyCems, Spain

For Chris

CONTENTS

PROLOGUE

'S mise fior chaisteil Chlann 'ic Leoid

I am the real castle of the MacLeods – not that upstart on the hill across the bay, built by the Mathesons on the site of the MacKenzies, but the real castle, built and fortified and maintained by the MacLeod chiefs of Lewis.

Where am I? Under No 1 Pier!

Who but the douce burghers of Steornabhagh would have used the ruins of the castle of their ancestors as part of the foundation of a new pier? For centuries I sat at the entrance to the harbour, enduring heat and cold, storm and tempest, crumbling into ruin through neglect while the merchants of Steornabhagh turned their backs on their history. I, who defied the Earl of Huntly, and Cromwell's colonels, to end up as rubble under a pier!

But at least I have the pier as a roof over my head now to shelter what is left of me, and I can smirk across the bay at the pretentious new Lews Castle – barely a century and a half in age, and falling into ruins already! The Victorians built for show and splendour, but I was built for strength, so long ago that no-one knows who built me first.

Was it the Iron Age people, who were here more than two thousand years ago, and who built the massive duns or brochs on their farms to impress the neighbours? When I look around the town now not much seems to have changed in that regard!

1. The MacLeod Castle

Or was it the Vikings, putting a fortification to guard the entrance to their harbour? They gave the place its name, Steornabhagh, said to be Steering Bay – and they must have been impressed with the natural harbour behind me, an ideal shelter for their reiving ships, coming from Norway, first to sack and then to settle in the Hebrides.

When Alexander III of Scotland defeated Haakon of Norway in the Battle of Largs in 1263 – though it was really the weather that defeated him! – Lewis became part of Scotland again, but since it was ruled by the Nicolsons, themselves descendants of the Vikings, that made little difference. When the MacLeods took over from the Nicolsons, as we shall see at Port nan Giuran, they made their base at Steornabhagh, and probably it was Torquil, the first chief of the MacLeods, who built the medieval castle here, about the time that his son Malcolm was slain at the Battle of Tuiteam Tarbhach in Strath Oykell in 1406. His grandson Roderick was buried at Uidh Church, as we shall see there, and so was his daughter Margaret, wife of Lachlan MacKinnon. Roderick's son, another Torquil, was granted land in Trotternish in Skye in a charter of 1498, and it is he who was praised by the bard, as recorded in *The Book of the Dean of Lismore*:

> Hoaris mak mir in taayr mach er flarhew ir neolyes
> A arcoll a eyg si agna is me ga chaddrew in loyss

In more modern Gaelic:

> Fhuaireas mac mar an t-athair, mach thar flathaibh ar n' eolas
> A airill 'aghaidh 'us aigne 'us mi 'g a chaidrimh an Leodhas

> The son has been found like his father, above all chiefs we have
>   known
> His bearing, countenance and mind, and with me he dwells in
>   Lewis.[1]

The castle remembered this Torquil only too well; he had sheltered his wife's nephew Donald Dubh, claimant to the Lordship of the Isles, in the castle. James IV of Scotland sent an army, led by the Earl of Huntly, who had invaded Lewis, captured and ravaged the castle, and defeated the MacLeods at Allt an Torcan, on the road to Acha Mor.

Torquil had disappeared from sight then, and his brother Malcolm, who took over as chief, had repaired the damage to the castle. In 1511 the king had granted a Charter to:

> Malcolm, son of the late Rory Macleod of Lewis of the lands and
> castle of Lewis and Vaternish within the Lordship of the Isles; the
> land of Assynt within the earldom of Sutherland; and of Coigeach
> within the sheriffdom of Ross, in the king's hands by forfeiture.[2]

2. Steornabhagh *c.*1880

From his stance overlooking the harbour, the castle had been able to view, with both surprise and suspicion, the number of Dutch ships frequenting the shores.

> No foreigners had fished off the island of Lewis until 1594, when the Hollanders began to fish in the seas about the island by virtue of a licence, which kept them, however, at a distance of twenty-eight miles from the shore. The man who discovered how to cure herring, and who thus has the credit of having been the founder of the greatness of the Dutch salted herring trade, and of the maritime supremacy of Holland in after years, was William Beuikesz, who about the middle of the fourteenth century lived in Biervliet, now a village in the southern part of Zealand.[3]

The Lewis fishermen, of course, objected; but with their smaller boats and poorer harbours, they found it difficult to match the scale of the Dutch fishery.

Roderick, who succeeded his father Malcolm, was to prove the last MacLeod chief of Lewis. He was married three times, each time with a legitimate son called Torquil, and a large brood of illegitimate sons, and they spent the next years fighting each other. Torquil Conanach was the eldest son, but his father repudiated him, and he was brought up by his MacKenzie relatives. Torquil Oighre was drowned and Torquil Dubh was executed. The castle was thoroughly sick of their continual fighting and the damage they did in the process. Fraser of Wardlaw was right when he said:

3. The MacLeod Chiefs at *Seallam!*

> The clan Torkil in Lewis were the stoutest and prettiest men, but a wicked bloody crew whom neither law nor reason could guide or model, destroying one another, till in the end they were expelled that country, and the Mckenzies now possess it.[4]

While the various sons were still squabbling over their father's estate, James VI took the chance to interfere.

> The King resolved to plant lowland men in the Isles, in imitation of Queen Elizabeth's course for civilising Ireland, so he made a beginning at the Isle of Lewis.[5]

The Fife Adventurers, tempted by the fishings and a vastly exaggerated description of the potential of the land, set up their new town near the castle, which they and the MacLeods fought over – which did no good to the castle, with all the destruction and consequent repair. MacKenzie, with a rather dubious claim through Torquil Conanach, played the MacLeods, the Adventurers and the King against each other, until the MacLeods were all dead, and the others gave up in disgust, and were happy to cede their rights to MacKenzie in 1613 – and with them the Castle.

The official genealogies pass the chiefship of the MacLeods to the MacLeods of Raasay, who were certainly related but probably not nearly so closely as is claimed. A claimant was traced in Tasmania, and his sons now claim to be the chiefs of Raasay and Lewis, though when we met them in *Seallam!* Visitor Centre in An Taobh Tuath they themselves appeared to treat their claim with a sensible degree of scepticism.

But there are several families in the Suardail area who think they have a far better claim than the Tasmanians.

The Castle never liked the new MacKenzie landlords; one of the first things they did on Lewis was to start to build a new castle for themselves on the shores of Loch Siophoirt, from which they took their title of Seaforth, and they also began a new castle on the other side of the bay from Steornabhagh. You would have thought that the MacKenzies would have learned from the experiences of the Fife Adventurers, but no.

Colin, first Earl of Seaforth, was clearly alive to the possibilities of the fisheries of the islands. He realised that assistance from outside sources was necessary for their development, so he turned to the Dutch for the needed co-operation, and encouraged a number of Hollanders to come to Lewis. He applied to Charles I for a Charter for Steornabhagh as a Royal Burgh, though unsuccessfully, but it was the Dutch link that led to the final fate of the Castle.

The future Charles II, while in exile, had even suggested that Lewis should be offered, with Seaforth's blessing, to the Dutch in return for their assistance, so it is hardly surprising that the Commonwealth took an interest in the island. Colonel Lilburne, General Monk's successor as Commander-in-Chief in Scotland, reported:

> I doubt nott but what wee may be able to doe upon that island, will soe startle the whole Highlands and islands that wee shall nott bee much troubled with them in such like case hereafter. Undoubtedly to make the Lord Seaford and his island (called the Lewes) exemplary will bee a very great advantage to the peace of this nation.[6]

Lewis was soon to feel the weight of Lilburne's hand. Under the command of Colonel Cobbet, a military force, with warships and provision ships, was sent from Leith to take possession of Lewis. It was thought that its seizure would deal a severe blow at the Dutch fishing industry, advance the trading interests of the Commonwealth and overcome the resistance of the neighbouring districts.

For a time the castle had to suffer the indignity of being occupied by the Commonwealth soldiers, but worse was to come. Seaforth made an abortive attack on them in 1654, and the English built new forts on the shore beside the castle, and on Goat Island, and demolished parts of the castle to use as building materials – as though it was no better than a quarry! A most undignified end for the castle of the Clan MacLeod of Lewis. Thereafter the castle was condemned to the role of a spectator – no longer a main actor in the story of the island.

The Seaforths did not attempt to rebuild the castle, but concentrated on their new Seaforth Lodge across the bay. There they managed to follow the family ability to back losers. Coinneach Mor, 4th Earl, was there at the time of Cromwellian invasion. His son Coinneach Og supported James VII after 1688, for which he was created Marquis of Seaforth – an empty honour, as he was forced into exile in France. His son Uilleam Dubh was involved in the 1715 Jacobite Rebellion, and he also had to flee to exile in France. Four years later, he was involved again in the abortive 1719 Rebellion, and was injured in the skirmish of Glenshiel – and had to head for France again, and to make his excuses to James Stuart, better known as The Old Pretender to distinguish him from 'Bonnie Prince Charlie', The Young Pretender.

To Prince James Francis Edward Stuart
Dec 22 1719
I will not pretend, Sir, to give you a details of things here, since you have not honoured me with the trust of any, only to assure your Majtie. that as there was no men engag'd in the action of Glenshell but mine, and those but a few (tho a great many standing by) so there are non more reddy on all occasions to shew there zeale for your service, when opportunity offers.

I am sorry I am forc'd to acquaint your Majtie. that your affairs here are brought to so low an ebb (by whose fault I wont say) that there nothing remains but every one to shift for him self, and yt. by ye. advise of him you honour with your commands, I still made it my studdy (upon which account I suffer most of any) to serve your Majtie to ye utmost of my power, and tho I be once more oblig'd to leave my native country, as in all probablity I must, to wander abroad, in what ever place fortune alots my abode, I shall always beg leave to subscribe myself, with the profoundest regret
Sir, Your Majties most dutifull subject
And most Obedient humble servant
Seafort.[7]

Friends at court managed to arrange for Seaforth to return to Lewis, though he had forfeited his title, and his son Kenneth had to be content with the courtesy title of Lord Fortrose. Kenneth had learned the lesson of history, and took no part in the 1745 Rebellion, though the castle might have caught a glimpse of the Prince when he was at Airinis, looking for a boat to take him to safety. But the burghers of Steornabhagh refused to have anything to do with him, and he had to head back for Uibhist.

Kenneth's son was restored to the title of Earl of Seaforth, but took little to do with the island, except as a recruiting base for his own army ambitions. He died in 1778 en route with his soldiers to India, without an heir, and having already sold Lewis to a cousin, who in turn died in India in 1783. The estate passed to the cousin's brother Francis Humberston MacKenzie, who again was able to obtain the title of Lord Seaforth.

The new Lord Seaforth at least resided in Seaforth Lodge:

> On an elevated situation on the other side of the bay, near and opposite to the town, is built Seaforth Lodge, for the reception and accommodation of Seaforth, the proprietor of this island, when he chose to come and visit this part of his estate, and where the present proprietor, Colonel Francis Humberstone MacKenzie, a gentleman universally known for benevolence and a public spirit, did reside for some years with his family; who, with his lady, when here, took pleasure in directing and superintending their people to habits of industry and happiness, until he was called away, at the commencement of the present war, to serve his King and country, by raising two batallions of infantry for Government. This mansion is delightfully situated, and commands an extensive view, both of sea and land.[8]

> [The drawing] was taken from an eminence near the building represented in the foreground, which is called Seaforth Lodge; this elevated point commands the most extensive prospect of any in the vicinity; it includes the whole of the town, with the loch; the remote sea view is bounded by the finely varied outline of Skye. The islet in the middle of the loch is called Elan-na-caul. In the

4. Steornabhagh 1819 – William Daniell

distance there is a house called Holme, the residence of Captain Reid, who commands the government cutter. The tall building in the foreground is erected over a fresh-water spring, chiefly for the supply of the shipping. Near to the pier head are visible the remains of a castle, built many centuries ago. The larger edifice seen on the left of the view is the church, a modern structure, which was opened for the first time in 1795; it is capable of containing a very large congregation.[9]

This was the period when recruiting began in earnest for the Canadian Fur companies, and the Castle remembered the fracas of 1811, when the agents of the Hudson's Bay Company and the North-West Company came to blows in the harbour in front of him.

Seaforth died in 1815, and the estate passed to his daughter, widow of Admiral Hood, and later wife of James Stewart of Glasserton, who took the name Stewart-MacKenzie. He had been full of plans to develop Lewis, but had neither the cash nor the ability to carry them through properly, and caused a great deal of hardship to the local people in the process.

In 1844 the estate was sold to Sir James Matheson, who immediately set about redeveloping the Lodge into his own fancy castle – a fake Tudor mansion, stuck on a Hebridean hillside! Even the fittings of the Seaforth Lodge were jettisoned, as one Hebridean exile found, many years later:

In 1925, when I was in Mull, I was staying in a tiny two roomed cottage, and one of the first things which attracted my attention was the grate in the kitchen. It was very old-fashioned, wrought in iron, with two high sides wonderfully decorated. It struck me as strange that such a fine bit of craftmanship should be gracing the humble kitchen of a Mullman's tiny home, and I asked the good housewife whence it had come. She replied that when the ruins of the old castle at Stornoway were being removed and the new building constructed, her father, who had been employed as a tradesman at the work of building, secured permission to keep the old grate which had been laid on one side during the dismantling. Thus the grate had been at one time in one of the rooms of Stornoway Castle and many generations of MacKenzies had probably sat warming themselves before its cheerful blaze while the winter storms raged round the old walls.[10]

Though the Castle didn't think much of the new Castle, he had to admit that the trees planted in the Gearraidh Chruaidh were spectacular – who would have thought that such magnificent trees could be grown on a Lewis moor? All that he could remember were a

5. Lews Castle

few trees at Allt nam Brog, where it was said that the country people used to put their shoes on, on a visit to the town. Seaforth had tried earlier, but without success:

> Here no woods grow to any useful height or size. The proprietor, some years ago, planted a variety of trees in a well-sheltered spot of ground near his house, which have all failed, except the allar, and mountain-ash or rhoddin tree.[11]

He had to admit, too, that Sir James had remodelled the harbour of Steornabhagh, with new quays and paved streets. He enjoyed all the bustle of a thriving sea-port around him, with the new sailing packets to Poolewe and Glasgow. Sir James died in 1878 and his widow's main interest seemed to be in keeping everything as it was in his time – there was another widow in Windsor with the same idea!

Lady Matheson came into dispute with the burghers of Steornabhagh about the rights to the foreshore, and so the piers and harbour. Eventually the rights passed to a Pier and Harbour Commission, and what was one of the first things they did? – they knocked down what was left of the castle! In 1882 what was left of him was used in the foundation of a new pier.

What an indignity! – but it was good to have a roof over his head.

Lady Matheson was succeeded by Sir James's nephew Donald, whose son Duncan sold Lewis to the then William Lever, later Lord Leverhulme.

6. MV *Loch Seaforth*

He redesigned Matheson's castle – leading to many structural problems in the future! – and brought the whole panoply of nouveau-riche society to Steornabhagh. According to his niece, Emily:

> My uncle had knocked the drawing-room and ball-room into one, and laid a new specially sprung dance floor. He had acquired along with the Castle some magnificent Gobelin tapestries which were on the walls and framed in white painted panelling and he had some very fine crystal chandeliers hung from the ceiling. All this made a ballroom which could have had very few equals in the Highlands.
>
> We were piped into dinner by Pipe-Major MacLeod in full regimentals, and he remained in the room throughout the meal, playing at intervals. This however precluded all conversation when he was playing. Actually I am very fond of pipe music in the proper place, but I am perfectly certain that that is outside, and not in a room.[12]

The Castle remembered some of the balls that were held there – not that he was involved, but Leverhulme was so deaf that the noise echoed all across the bay. But that era passed, too; Leverhulme ran out of both money and patience, left Lewis and gave the castle, with the rest of the Parish of Steornabhagh, to what became the Stornoway Trust.

Still the traffic overhead continued: ferries like the *Sheila* and later the *Loch Seaforth*, and tenders for emigrant ships like the *Metagama*. Recently a new pier was built towards Newton, and a new ferry terminal, so No 1 Pier had become much quieter – indeed rather lonely.

But the new castle, without any source of income, was a liability, and it was with a certain grim satisfaction that the Castle watched its rival deteriorate. It was for a time used as a technical college – Lews Castle

College – but this later had to be replaced by a new purpose-built college to the rear of the castle.

It was rather amusing to think that it was a student at the Technical College who stumbled upon the 'Shoeburn Hoard' – why couldn't they have left the name as Allt nam Brog? – a collection of coins from dates up to 1669, so probably buried soon after that date. That could have come in useful in paying for repairs for Lews Castle.

Now, unless major repair work is undertaken soon, the whole fabric of the building is in danger. Comhairle nan Eilean Siar is trying hard to find a solution to the problem of what to do with Lews Castle in such a way as to preserve the structure and find sufficient income to maintain it.

And all the time, the old ruined castle lies under its pier, remembering its past, and wondering what else the future may hold – perhaps even a proper memorial, rather than just a small plaque to say where he used to be:

Air an larach so bha seann
CHAISTEAL STEORNABHAIGH
an daingneach aig cinn-fheadhna
CHLANN MHICLEOID
LEODHAIS o shian

On this site stood the old
CASTLE of STORNOWAY
The ancient stronghold of the chiefs
of the MACLEODS of the LEWS

PART 1 – SGIRE BHAC (BACK DISTRICT)

Sgire Bhac has been used to denote the whole area from the outskirts of Steornabhagh, through Tunga, Col, am Bac and Tolastadh to the boundary with Sgire Nis. Vol. 1 of this set deals with the west coast from Nis to Uig.

The area varies from fertile machair and black-lands to skinned land, once covered with peat, peat-hags and the rolling hills of Muirneag and Beanntan Bharabhais. When the poet wrote of 'Muirneag ainmeil is Beanntan Bharabhais', he was referring not so much to the height of the hills themselves as to the way that, seen from the sea, they dominate their low, rolling surroundings.

To the east, Sgire Bhac is bounded by Loch a' Tuath – Broad Bay – in its day a fruitful area for sea-fishing, so it is hardly surprising that the story of the area is so largely the story of the fishing community.

7. Loch a' Tuath

Filiscleitir

We can begin, as we did in the first volume of *Lewis in History and Legend*, at Filiscleitir, on the moor between Nis and Tolastadh – and I have to begin with a mea culpa! I had always heard of Iain Fiosach's church there as an Eaglais Bhaisteach, and had carelessly translated this literally, and assumed that he was a Baptist, when in fact he belonged to the Brethren. But whatever his religious affiliations, the ruins of his house are still there, overhanging the cliff, and giving us the starting-off point for this volume also.

The gap between the peat roads of Tolastadh and Nis is only five miles, and there have been many plans to plug the gap, among them one of Lord Leverhulme's schemes, but none have ever come to fruition. What I remember as a vague track is now a Heritage Trail, well-marked, but in some places churned into bog by over-use by heavy cycles. I suppose that one of the reasons why the road has never been made is that it would only make a minimal difference to the length of journey from Steornabhagh to Nis, and none of the land along the way would be very suitable for settlement, even if there was road access. But it is a beautiful walk, with lovely views on a good day over the cliffs towards Sron an t-Seileir – I refuse to use the bastardised English form of Cellar Head!

William Daniell tackled the moor between Tolastadh and Nis on his tour of the island in 1819.

8. Sron an t-Seileir

On the following day, although the weather was very unpromising a guide was procured for the purpose of traversing the extensive tract of moorland between this place and the northern extremity of the isle. In no part of this summer's excursion, nor indeed at any remembered period since the commencement of the voyage, has there occurred a day of such fatigue and discomfort. There was a dense drizzling rain, usually called a Scotch mist, throughout nearly the whole way (path indeed there was none) which lay over an expanse of quaggy peat, mostly ankle deep in wet, intersected by frequent ravines and gullies both narrow and broad, requiring an equally frequent interruption of the regular travelling pace, by the ambulatory variations of striding, skipping and leaping – variations which in their occurrence afforded no very perceptible relief to the uniform drudgery of walking.[13]

I know exactly what he means – the ground looks so flat, and yet every step is either a step up or a step down, and any idea of a regular stride has to be forgotten. Moor-walking is indeed a very different technique from street-walking! (For some reason, my wife Chris thinks I should re-phrase that.)

George Atkinson, on a visit to Lewis in 1833, set off also from Tolastadh, with no better success.

The morning had commenced with rain, and then it came on fine, but changed just as we landed, thickening most suspiciously and settling in gradually to a splendid Scotch mist. Never mind, we had a guide and a compass, certain whisky and a bottle of cherry brandy, so we need not fear a wet coat, and off we set, the day becoming worse with each step. It was a thick mist and through it, impelled by a sharp, cold northeaster, drove a heavy pelting and incessant rain. We kept on confidently by our guide's direction till 4 or 5 o' clock, and then began to feel impatient at not having reached our destination, which was only called twelve miles from Tolsta where we landed. We began to consult our compasses and, after noting our course by them for 10 minutes, found to our extreme provocation, though a little to our amusement, that our friend Donald was rambling about quite at random in the thick fog. The mist cleared, we saw houses at two or three miles distance – it was the village of Ness, so we dedicated some few minutes to the conclusion of a bottle of cherry brandy and some cold food.[14]

Atkinson's view of Lewis was perhaps prejudiced by this forced wandering.

On the whole there is little in Lewis to induce a tourist to visit it. It
is, I think, almost the only spot my ramblings have led me to, that
I should not feel desirous of re-visiting to see something more of. I
have seen nearly enough of Lewis and formed the general conclusion
that its north part is chiefly level, uninteresting moor, interspersed
with numerous, boggy un-picturesque lakes.[15]

I have walked the track here many times, always starting from
Nis and heading south, and, as it happens, always in good weather!
The moral would seem to be: always do the walk starting at the Nis
end – and never take a guide!

From Filiscleitir, the track runs south along the upper edge of the
valley of Maoim – the bottom of the valley can be very wet and is better
avoided – but it is a great place to see birds of prey, dashing through the
valley. So we come to the steep glen of Dibeadal – a good Norse name
meaning deep valley. Here, and at neighbouring Cuibhleatotair there
are the ruins of houses, too substantial to be merely shielings, and oral
tradition tells that some families evicted from Cnoc Ard in Nis could
find no better place than this to live, until they were able to obtain
crofts in Tolastadh.

The shieling system was an integral part of the agricultural life of
the islands. When the time came for ploughing and sowing the arable
lands around the townships, the cattle had to be cleared out of the
way. At the same time, the grass was beginning to grow again on the
moors, so it made sense to take the cattle off the crofts to pasture on the
moors. Each township had its own area for *airighean* – shielings – and
the women and children would go out there with the cattle, leaving the
men at home to plant and tend the crops.

The Tolastadh people had many shielings in the area to the west
of the track, along Loch Langabhat and Loch Bhataleois, under the
slopes of Bein Dhail, where the Niseach shielings were their near
neighbours – and a favourite place for romantic dalliance in the long
summer evenings!

But the land here can be very dangerous too – I remember venturing
too boldly into the moor around Blar an Domblais, and getting the
fright of my life when I realised that what I had taken for firm tussocks
of grass were in fact floating on the surface of a very liquid peat-bog,
and every step took me calf-deep in stagnant water! Carrying on was
not an option, but retreating was almost as bad, as the 'stepping-stones'
I had used earlier were now under water as well! Luckily I was wearing
hiking boots rather than wellies, for I am sure that the wellies would
have been sucked off my feet long before I got back to terra firma. I
discovered that day that a smooth green plain of grass in the middle

9. Near Dibeadal

of the moor should be taken as a warning, not an attraction. Many an incautious sheep must have met its end in such a mire, drawn in by the lushness of the grass. I have learned since then to pay more attention to the feel of the ground under my feet, but then I was the typical walker, thinking that all you needed was a map and a compass!

South from Dibeadal the track wanders through rather featureless moor, coming near the shore again at Dun Othail, the scene of one of the more grisly folk-tales of Lewis!

The deep ravine dividing Dun Othail from the mainland is called Leum MhicNeacail – MacNicol's leap. MacNicol, for some misconduct, was sentenced by the Chief of Lewis to be mutilated. In revenge, he ran away with the only child of the chief. Being pursued, he leapt over the chasm to Dun Othail with the child in his arms. Persuasion was used to get him to deliver the child, but he refused until the chief would undergo the same operation as he had gone through. Several subterfuges were tried, but in vain, and to save the child the father consented to be mutilated. When MacNicol was sure

10. Dun Othail

11. Bridge to Nowhere

that this had been done, he sprang with the child in his arms over the cliff into the sea – saying in Gaelic 'Chan eil oighre agamsa 's cha bhi oighre aigesan' – If I have no heir, neither shall he![16]

Then south again brings us to the 'Bridge to Nowhere'! This was part of Lord Leverhulme's scheme of a road to fill the gap to Nis, but like so many of his schemes, the road came to nought, and the bridge remains as a reminder of what might have been.

12. Caisteal a' Mhorair

Not that Leverhulme was the first to think of the road – as seen from an instruction from Seaforth in October 1830:

> The road from the Tong Road to Tolsta must be pitted and lined off by Francis MacBean as soon as he returns. He will do well to go over it all at once, as far as Gress, in the direction pointed out by Seaforth – from there to Tolsta, with a view to a line of road to Ness as well as conveniencing for cultivating the moor of Tolsta.[17]

The bridge crosses Abhainn Geireadha – Garry River – which flows into a beautiful sandy beach, beloved of campers and caravanners. At the south end of the beach are two natural stacs, which have gathered to themselves stories, such as that of Caisteal a' Mhorair – the Chief's Castle.

> Caisteal a' Mhorair attains an altitude of seventy feet, and is pierced from east to west by a natural tunnel through which the sea rushes in rapture with the flowing tide. The smaller apertures, occurring approximately in the north and south of the interior of this stack act as would windows in a transept. Thus Caisteal a' Mhorair may be likened unto a Norman abbey with nave and transept, and with dulse-covered pews on which the writer has found groups of seabirds congregated in silence at low water. The interior is lofty and spacious; within this veritable sea-abbey clans of feathery bipeds commune at the close of day; and the music of the sea reverberates through its aisles as would an organ softly played at evensong.[18]

Who but Alasdair Alpin MacGregor could have penned so 'over the top' a description? On the other hand, who else was bothering to visit the more remote parts of the islands then, let alone write about them? – and some of his photography is quite amazingly effective, as we shall see when we come to Griais.

In more prosaic terms:

> The flat oval summit measuring some 60 feet from east-south-east to west-north-west is defended by a wall 4 to 6 feet wide and now 1 ½ feet high built round the precipitous edge. The greater part of the summit towards the north-west is occupied by a roughly rectangular chamber 32 feet long and 14 feet broad, entered 11 feet for the north-western end by a passage in the south-western flank 2 feet 9 inches broad and walled for a length of 14 feet. Access to this entrance is obtained by climbing a dangerously steep rib of rock opposite it, the cliff otherwise being unclimbable.[19]

It has always bothered me that so many of the defensive sites around the coasts of the islands are so difficult of access. Did the inhabitants use a Blondin – a rope slung between posts on either side – which could be cut if necessary? I first became aware of its use among the less accessible peat-banks in Harris, and was fascinated by the derivation from Blondin the tight-rope walker, though I believe the name is used in the army also.

Beyond the Caisteal, we join the road for Tolastadh and on towards Steornabhagh.

Tolastadh (Tolsta)

Tolastadh is a group of villages, sitting high on the moor some 80m above the beach and harbour of Gioradal to the south and the wide sweep of sands of the Traigh Mhor to the north. The sands can be particularly beautiful on a sunny day, especially as seen from the road at the west end. Nearer to the east end is the graveyard of St Michael.

> Cladh Mhicheil shios ri taobh na mara
> Cladh Mhicheil shios an glaic an t-sail
> 'S ann ann a dh' iarrainn siorruidh cadal,
> Nuair thig orm cabhaig 's neart a' bhais.
>
> Tha gathan oir na grein' 's a' mhadainn
> A' laigh ort dluth bho shlios na h-Aird;
> Is guth a' chuain gu buan air gainneamh
> Ri cluais gun aithne luchd ar graidh.

13. Traigh Mhor Tholstaidh

Tha tuilleadh bliadhn' thar bliadhn' ag imeachd
An t-slighe nach imich iad nas mo,
Gu laighe 'n tathaich Cnoc nan Curran
Ri duan an t-sruthain 's a' chuain mhor.

An Reidhlig Mhicheil taobh na mara,
'Sann ann tha mairbh ar baile tamh;
'Sann ann a dh'iarrainn cuideachd laighe,
'S sin fath mo ghuidhe is mo dhan.[20]

As usual in these books, we have appended a rough translation of the meaning of the words, where necessary, though well aware that in doing so the poetry is lost irretrievably.

Cladh Mhicheil down beside the sea, down at the hollow of the ocean – it is there that I would want to sleep when death comes to me. Golden rays of the morning sun lie on you under the slope of the Aird, and the sound of the sea stirring the sands comes to the unhearing ears of our ancestors. Michael's graveyard beside the sea, it is there that the dead have their resting place, and to lie there also is the theme of my prayer and song.

Martin Martin in his *Description of the Western Isles* in 1703 mentions the church of St Michael at Tolastadh, but T S Muir, visiting the site in 1885, noted:

the burying ground of St Michael, on a grassy slope overlooking a long stretch of smooth sandy shore, but in it no traces of the church under the dedication mentioned by Martin.

Donald MacDonald in his *The Tolsta Townships* of 1984 notes that the large foundation stones of the chapel can still be found, but the slopes of the shore are now so overgrown with *gallan* – butterbur – that it would be difficult to find anything there.

Martin Martin mentions that in Uist there were horse races held every St Michael's day, and the shore at Tolastadh would be an ideal place for similar exercises. The dedication to St Michael could be a link, though I have never heard of such an occurrence in Tolastadh.

For much of its history, Tolastadh has been split into Tolastadh bho Thuath – North Tolsta – and Tolastadh bho Dheas – South Tolsta. In a rental of 1716[21] the tack of Tolastadh bho Thuath was let to 'Alexander MacEiver' and Tolastadh bho Dheas to his son Rory. Rents in these days were largely paid in kind, and in 1726 each farm was liable to pay 6 muttons, 3 stones of butter, 1 bushel of meal, and £113.17.4 Scots money – which seems a lot, but a pound Scots then was worth only one-twelfth of a pound sterling!

Although the farms were let directly to the tacksmen, they in turn sublet part of the land to subtenants, to provide a labour force for the farm. In a Judicial Rental of 1754[22] we find that both parts of Tolastadh were held in tack by Roderick MacIver, but that Tolastadh bho Dheas was sublet to sixteen subtenants, while Tolastadh bho Thuath was kept in the tacksman's own hands. This is surprising as the rental goes on to state that:

> North Tolstay is much abused by Sand Drift, and not so good as South Tolstay

– much more commonly the tenants were on the poorer ground!

The houses of the subtenants would have been gathered together in a *seana-bhaile* – literally, old village – and the land would have been shared out among them on a run-rig basis, with the tenants balloting every few years for a redistribution of the land, so that every tenant got a chance of the best land. The rent also would have been shared in common, which had the advantage that a tenant in poorer circumstances could take a lesser share of land, and therefore of rent, until he came to better times. It had the disadvantage though that, since you were going to move to new pieces of land fairly regularly, there was little incentive to improve or even look after the land you had at any one time.

Roderick MacIver, tacksman of Tolastadh in 1754, is said to have had three sons, two of whom may have gone to America. He was succeeded at Tolastadh by his brother Donald, father of Ready-Money John MacIver of New York and grandfather of Alexander MacKenzie, the Canadian explorer. Donald in turn was succeeded by his brother John, whose daughter Ann married Kenneth MacIver of Col. Kenneth became the last tacksman of Tolastadh. He and his wife did not live there, but in Point Street in Steornabhagh, where they are primarily remembered for having had at least twenty children.

In 1829, the MacIvers lost both tacks, which were then let directly to crofters, holding their land direct from the landlords – the Seaforth Estate – instead of through the tacksmen. Crofting was a new system whereby each tenant had his own piece of land to hold for as long as he could pay the rent, for which he was wholly responsible. This certainly gave more incentive to improve the land, but the real reason for the change was that it allowed the landlords to get more people on the same amount of land – a response to the new kelp industry, which was very labour intensive.

Tolastadh bho Thuath was let mainly to new tenants coming across the moor from Nis, while Tolastadh bho Dheas went mainly to the former subtenants of the tack and their families.

One family, however, came from Mealabost, outside Steornabhagh. These were the brothers Donald and John Martin, of a family known as na Sealgairean – the hunters. John's son Norman certainly lived up to his by-name, for he went off to Canada with the Hudson's Bay Company. There he married a First Nation lady, whose name we have never been able to discover, and they had a son, also called Norman. When his tour of duty ended, Norman returned to Tolastadh with his wife, whose prowess with a gun is still remembered locally: 'we were all well fed that winter!'

Unfortunately Norman was drowned, returning from a voyage to Wick, and his widow after a time decided to return to Canada. Some years later, her son decided to come to Lewis, but he died of a heart attack at Liverpool and never returned to the island where his mother had lived.

According to oral tradition, there are three First Nation wives buried in Cladh Mhicheil, but although we know of other Tolastadh men who married in Canada, we have no trace of others returning with families.

The boom period of the kelp industry was during the Napoleonic Wars, but the availability of other sources in the peace-time which followed the Battle of Waterloo in 1815 led to the decline and finally the collapse of the industry. The kelping labour force was now redundant, and the landlords turned to sheep-farmers as their preferred tenants.

John Munro MacKenzie, the factor of Lewis in 1851, debated whether Tolastadh should be cleared.

> The Tolsta people are much in arrear of rent and I fear can never pay. They seem a lazy and indolent set & many of them shew no anxiety to pay rents. There are several fishermen among them, and Tolsta is a

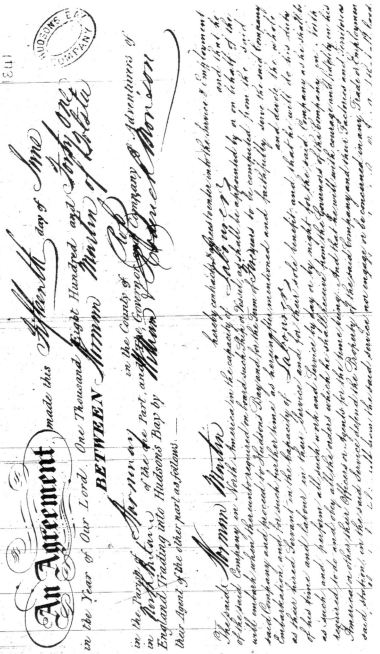

14. Contract between Norman Martin and the Hudson's Bay Company

good fishing port, but like all others who depend entirely on the Cod
& Ling fishing they draw their earning in meal and shop goods and
little or nothing of the produce of that labour goes to pay rent. What
the fishermen pay mostly comes from Caithness. The Tolstas would
make a good sheep farm if cleared. If the people could or would pay
I would not recommend this. I addressed them and warned them if
their rents were not better paid up by Whitsunday they might look
out for a change.[23]

In 1852, Tolastadh bho Thuath was cleared to make a farm. Many
of the former tenants were settled on new crofts made for them on the
peat-lands surrounding Tolastadh bho Dheas, and others emigrated
to Canada.

The first tenant on the new farm was Roderick Nicolson, but he
was soon replaced by Thomas Newall and his cousin Samuel, who
later moved to Aignis farm. After them the tack changed hands a few
times before being broken into crofts again in 1922 as part of the land
settlement schemes of the Leverhulme era.

For some reason, it became the habit, once the old Tolastadh bho
Thuath had gone, to refer to Tolastadh bho Dheas as Tolastadh bho
Thuath – perhaps to distinguish it from Tolastadh a' Chaolais near
Carlabhagh, which is in fact west! That was all right until the farm
of Tolastadh was once more broken into crofts in 1922 and given the
name of New Tolastadh – am Baile Ur. So now we have New Tolsta
which used to be North Tolsta, and North Tolsta which used to be
South Tolsta!

Being at the end of a road, Tolastadh developed differently from
the townships closer to Steornabhagh, and was especially known for
buidhsneachd – witchcraft. The Tolastadh people will tell you that this
all developed from a humorous article in a newspaper in the 1930s, and
the joke got out of hand, but my wife remembers a Tolastadh family
in her own village who would never leave their house without making
a particular arrangement of stones and pieces of iron around the gate –
presumably to keep off the fairies!

Whatever the Tolastadh folk may have thought of the *buidhsneachd*,
the rest of Lewis firmly believed that the Tolastadh folk believed in
it! I remember hearing when I came to the islands first about an old
cailleach in Tolastadh who was waiting for a phone to be installed in
her house – this was just at the start of the house phones in the area,
and there were plenty others waiting as well. The engineers arrived with
their van and went up to the house, only to discover that it was the
wrong house, and the phone they had was actually for another house in
Tolastadh – at which she was far from pleased. They went back with it

to their van – and nothing they could do would get the van to start. In the end they sent for an engineer from the garage in Steornabhagh, but nothing he could do would start the van either. As they were standing around wondering what to try next, a Tolastadh man came along the road and asked what was the trouble. When they told him, he asked if they had annoyed the *cailleach* in the house. When they agreed that she had been less than pleased, 'Right', he said, 'just you push your van past the fence at the end of her croft, and then it will be all right.' So they pushed it up the road past the end of the croft, and as they got there, the engine started. Nothing would convince them that it was pushing the van that started it – it was getting it beyond the power of the *cailleach*!

Even the Tolastadh people themselves are very conscious of their reputation. I remember one occasion when Chris and I were doing a talk in Tolastadh about the families who emigrated to the Eastern Townships of Quebec. We had a series of slides from that area, including some of floats at a carnival procession. There is a township in that area still called Tolsta, and there was a float for timber-workers from Tolsta. Timber-workers in French are *bucherons*, and as soon as the placard with their name came up, you could hear the intake of breath from the audience – they thought it was going to be Buidhsneachd, and that the reputation had even crossed to the other side of the Atlantic!

Although Tolastadh was a crofting township, most of its livelihood was taken from the sea, with the beach of Gioradal used in place of a harbour. Tolastadh was very favoured in having its own historian – Donald MacDonald, of the Buidhe MacDonalds who were at Cuibhleatotair – and his description of the launching of a boat is well worth quoting at length, to show the amount of sheer labour involved.

It was always exciting to see the fishermen, singly or in groups of two or three, making for the shore. On arriving there the 'sguils' (baskets of baited lines) were deposited near the water's edge and the labour of launching begun, never an easy task owing to the shallowness of the beaches and the distance boats had to be man-handled from their resting area. Because of the softness of the sand 'lunnan', six-foot lengths of wood, were placed at intervals, like railway sleepers, along the boat's proposed track. The first of these lunnan was placed under the boat's keel, and then she was pushed over them by the crew ranged on either side of her until she had cleared most of her rollers, when a halt was made and while some held her upright, the rest collected the cleared lunnan and placed them, as formerly, in the track ahead. This process of depositing, pushing, halting and depositing continued until the sea was reached. Seaweed was often

15. Bucheron Tholstaidh

placed on the lunnan, or even bits of fish, to make it easier for the keel to slide over.

The boat, except in stormy weather, was always launched stern first, so when the sea was reached she was allowed to lie on her starboard side for her plug, linen wrapped, to be fitted into the plug-hole on her port side. She was then pushed forward until she was practically afloat. The skipper and the mate then went aboard, the former taking up his position in the stern and, with his boat-hook thrust deeply into the sand, held her from going broadside to the oncoming waves, while the latter placed the ballast, mostly amidships, and placed the sguils and the boat gear in their proper places, with the mast and sails in the bows. The boat was pushed further to sea, and when the oarsmen thought fit, they went on board and took their places on their thwarts, facing shorewards, while the bowman still on shore gave her the extra push that made her sea-borne, although still anchored to the land by him, who, although up to his armpits in the sea, kept her so by sheer strength. Whenever the skipper saw a fiath, a calm stretch, he gave the order to let her go, and the four oars dipped like one, the boathook was given a final push, and so did the bowman and away she went while the bowman, with the boat at times so high above him that he could only touch her gunwhale with his fingers, somehow managed to heave himself aboard. Once clear of the breakers, the boat was turned round sunwise and, with the minimum of fuss and the dexterity of long practice, the rudder was

16. Launching *The Brother's Delight*

fitted, the tiller fixed, the ballast placed to the mate's satisfaction, the mast stepped, the lug sail set, and with hardly a word of command, course was set for the fishing grounds.

It was not the work at sea that was so killing on the men, it was the launching and the beaching, back-breaking labour, which aged them while they were still young. Many suffered from rheumatism and hernia. When one considers that the sgoths weighed almost 6 tons in some cases, and that a ton of sand and a similar amount of stones for ballast, along with the weight of the boat's gear and fishing gear, had to be pushed into the sea by six or seven men, this is not to be wondered at.[24]

We will tell more of the story of the *Iolaire* and its wrecking off Tolm on New Year of 1919 when we come to that area, but Tolastadh like all Lewis townships had its losses from that disaster. There is the story of Norman MacLeod who, when he heard of the disaster, headed off to Steornabhagh to see if any help could be given. When he heard the full scale of the disaster, he headed home again, but on his way across the moor he met his brother Calum, seeking news of his two sons. Recognising from Norman's face that the news was bad, Calum asked 'Cò fear ac' a th' ann? Ni Dòmhnall a th' ann?' – Was it Donald? – but got no reply. 'Ni Calum a th' ann a rèist''? – Was it Calum? – still no reply. The truth dawned on him – 'A bheil an dithis ann?' – It was both! he cried, and turned away in the fullness of his grief.

Another tale of the war from Tolastadh is that of John MacLennan – Iain Scodaidh – and his song, still well-known in Lewis:

Gu 'n dean mi rann, 's mo chridhe trom
Is mi fo chuing dha m'aindheoin
Air bord nan luing 's mi sgith is tinn
'S an cuan fo thuinn dol seachad.

Tha 'n geamhradh fuar 's an reothadh cruaidh
'S tha smuid a' chuain gam dhalladh
Gun d' toirinn duais bhi 'm blaths mo luaidh
'S i thogadh gruaim fo m' aire.

Nuair bhiomaid cruinn an tigh MhicAoidh
Cha b' fhad' an oidhch' dol seachad,
Ged bhiodh e uair cha bhiodh oirnn gruaim
Ag eirigh suas 's a mhaduinn.

Bheir mi gu ceann am beagan rann
'S mi cluinntinn fear le feadag,
Toirt orduigh teann bhith suas air ball
Tha long leinn fagail caladh.[25]

I will make a song, my heart so heavy and imprisoned against my will, on board the ship, tired and sick, and the billows of the sea going past. The winter is cold and the frost is hard, and the foam of the sea blinding me. I would give a reward to be within the warmth of my love, and she would lift the heaviness from my mind. When we would be gathered in MacKay's house, the night wouldn't be long in passing; though it would be one o'clock we wouldn't be worried about rising early in the morning. I have come to the end of this little song, and I am hearing the sound of the whistle, making me run quickly on deck, and the ship is leaving the harbour.

My friend Donald Murray – Domhnall Mhurchaidh Chlaoid – himself no mean historian, told how Iain had written the song not long before he was lost on the *Boreas* in 1940, and the song was found among his papers when they were brought home.

My wife's father used to tell that the first time he heard the song was when he was on the *Cameronia* in port in Alexandria. Another ship was passing, and on board her Finlay Nicolson from his own village was singing the song – an example of just how quickly a good song could travel, especially at sea.

The song is usually sung to a tune which seems to have its ultimate derivation from the English song 'Barbara Allan', which shows just how international a good tune is; but then Samuel Pepys in 1662 mentions 'The little Scotch song of Barbary Allen' – so where did it come from originally?

Listen to it as sung by Ishbel MacAskill, so recently and tragically lost to us, and I defy you not to be moved.

Although John MacLennnan the bard was from Tolastadh itself, his people came from Gleann Tholastaidh, a little valley on the boundary between the farms of Tolastadh and Griais. Originally this had been a stance for a boundary shepherd, but when the Leumrabhagh area of na Lochan was cleared in 1850, five of the dispossessed families were settled on crofts in the Gleann – MacLennans, MacMillans, Carmichaels and MacInneses, all very alien names to find in Tolastadh!

Griais (Gress)

On the moor side of the road in Griais lies the graveyard of St Aulay and the remains of the old church, referred to by Martin Martin as 'St Aula in Grease'.

T S Muir refers to it as

> standing in an open though cleanly burying ground a little way up from the shore; it is a very small building, the internal length being barely 19 feet, the walls nearly entire, but without any peculiar features. Above the entrance are the figures '1681 – IB MK'.[26]

Rev. William Matheson in an article in the *Stornoway Gazette* in 1952 notes a Sasine of Gress in 1673 in the names of John Bayne and his spouse Isabella MacKenzie. No doubt it is their initials in the inscription, which will refer to a rebuilding of the chapel by them.

After the Baynes, Griais passed into the hands of another family of MacIvers, descended from a Rev. Evander MacIver of Fodderty in Ross-shire, whose grandson John is on record in Griais in 1726, and this John was the father of Evander who had Griais in the 1780s. Evander was in turn the father of Lewis MacIver, the last tacksman of Griais, and one of those larger-than-life figures occasionally thrown up by history.

As well as being tacksman of Griais, Lewis MacIver had a business in Steornabhagh, where he is remembered as having fought the last duel to take place on Lewis. A note in the Seaforth Papers in 1835 tells how he

> attacked Alexander Stewart, the factor, on the Stornoway Quay while the latter was engaged in transacting business about harbour dues. MacIver had a vessel taking on board cattle, and on hearing about harbour dues, struck Stewart and got a mainland ruffian to attempt to strangle him, and he himself later tried to throw him over the pier.[27]

17. Griais Church

In the same year,

a hostile meeting took place at the northeast end of the Goathill Grounds, between Collector MacLeay and Lewis MacIver, the former supported by the Comptroller, the latter by Mr William Fairbairn, and after exchanging shots once, the parties separated. The Collector rents MacIver's house in Kenneth Street and being somewhat troublesome as to repairs and alterations, workmen were employed in taking a floor out of one of the rooms and putting in a new one.

MacIver called, grumbling and complaining at the expense, words of an unfriendly nature were exchanged, and the Collector attempted to strike MacIver with his stick. The consequence was a message by Mr Fairbairn to the Collector and the meeting just mentioned. Nobody was hurt, fortunately, for there was no surgeon present.[28]

In this case MacIver does not seem to have been the aggressor!

Lewis MacIver was the father of Evander MacIver, later factor of Scourie in Sutherland, whose *Memoirs of a Highland Gentleman* contains some interesting references to his youth at Griais – though the first of these can hardly be termed a reminiscence:

On the occasion of my birth, when my mother took ill, she was attended by a well-known wise woman of the profession; the wise woman was of the opinion that my father and my grandfather should leave the house and take a walk. My father proposed that they should go to the Gress River, and try to get a salmon in the rock pools, where the fish rested on their way to the loch from which the river issued. The peculiar way of catching them was by getting into the pool and ascertaining with the naked foot whether any salmon were resting there. The salmon submitted to be touched and scratched by the human foot. A strong string or hand-line with a loop on it was procured, and they got the tail of the salmon into the loop, which was drawn by degrees so that it could be hauled out. They found on this occasion that there was more than one salmon, and succeeded in securing two by this strange mode of capture; and returning home with them, they found that I had appeared, and it was immediately predicted by the wise woman that I would prove a lucky boy.[29]

I am sure that it was a very good way of getting the men out of the way, but somehow I cannot see a poacher being allowed to try the defence that he had stood on the salmon!

Evander MacIver tells us that Griais was never a profitable farm:

Gress, vast, scant dreary – it never procured what it did not swallow up. In short, it was never a source of profit. My grandfather, after whom I was called, was ruined in a singular manner. There was a considerable extent of arable land, from the produce of which a large fold of Highland cattle were wintered in byres. A stackyard adjoined, and they consumed the straw; a swarm of rats landed at Gress from the sea, came to the stackyard and ate up the grain, riddling the stacks to such an extent that they fell to the ground, and what was left by the rats rotted away, and was rendered useless for the cattle. A very severe spring followed, and a large number of the cattle died of starvation and poverty; such was the loss that he was never able to recover and when he died he left debts behind him. My father was a man of much ability and great natural talent, and by good management, industry and economy, he became prosperous; he speculated in cattle, fish-curing, ship-owning, and rose to be the leading man of the island, carrying on extensive business in Stornoway and acquiring house property there.[30]

It is rather difficult to reconcile this description with that of Lewis the dueller!

W Anderson Smith appreciated Griais:

About eight miles north from Stornoway, finely situated amid undulating downs, lie the farmhouse and shooting-lodge of Gress. It is acknowledged to be one of the loveliest spots on the island, lying, as it does, on the finest bay on the coast, and commanding pleasant prospects both seaward and landward from its cheerful green-fringed garden.

18. Shooting Pigeons near Griais

On the shore close by is the fishing-station of Gress, giving life and animation to the neighbourhood, and studding the waters with dancing boats, from the small cod and ling or stout herring-boat, to the more important-looking smack.[31]

Attached to the farm was a mill, serving the whole area north of Steornabhagh as far as Tolastadh. Tenants using the mill paid a twelfth share of their meal to the miller, and even tenants who did not use the mill had to pay a 'dry multure' towards the cost of running and upkeep of the mill.

One of the last local millers there was a John MacKenzie, whose family later moved to Col and then to the Eastern Townships of Quebec. There I met his grandson Johnnie – Seonaidh Mhurchaidh a' Mhuilleir – and his wife Chrissie. They were living then in the town of Scotstown in Quebec and what struck me most about their house was that outside their door we were in Canada, but as soon as we stepped inside, and the shutters were closed on the windows, we were back in Lewis – and in a Lewis that neither of them had ever seen!

19. Griais Lodge *c.*1875

20. Lac MacKenzie

The last time we saw Johnnie he was just short of one hundred years old, and he was telling us a yarn about Domhnall Choinnich Bhreabadair – Donald Murray – and how he had brought fresh-water *sgadan* (herring) in a can and set them in Lac MacKenzie, and how you could never catch them in a net, only on a line.

Chris recorded his story and we were playing it one night at a talk in Tolastadh when Domhnall Mhurchaidh Chlaoid said 'But we have the same story here!' That was where Domhnall Choinnich had come from.

But at least that was better than the bodach in na Lochan who reckoned that the only way to catch some fish was to wait till they jumped and then shoot them!

21. Seal Cave at Griais

Of greatest interest to the visitors to Griais was the Seal Cave. Geologically, Griais is at the joint of the softer Steornabhagh Conglomerate beds with the hard basic gneiss of Lewis, and a series of caves have been hollowed out along the shore of the join. The Seal Cave was described in some detail by Rev. John Cameron of Steornabhagh in his article for the New Statistical Account of Scotland in 1833:

It is about a furlong in length from the entrance to high water-mark in the interior. The cave at the mouth is about ten feet wide; it gradually decreases to four feet in breadth; and after this, it widens and terminates in a spacious semi-circle, irregularly arched, and containing a deep bason of water. Here the roof is very lofty, and resplendent when viewed by torch-light. There is a small apartment in the interior, which by torch-light produces a fine effect; the pearly icicles of stalactite suspended from the roof reflect the light as from so many diamonds. The sides and roof of the cave are lined with this concreted matter. The natives, and strangers who have visited the cave, broke and carried away many of the finest icicles; but with a short respite, the plastic power of nature can restore the injury done by man.[32]

22. Griais Farm

Griais was the scene of one of the major land raids of the Leverhulme era. Leverhulme was determined that the farm should be kept as a source of milk supply for Steornabhagh, but the raiders were equally determined that the land should be broken into small crofts. The raiders won in the end, and in 1922 Griais was broken into 46 crofts. We will look at this period in more detail when we get to Col, but it is worth noting in passing that Griais was unusual in the land raids in that the farm had never been crofted and cleared, but had always been a farm.

About 1 ⅞ miles north-west of Gress Lodge at an elevation of 275 feet above sea-level, on the southern hillside slope of Druim a' Chairn, about 500 yards north-east of the Gress River, is a large cairn of stones, Carn a' Mharc, measuring 92 feet from north-east to south-west and some 77 feet from north-west to south-east and 10 feet in height. Occupying a small plateau which seems to have been excavated on the higher side and banked up slightly on the lower side, it commands a wide vista of peaty muirland, and of the mountains on the mainland beyond the Minch. The cairn has been much despoiled, and on the south-east side, extending over a length of 33 feet from the edge towards to centre, there is a large number of big slabs dislodged and tumbled about, which probably formed the burial chamber and the entrance passage leading into it. Round the south-western edge of the cairn is a number of large, pointed stones placed on end, apparently the remains of a marginal ring of such standing stones.[33]

The modern view of such cairns is that the central burial chamber and the access passage would have been built, and then stones heaped at random to cover them within the limit of the kerb circle, as can still be seen at Barpa Langais in Uibhist. The technology involved in erecting the stones of the chambers is impressive, but even more so the ability to organise the numbers of people needed to gather and place the shroud of loose stones.

Even older remains are recorded at Griais Lodge itself:

Under the lawn in front, that is east of Gress Lodge, is an earth-house which was discovered many years ago, but is now covered up with blown sand. The entrance to the house was only a few feet above high-water mark on the beach. There was a circular chamber near the entrance and a guard chamber on either side of the passage a few feet before this passage was reached. A narrow passage ran some 40 to 50 feet in a north-westerly direction towards Gress Lodge, when another circular chamber was reached. From this a passage branched off towards the north-east, and at the end of this branch there was another circular chamber. Mr Peter Liddle, farmer, Gress, got a pick of stag-horn near the latter spot, having dug down at least 15 feet from the surface. Querns and bones were also found in the earth-house.[34]

One of the shooting tenants at Griais Lodge in the 1870s was Daniel MacKinlay from London. He was of a Lewis family and, surprisingly for a member of the huntin', fishin' and shootin' gentry, wrote a book[35] supporting the crofters against the landlords and in particular against Donald Munro, the factor, of whom we shall hear more when we reach Steornabhagh.

Another shooting tenant was John Bickerdyke, whose book *Days in Thule with Rod, Gun and Camera* – who but a Victorian would have penned a title of that length? – contains a wealth of detail about the fishing, and some very fine photography. He was fascinated by the hundreds of lochs scattered about the moor:

It was a land of enchantment for the trout-fisher, with lochs never yet struck by the angler's flies. We decided to try a loch some three miles distant, which the head-keeper said no one in living memory had ever fished, but which he knew held trout, as once, when resting by its banks after a long tramp over the moor, he saw several good fish rising. – Loch an Fheoir Grinnavat. Long Murdo, who went with us, did not know the way, but he was given directions and we took with us a good map and a compass, without which I doubt if we should have found the loch.

I am glad to be able to give a portrait of our most worthy Murdo. He was an excellent gillie, though somewhat lacking in cheerfulness, the result of having faced death one winter's night in the Minch, when the boat he was on foundered.

23. Murdo

24. On the moor

The loch of the grassy banks, to give it its English name, lay high among the hills. Up, up we went, and suddenly found ourselves enveloped in mist. This was awkward, for the saddle between the twin tops of a certain distant mountain had been our mark. Fortunately we had the compass, and taking our bearings very carefully, we went on and soon struck the lower end of a considerable piece of water known as Loch Langabhat. We slightly altered our direction and in about half an hour reached the mysterious loch where living man had never yet cast a fly.[36]

25. Kennie

On another occasion, Bickerdyke decided on a trip to Tolastadh to shoot rabbits:

On the way we passed two strapping girls who, with feet bare, were stepping out on their way to do some shopping in Stornoway. A little matter of twenty-two miles there and home again. One of them had thrown back the peculiar head-dress which they mostly wear as a protective in that windy and wet part of the kingdom.

Leaving the moor, we passed through the great peat-bog which affords fuel to the inhabitants of those curious crofter townships peculiar to the Lews. Just on the edge of the bog was a picturesque group consisting of an old crofter or fisherman-farmer, a weather-beaten, smoke-dried, sturdy woman, attired in the dress of the country, and a sleek cow, which the man was leading about by a halter. I was fortunate in being able to obtain a photograph of this interesting little scene. The illustration shows very clearly the soleless stocking which the women wear. The country is too wet for leather boots, and (most of the year) too cold for bare legs. This peculiar stocking is a compromise.[37]

I cannot resist one more example of Bickerdkye's photography:

A capital fellow was Kennie, but as a boy, so the story went, he was the terror of every gamekeeper in the district and as much at home in the river as out of it. He commenced by being a fisherman-crofter, like most of the men in the island, but his boat was wrecked and he was all but drowned, so, having a wife and family to support, he was thankful when Donald very judiciously made him a river-watcher. He was a merry little man, notwithstanding his misfortunes, with bright, twinkling black eyes, an intelligent face, and no English to speak of.[38]

Between Griais and am Bac lie wide saltings, a grand place for seeing waders, especially those on migration transit – godwit and the like.

The wild goose, rain-goose, swan, teal-duck, common wild duck and drake, wigeon, sheldrake, puffins, guillemots, solan goose, plover, wild pigeons and grouse in abundance are found here. A few robins, numerous larks, thrushes and starlings. The cuckoo visits us, but makes a very short stay. The sand-martin is the only one of the swallow tribe that visits the island. The common house-sparrow has only of late visited the island. There are two pair just now in Stornoway, hatching. The gardens miss them very much, for the caterpillar, which has been unknown in this parish twenty years ago, is now a great plague. If this small bird could thrive in Stornoway, it would be a considerable boon, for it has been found, by actual observation, that two sparrows carried to their nest forty caterpillars in an hour.[39]

Anderson Smith appreciated the bird-life for a different reason:

The curlew is everywhere abundant. Before it has taken up its permanent residence on the sea-coast, and become a little fishy, there is no more delicate bird for the table, and we consider a slice from the breast of a curlew in good condition superior in every respect to a golden plover in the short days. Grey herons are exceedingly common, as might be anticipated in such a land of fish-haunted pools. They are generally believed to be in the best condition during the full moon, when they have most success in their piscatory excursions. Their oil is considered capital for guns, and is obtained by the primitive mode of burying them in a manure heap, with their bill stuck in a bottle, into which the oil distils.[40]

Obh, Obh! – an RSPB!

Am Bac (Back)

South again from Griais we come to am Bac and Bhataisgeir, two townships which fit into each other like jigsaw puzzle pieces. Historically am Bac had been linked with the farm of Griais, while Bhataisgeir was linked with Col. I suppose that in their earlier days, Bhataisgeir was more fishing and am Bac more crofting, but both townships spread inland until they intersected. To me they now form a large built-up area, which, although close enough to Steornabhagh to be commuter-friendly, nonetheless has the feel of a distinct unit of its own. (Of course the Bacaich and muinntir Bhataisgeir will throw up their hands in horror and point out to me how different and distinct the two townships are!) But am Bac has its own church (which is actually in Bhataisgeir), its own school (also in Bhataisgeir) and even a shop and petrol filling station (and guess where they are?).

On the moor side of the townships lies Cnoc an t-Solais (Lighthill), where the crofts on the west side of the street are in Bhataisgeir and those on the east side in am Bac. I am told that it got the name because there were two weavers there in the old days who had particularly bright lights above their looms, but I am not sure that I am wholly convinced!

Another extension of am Bac is called very prosaically New Street in English, but in Gaelic am Poileagan because, I am told, of its fancied resemblance in shape to the Polygon Bastion, a defence-work in the Boer War. When I tried to check this on Google, I could only find a reference to a Polygon Wood, the site of a major battle four miles east of Ypres in Flanders in 1914 in the First World War, along with a reference to a Polygon Barracks in London, but no trace of one in the Boer War. Local sources told us that the name at am Bac was coined by one of the first settlers there – an Diuc – Angus MacDonald, originally from 27 Bhataisgeir, who had been in the Boer War.

One of my best sources for oral history in am Bac was the late Seoras Sheoyan – George Stewart. He and his colleagues in the Comunn Eachdraidh there did a tremendous amount of work in gathering local history, though a lot of their material was dissipated when they lost their premises. Although there were other Stewarts in the area, as we shall see

26. George Stewart and Margaret MacDonald at Bac Comann Eachdraidh

27. Clann-nighean an Sgadain

in neighbouring Col, Seoras belonged to an incoming family, deriving from a George Stewart, a fish-curer who came from Banff in the 1750s, from whom he derived the name George.

Another family in the area were Martins, but not, so far as we can trace, the same Martins as the Sealgairean in Tolastadh. According to oral tradition Norman Martin was one of the old soldiers of Uig, whom we mentioned in the first volume of this set, but was killed in action in India. MacIver, the tacksman of Griais, gave his widow and children a site in Gleann Tholastaidh as boundary shepherds, from which the family still have the by-name Buachaille – herd. There are many of their descendants in am Bac area today, and many more in Canada, where part of the family settled in the Eastern Townships of Quebec.

One of these Martins – Domhnall Thormoid Dhomhnaill Bhuachaille – giving evidence to the Napier Commission in 1883, had plans for the improvement of the fishing, on which, like Tolastadh, am Bac depended to supplement the meagre return from the crofts:

> In the place where I live the way the fishing is being prosecuted is sufficient to make an old man of one while he is yet young; for in winter we have to leave our homes for the fishing at ten o'clock at night and on through all the hours of the morning according as the weather will allow. We, then, six of a crew will have to launch a boat over a 100 yards of dry ground, and we have to do the reverse process when we come home again. We have to put a ton of stones into her along with the sailing and fishing material. Now, if we had harbours we could work bigger boats than we have, where we could have greater safety on sea, and that would be less difficult to manage

when we came ashore; and if we had that we could go three times further away to the fishing ground than we can now with the boats we have.

I think that there are various places where it would not be difficult to make a good anchorage, but because there is a fishing station at Gress, I believe that would be as suitable as any. I mean a place of shelter protected by a breakwater, that a boat might enter in all weathers and at all states of the tide. They would not require to be anchored – they could be fastened to a quay within the harbour – sixty or eighty boats perhaps.[41]

A new harbour was eventually built – not at Griais but at Breibhig in Bhataisgeir – and the local fishermen had to argue for years to get the new harbour adjusted so they could use it safely.

It was not just the men who followed the fishing – as the men followed the shoals round the north and east coasts, the women went with them, as gutters, salters and packers. Wick, Peterhead, Fraserburgh, Eyemouth and Yarmouth – clann nighean an sgadain (the herring girls) would be there in the season, and if we cannot find a marriage record for a Lewis couple, these are the places we would look next.

And fishing was not the only type of sailing for the men of Lewis: the merchant navy had its place too, and Lewis men were to be found on ships all over the world – like Alexander Martin ('Fradhlaic') from am Bac, on board the *Port Hardy*:

28. Fradhlaic – Alex Martin

Nuair dh'fhag sinne Auckland 'n dol fodha na h-oidhch'
'S a fhuair sinn fo ordugh na ropan thoirt innt'
'Thainig poidhleat air bord innt' le ordugh bhon chinn
'S gun deanadh e stiuireadh le shuil air an rinn.

Tha nise 'n uair a' tighinn fagas dhol dhan bharaille 'n aird
Gu cumail oirr' faire bho sgaradh an la,
'S nuair bhios mise gam dhalladh aig cabhadh an t-sail
Thoir mo dhurachd-sa dhachaigh gu cailinn 'n fhuilt bhain.[42]

When we left Auckland at nightfall, we got orders to untie the ropes,
a pilot came on board with orders to steer us out to sea. The time is
drawing near for me to go to the crow's nest to watch over her until
dawn; when I am being blinded by the billows, take my greetings
home to the fair-haired girl.

Bhataisgeir (Vatisker)

In Bhataisgeir was a family of Beatons; historically, the Beatons had
been the hereditary physicians of the isles, but the Bhataisgeir family
had a different claim to fame as they were na Piobairean – the pipers.

Rather surprisingly, there were Harris families there too, who came
to Bhataisgeir in the 1820s as boatbuilders – MacLeods and Morrisons.
Neil Morrison came from the Isle of Tarasaigh, and I remember his
great-grandson Murdo telling that the family were known in his youth
as 'Tarasaich Lapach – handless Tarasaich' – a by-name no doubt given
to them by boatbuilding competitors.

A John Murray in Bhataisgeir appears in the Seaforth Papers in a

List of Soldiers now alive, and the representatives of those dead,
belonging to the late 100th Regiment of Foot, who were at the
capture of the Dutch ships in Saldannah Bay in the year 1781.[43]

The capture of the Dutch ships was hardly a glorious achievement.
It was part of the British war against the Dutch East India Company.
Cape of Good Hope belonged to the Dutch at the time, but it was too
strong for the English fleet to take. A Dutch fleet of six merchant ships
were concealed in Saldanha Bay, but an English ship, flying French
colours, had intercepted another ship and learned of the whereabouts of
the Dutch. The English fleet, still flying French flags, entered Saldanha
Bay, and attacked the Dutch, burning some of the ships and taking
others as prizes. Two questions arise – why were the English ships
flying French flags, and what were 24 Lewis soldiers doing on board
the English ships?

A John Murray appears twice in the list, first as representative of his grandfather John Bain and then as representative of his uncle Kenneth Bain. We know from our genealogical records at *Co Leis Thu?* that there was a John Murray of Croft No 20 Bhataisgeir, who was born in about 1786, and was the son of an Alexander Murray – Alasdair Ruairidh Ghobha – and his wife Isabella Bain. I wonder whether she was any relation of the Baynes who rebuilt the church at Griais? Or was she just Iseabail Bhan?

One of the first major emigrations from Lewis was in the 1770s, to Pennsylvania and New York States. There had been a series of years of bad harvests all through the north of Scotland, linked to an eruption of Hecla in Iceland in 1756 and the subsequent ash-cloud, causing *Bliadhna an t-Sneachda Dhubh* – the year of the black snows. At the same time there were many persuasions to emigration, as pointed out by John Knox in his *View of the Highlands* in 1784:

> The Highlanders, who had served in the American War, being, by royal proclamation, entitled to settlements in that extensive country, were desirous that their kindred and friends should partake of their good fortune. Some transmitted their sentiments by letters; others, returning from thence to pay a farewelll visit to their native land, delivered their opinions personally, and all agreed in the enconiums upon the new world. They exhorted their countrymen to exchange their barren heaths for the boundless plains of America; they declaimed upon the softness of the climate, the fertility of the soil, the abundance of provisions, the exemption from taxes, the opulence, ease and luxury of the people.
>
> The Highlanders now first began to look on their native country with contempt, and upon their oppressors with indignation – Shall we, said they, remain in these miserable huts, the objects of derision, without the common necessaries of life, or the prospect of better times? No! We will depart to the great country beyond the ocean, where our labour will be rewarded, and our families comfortably maintained.[44]

One of the emigrant ships of that period was the *Friendship* of Philadelphia, master Thomas Jann. He was recruiting emigrants in Stornoway, and at the same time the Seaforth Estate was trying to dissuade them, to the extent of taking court action to prevent them. This was during the days of the boom in the kelp-industry, and Seaforth was afraid that he would lose too many of his work-force.

Seaforth tried a scare campaign:

> Which Thomas Jann and emissaries employed by him are busy decoying, enlisting, indenting, or otherwise seducing the ignorant

Inhabitants of this Island to emigrate to foreign parts in order, as is believed, to sell and make merchandise of them.[45]

He even claimed that Jann was virtually kidnapping 'Children under Age without the Consent of their Parents'. There were certainly a lot of youngsters on the *Friendship,* but we have to remember at how young an age people began work at that time.

Probably more important to Seaforth:

> by which means the Country is exposed to be drained of useful Inhabitants, and numbers attempted to be carried off by this illicit practice who are under Lease with the proprietor of the Island and his tacksmen's servants who are engaged in actual service and people that are due lawful and just debts, to the manifest loss of the country in general & of the proprietor and lawful creditors in particular.[46]

Among the passenger families were Alexander Campbell from Bhataisgeir, his wife Margaret Morrison, and their children Neil and Isabella.

And like all the other passengers, their reason for leaving was:

> In order to procure a Living abroad, as they were quite destitute of Bread at home.[47]

Like almost all the other emigrants of that date, the Campbells disappear from trace into the wilds of America, especially after the American War of Independence. But who knows who may crop up sometime among the clients of *Seallam!*?

A later emigrant from am Bac was Kenneth MacAulay of Croft No 38, who was among the settlers at Killarney in Manitoba in 1887. A report in November 1889 notes that MacAulay had by then built a double-boarded house with a log extension and a log and turf stable, and had a stock of a yolk of oxen, a cow, a yearling, a calf and two pigs, and had cropped 120 bushels of wheat, 60 bushels of potatoes and 30 loads of hay.

> I am quite satisfied and will have sufficient seed. Other settlers are not so advanced here as we are in less than two years. If half the Island of Lewis would come here, they would be alright.[48]

Others of the emigrants found the transition from being a fisherman in am Bac to becoming a farmer on the limitless prairies too difficult to cope with, and some drifted south to the cities of the United States, or like Neil Munro from No 40 am Bac returned to Lewis – but then he went out as a bachelor!

29. Passenger List of *Friendship* of Philadelphia

Col (Coll)

Col was another farm held by MacIvers – the family gained many good farms in return for their support of the MacKenzies against the old MacLeod chiefs.

The last tacksman was Colin MacIver, who emigrated, with several of his large family, to a farm at Melbourne in the fertile valley of the St Francis River in Quebec. He took some local men with him as farm-workers, but several of them took the chance of free land in the neighbouring hill country, where they formed the nucleus of the later Gaelic-speaking community in Bury and Lingwick Townships.

Col was crofted in the 1820s, the first township in Sgire Bhac to be so divided, but we can be sure that, even previous to this date, a large part of the township would have been occupied by subtenants, with the farm restricted to Col Uarach, on the south side of the river. Even a part of the farm – Gearraidh Ghuirm – was crofted in 1830, mainly for crofters from Borgh on the west-side of Lewis, but this settlement was not successful, and the tenants were cleared in 1843 and the area added back to the farm.

Among the families in Col were Stewarts, who claimed a more aristocratic lineage than those in am Bac. Roderick, last chief of the MacLeods of Lewis, in 1541 married as his second wife Barbara Stewart, daughter of Andrew Stewart, Lord Avondale. As was usual in such cases, some of her relatives were brought across to Lewis to safeguard her rights – which in light of Roderick's reputation, may well have been a very necessary precaution. The Stewarts of Col claim descent from her supporters, and cite the family names of Barbara and Andrew as proof. The first of the family to appear in written records is Andrew Stewart, born in about 1750; very few records exist for Sgire Bhac prior to this date but, as all historians should know, absence of evidence is not evidence of absence! There may not be any proof of the descent, but there is no reason to doubt it either, and oral tradition is a very reliable source in such matters.

A later member of the Stewarts of Col was Murdo Stewart – mac Neill Mhurchaidh Neill (son of Neil of Murdo of Neil) – of No 35 Col. His sister Mary had married Allan MacLeod – mac Chaluim Dhomhnaill – of No 17 Col at the fishings in Shetland, and Neil went with them in 1888 to the Killarney settlement, south of Brandon in Manitoba. Killarney was a station on the newly-built Canadian Pacific Railway, so there was a good market for crops there, as well as paid work for the settlers to supplement the income from their farms.

The Report of 1889 shows that Allan MacLeod had built a double-boarded house 14 ft by 16 ft, packed between boards with soil, etc., with

30. Murdo Stewart

a double-boarded roof with tar paper and a log and turf stable. He had stock of one yoke of oxen, one cow, one yearling, one calf, two pigs and a few fowls, and had taken off crops of 48 bushels of wheat from 9 acres, 19 bags of potatoes from 5 acres sown, and 8 loads of hay.

Murdo Stewart had married Isabella Martin – ni'n Dhomhnaill Thormoid Dhomhnaill Bhuachaille – of No 63 am Bac soon after arriving in Manitoba, and he was living on his own homestead, with 5½ acres ploughed and a house erected, value $55.[49]

Many of the settlers were young fishermen with little experience of crofting, never mind farming, and many of them are said to have had a hard time settling in the Prairie environment – but to judge from his picture, Murdo Stewart never had a hard time in his life! The photograph was supplied to us by his great-grand-daughter Lois Klaasen, and we have used it ever since as part of our exhibition at *Seallam!* in an Taobh Tuath – it is such a happy picture!

We included it in our exhibit for the opening of *Seallam!* in 2000, and we had just finished the official opening and were tidying up when a Canadian couple arrived and asked if they could have a quick look around. The lady came in, took one look at his photo and cried 'But that's great-aunt Isabel's husband' – and so it was!

Another ancient branch of the MacLeods in Col are the Baranntaich.

The early written records for Lewis are of course all written in English, with clerks doing their best to write down phonetically what Gaelic-speakers said to them. So the Baranntaich appear under many guises – from 'Baron' to 'MacWarrant'. It is not until the 1820s that the Baranntaich start to use the MacLeod surname, nor is it known why the change of name was made then or by whom.

Another such change of name is that of the Portairean. Portair in Gaelic could refer to a ferryman, or perhaps more accurately the person in charge of a ferry. Murchadh mac a' Phortair in Col was married to a daughter of Alexander MacIver, tacksman of Tolastadh, so the family would have been of some consequence. They appear in records as 'MacPhortair' or even 'Forster' before settling in the 1820s as MacDonalds.

Col Uarach – Upper Coll – was a farm until the Leverhulme years, when it fell within the attention of the land-raiders. This story has been told many times before, from varying points of view, and most recently – and very fairly – by Roger Hutchison, in his *The Soap Man*. Lord Leverhulme, who had recently purchased the island, had ambitious – some say over-ambitious – plans for reforming the economy of Lewis, and these included the retention of the farms of Griais and Col Uarach as a supply of milk to Steornabhagh. The land-raiders, recently returned from the war, wanted the farms split up into crofts for themselves. The arguments on the land question are still politically highly charged, but perhaps a fair assessment comes from Colin MacDonald, who was involved as an official of the Board of Agriculture.

> His failure to understand and meet the views of the people led to the failure of all his projects. A little mutual compromise would have enabled both sides to attain, substantially, their particular ambitions. But Lord Leverhulme refused to compromise until the very end – and then it was too late.[50]

Col Uarach was divided into 42 crofts, on either side of the road to Col itself, and including the former lands of Gearraidh Ghuirm, though that name has now been transferred to a nearby housing development.

Tunga & Aird Thunga (Tong & Aird Tong)

Although Tunga and Aird Thunga now run into each other, they were at one time two different townships with very different histories. Aird Thunga was much the older, and even when crofting came there in the early 1800s, Aird Thunga retained its own individuality, as most of the crofts had pieces of land in different parts of the township.

Among the early families in Aird Thunga were Sliochd a' Chaiptein –

the people of the captain – one of the many branches of MacLeods. There are many stories about how they got the name, including one deriving them from a Swedish captain whose ship was wrecked off the coast. I prefer the story that links them to Raasay, and the harrying of that island by Government forces after the defeat of Culloden. We know that some families fled from Raasay and came to Lewis at this time, and I suspect that Sliochd a' Chaiptein were followers of Captain Malcolm MacLeod of Eyre, who had been deeply involved in the Rebellion, on behalf of his uncle, the chief of Raasay.

Angus MacLeod of Aird Thunga, giving evidence to the Napier Commission:

> I have seen my mother selling grain to the distillery here and paying the rent with it, and selling butter at 6d the lb and cheese at 2½ d the lb. And now, since the population has become increased, what I see is that much of the food of the people has to be brought from other countries, and their kitchen also. Undoubtedly, much money comes into the country now that did not when I was young. The herring fishery, which did not exist then, brings money to us, and the Royal Naval Reserve brings money into the country. But there is none of the money that is in these ways brought into the country but must be expended upon food brought into it from other places, instead of the food that was produced in the country before.[51]

I remember as a youngster visiting Murdo Morrison in Troon. He was of the Tarasaich Lapach we mentioned in Bhataisgeir, but his grandfather, also Murdo, was drowned as a young man coming back from Wick in 1849 with a cargo of flagstones, and his widow had returned to her family's croft in Tunga. The older Murdo may have died young, but his grandson certainly did not – he lived till the age of 103 – and I remember him gleefully pointing out that he enjoyed a pension for more years than he had been working as a school inspector!

Tunga itself – more accurately Druim Thunga – was a much more recent settlement. Until the 1820s it had been an outlying part of Tunga Farm, which at that time was held as a glebe by the minister of Steornabhagh. When the little townships of Buthainis and Ailtinis on the south side of Loch Sealg in na Lochan were cleared, their people were relocated on new sites on Druim Thunga.

Mr Craig, who visited the site in 1828 was very scathing about it:

> Until I saw the actual situations of the new lotters in the Aird of Tong I had no idea of the great hardship and privation that the poor people endure who are forced into new allotments, without matters being previously arranged for their moving. The situation of the

new lotters at Aird of Tong, at this moment, beggars description. It is worse than anything I saw in Donegal, where I always considered human wretchedness to have reached its acme. The roofs of the present hovels on the Estate might, in general, stand for a few years if they were let alone, but the act of taking them down breaks and injures them so much that they are of comparatively little value in roofing their new homes – fresh timber is therefore necessary, and the exorbitant price demanded is so great as to more than exhaust their means . . . To erect their cabins, the sward has been taken off the whole line of the intended road, which has now become a morass, dangerous for both man and beast to set their foot upon; how the children contrive out and in of their cabins baffles my comprehension, for the men have literally to step up to the knee in mud, the moment they quit their threshold.[52]

However, the crofts there were rented in 1826 at around £3 each, which was high for a croft in this area, and the area is now looked on as good agricultural land. Perhaps Craig went there after a particularly wet period, or perhaps like many other visitors he had a tendency to exaggerate. On the other hand, five of the original crofters left within ten years, so perhaps the first few years of trying to break in peat-land were pretty desperate for crofters used to the free-draining hills and valleys of Loch Sealg.

Like most of the crofters in the south end of the Pairc, the crofters of Buthanis and Ailtinis had come originally from Harris; indeed the factor of Lewis reacted to complaints by pointing out that 'they being Harris people should and must be content with what they are given'. Among them were the brothers Campbell – John and Colin – who led the local opposition to the doctrines of their non-evangelical minister, Alexander Simpson at Ceos.

One day affairs came to a height. It was the communion day, and when he spoke of salvation depending entirely on men's friendliness and kindliness, four protestors rose up and called him a murderer of souls, and walked out of the church. The upshot was a law case. The men were prosecuted in the Sheriff Court and lodged as criminals in Dingwall Prison. When the Dingwall Prison was opened and they walked out they were conveyed in triumph to the Highland Capital and arrayed in new suits, Many other tokens of regard and admiration were showered on them.[53]

Most of the records of these days refer to the men of the times, but Tunga has at least one record of a woman who made a name in her own right. She was Mrs Isabella Thomson, and her story was published in *Tong – the Story of a Lewis Village.*

31. Tunga Local History Society

This was one of the earliest projects on which I worked along with a local historical society – the term Comunn Eachdraidh hadn't yet been invented! I made many good friends there, like the late Miss Morag Smith, Kenneth MacLennan and John Alex MacKay, and their knowledge of local oral tradition combined with my own knowledge of early written records was used to build up a most interesting book. The Tong book includes an article on Mrs Isabella Thomson, and although it is perhaps rather larger an extract than one would normally take from another publication, the story deserves re-telling in full, and the Tong book has been unavailable for many years.

I was married at Stornoway on the 27th April 1877. My husband, having come home from Canada on a visit and having to return almost immediately afterwards, I was exceeding anxious to accompany him on his return. The country at this time was very unsettled – the Indians had been put into a state of unrest, by raids and other troubles, and I was strongly advised not to accompany my husband out there.

Dr R Millar, who was the agent for the Hudson Bay Company at Stornoway, did all he could to prevent me, telling me that the cold in Western Canada was most severe in winter and that the heat of summer would be very trying for one like me. Still, my husband had been out for thirteen years, he was well acquainted with the country, he understood the Indians, their language and their customs, so I was not a bit afraid to venture. However, much against my will, and in no way discouraged, I was forced to forego my project, and it was three years afterwards before I got away.

My people redoubled their efforts to dissuade me from going – telling me that I would surely be killed by the Indians, and that my husband would be killed on my account. My mother, especially, gathered all the wild rumours she could about Indians and such like, but I would listen to no-one, my mind was made up, and go I must.

In the middle of April, I embarked on the ss *Clansman* on a Monday and arrived at Glasgow on Thursday, intending to sail from Glasgow on the following Saturday. But as I had hardly any English, and as I did not know any Gaelic-speaking people going by that boat, a friend advised me to wait for a week. A boat with a Gaelic-speaking Captain (Captain Maclean, afterwards provost of Govan) was due to sail in a week, and my friend spoke to the captain on my account. Every afternoon during our voyage, the captain sought me out and greatly encouraged me for my venture. Also before the voyage came to an end at Quebec, he sought out among the passengers a Gaelic-speaking man by the name of MacKay, from Kintail, who was going to Winnipeg to search for work.

The Captain entrusted me to this man's care, and while he was of great service to me as interpreter, I was at the same time useful to him. He had sent out his money to Winnipeg in advance, under the impression that his ocean ticket supplied him with everything he needed on the train journey as well as on sea. This, of course, was not the case, but as I was well provided with funds, I was able to see us both through.

After a short stay at Quebec, we entrained for Winnipeg, but, as some sections of the CPR had not yet been finished on the north side of the Great Lakes, we had to go through the United States. Leaving Quebec in the early morning by the Grand Trunk Railway, our route lay upland, through Montreal, Toronto, Missouri, Minnesota and Dakota – never once leaving the train from the time we entrained at Quebec until we arrived at Winnipeg.

On my arrival there, I was disappointed at not finding anyone meeting me, and as Fort Garry (the headquarters of the Hudson Bay Company) was nearly two miles from the railway station, I got the Kintail man to accompany me to the Company's office, where I called on Mr Christie and found him most considerate.

32. Upper Fort Garry

He told me that my husband was on duty out on the lake at Fort Alexander and would be back in a day or two. In the meantime he placed me in an hotel close to Fort Garry, and told me to want for nothing as he would arrange everything for my comfort.

With my husband was his cousin John MacInnes from Tong, and Angus Morrison from Stornoway. The latter was then the oldest pilot on Lake Winnipeg and second in command of the Company's steamer which was to take us out on Lake Winnipeg to the mouth of the Saskatchewan River.

Our meeting was a most happy one, and for a week we had an exceptionally fine time of it, meeting the many Stornoway and Lewis men who came to see me and enquire about the Old Country and the folk at home. These were all retired servants of the Hudson Bay Company, and they told me that there were no Stornoway or Lewis women in Winnipeg at that time, at the same time impressing on me that my adventure was only beginning then – a truth which I found out for myself.

Thus in the beginning of June 1880, we boarded the steamer *Colville* of the Hudson Bay Company, with Angus Morrison second in command and John MacInnes, my husband's cousin as steward, and began to descend the Red River. The view as we passed down by Kildonan and St Andrews was magnificent – pretty cottages nestling in sweet glades on each side of the river and a charming countryside stretching away on either side. I was told that the settlers who lived there were descendants of Gaelic-speaking people brought out from Sutherlandshire by Lord Selkirk many years before.

In the evening we arrived at Stone Fort, a large square closed in by walls twelve feet high and most strongly built of stone and lime. This enclosure was one of the wonders of the Hudson Bay territory, being very imposing and picturesque, and to me exceedingly interesting as it was the work of a Stornoway man of the name of MacRae, from Melbost.

Here, at Stone Fort, some goods were taken on board for use in the Northern Department's trade, and we then passed down the river to Selkirk, where most of the goods for the outlying districts were shipped.

Now was hustle and bustle loading the *Colville* working day and night until she was loaded down to a dangerous point according to Angus Morrison, and he knew the River and Lake Winnipeg better than anyone, but at last all was ready and we left Selkirk for the Lake about five miles distant.

There was a strong breeze blowing from the west as we got to the mouth of the Red River, and this had the effect of driving the water in a measure to the other end of the lake. The mouth of the river had not then been deepened or dragged, and the steamer often ran aground, making it impossible to get out on to the Lake. We were in a fix, and there was nothing for it but to turn back to the river, discharge part of the cargo, and try again.

After getting rid of some stores, we tried again, and were successful, getting on to the waters of the Lake, and passing along the North Side to the mouth of the Saskatchewan River. But we could only get two miles up the river, for we were told the *Colville* could get no further owing to an obstruction called the Grand Rapids and that the *Colville* had to return to Selkirk. There was a portage of two miles to the other side of the rapids, and all the goods were carried this distance to where a large Company steamer, the *North Castle*, was going up the Saskatchewan River.

Two days later we boarded the steamer and began to ascend through Cedar Lake, Moose Lake, La Passe, Cumberland Fort and Fort-a-la-Corne, above which the Saskatchewan forks into two branches. We took the north branch, and after a while came to Prince Albert where a few small houses could be seen scattered here and there. I was told that there was to be a town there soon, but as yet there was little appearance of it.

It took us a long time to get from the Rapids to this place, as the river was full of sandbanks and the current was very swift and strong, while huge pine trees, some 90 and 100 feet long, fallen from the river bank and floating downstream, made the going very difficult.

From Prince Albert we came to the great Fort Carlton, the capital of the North West Territories, where all the chief factors and traders from the far west MacKenzie River District, the Athabasca District, and the Isle-a-la-Crosse District came every summer to hold counsel as to how to carry on the work of the following winter. Fort Carlton was a formidable place, built of solid logs to a height of twenty feet all round, so as to protect the white traders from the savage attacks of the Indians. I was frightened on being shown the marks of the lead balls fired into the Fort by Indians in olden times.

Here my husband's Chief Deputy, Mr R Ross MacFarlane, a Stornoway man, and a man of high distinction in the district, came to see me and complimented me on my courage in venturing far west. He said that, although I had a hard part of my journey still in front of me, he was not a bit afraid that I would not accomplish the rest as well. And as he had had a hand in allowing me to come so far, he was to ask me to undertake a delicate mission for him – no less than to take a cage of six tame hens and a cock to Fort Chipewyan, a distance by the route we would take of, I was told, 1,500 miles.

I was to get a pony and trap for myself, and all the requirements for the hens were to be given to me, while carters and boatmen would be given instructions to assist me at all times when necessary. We were here on the border of civilisation and for the rest of our journey there would be no trains or steamers, our only means of travel would be by carts and York flat boats.

This, then, was the third stage of my journey, and preparations had to be made for a rough trip, the like of which I never so much as dreamt of.

Flint-lock guns had to be cleared out; powder and shot to be got; tents, poles, pegs; tea and sugar, kettles and pans had to be got ready, axes had to be sharpened and handled, and innumerable things had to be made ready for this part of the trip. As I faced this wild unknown I felt a quiver of uncertainty for the first time, and saw the wisdom of those who tried to dissuade me from entering the Wild West, but I was as determined as ever to go.

We crossed the river by flat boat, and struck due north, our train consisting of ten carts all in charge of a Red River District man, William Sinclair, who knew every part of the route.

Next morning we were off! The drivers shouted and laughed as they yoked the animals to the carts and fixed the baggage up, for everything had to be secure.

My place was in the rear with my pony and trap, and this enabled me to see the country on every side – wide, undulating country not very thickly wooded, but covered with the richest vegetation. For seven days we trekked through this land of plenty, stopping for

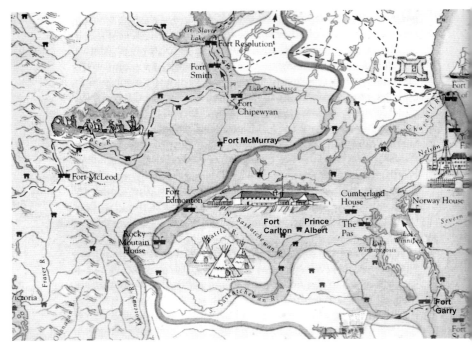

33. Detail from Map of Hudson's Bay Territories

dinner amid a cheerfulness and good fellowship which to me was good to see. There was plenty of game to be got – wild swan, wild duck, moose, beaver, and all sorts, so that we were never short of fresh provisions.

After seven days, we came to Green Lake, where we met six boats that were ready to carry us across the Lake. We then went down the Green Lake River, through Waterhen Lake and River to Isle-a-la-Cross Lake, Deep River, White Lake, Buffalo River and Lake, Methie River and Lake, and from there to the long portage called the Methie Portage. Here we were at the highest point of land and the Methie Portage is a connection between the water that falls into Hudson Bay (through the English and Churchill Rivers) and the water that falls into the Arctic Ocean (through the Clear Water, Athabasca, and MacKenzie Rivers).

This portage of twelve to fourteen miles took us a whole day to cross without horses and carts, and at evening we camped on fine high ground overlooking the Clearwater River. The view was extremely fine as far as Fort McMurray – the background of the

34. 'On the River' by Frances Anne Hopkins

mountains and the plains with the occasional patch of woodland forming a lovely picture.

Here again the York boats were ready to take us down to Fort Chipewyan, my destination, and they were in charge of a middle-aged French Canadian who knew his work well – he was called the Guide of the Brigade.

We left the long portage early in the morning, and I was placed with my charge in the Guide's boat. We were going downstream rapidly, gliding smoothly over the surface until in the afternoon there was a call from the guide for all the boats to land, and for all the steersmen to come to his boat for a consultation.

I saw that something unusual was going to happen, for all the boatsmen were stripping themselves to the very skins, and tying handkerchiefs round their heads. All the time, I could hear a loud, dull roar which seemed very terrifying but which, I was told, was caused by falling water. We were in fact, to run the Rapids.

The guide told the steersmen that every man had to do his part as he was told, the boats were to keep a certain distance from one another, and if any mishap were to befall any boat, all other boats coming behind were to go to her assistance as those in front could not turn back in the rapid current.

My husband, who had passed several times through these rapids and who understood all that the people were saying, told me all this, and at the same time, told me to fear nothing, as the going was perfectly safe.

Soon we pushed off from land, and in a short while the roar of the falls could be heard growing louder and louder as we rapidly approached the ledge. Before coming to the larger falls there were occasional smaller falls which the boats ran down, giving the boatmen a most exciting time as they rowed with all their might on one side of the boat and backed water on the other side, thus causing the boat to spin like a top in midstream.

All this time the roar of the cascade was terrific, and it was impossible to hear a word unless spoken at the top of a person's voice. The spray from this immense body of water falling 70 to 80 feet right down, then high above the trees on either side, and at first I thought the boats were going to shoot down this awful drop, which, of course, no-one could do and live.

The boats were landed above the big fall, all the cargo was carried by the men across a small neck of land in front, and the boats were dragged ashore and pulled across a small strip of land into the water below the great falls and so into smoother water behind.

It was a long time before I forgot the look and the roar of that giant fall or the majestic sight it presented to me when I viewed it for the first time. On our way down to Fort McMurray we passed as many as five of these rapids and at each one the cargo was taken out of the boat and carried across by the men.

It was a wonderful experience and a delightful sensation to me as the empty boats ran down the rapids towards Fort McMurray where the Clearwater River joins the Athabasca River. I was told I was the first Scotch woman, and I am certain that I was the first Lewis one, that got down these rivers, for although at all these trading forts and stations, Lewismen were everywhere in evidence, no Lewis women were to be met anywhere.

We left Fort McMurray after landing supplies for the next winter, passed down the Athabasca River to the lake of that name, crossed the end of Lake Athabasca and arrived in the first week of September at my destination – Fort Chipewyan in the North West Territories,

35. Fort Chipewyan

established by the famous traveller Sir Alexander MacKenzie, a Stornoway Man.

The Deputy Governor, Mr R R MacFarlane, who had arrived by canoe before us, came to see me and congratulated me on my success in coming through so many hardships – and in bringing the cage of hens safe and sound to Fort Chipewyan.[54]

An intrepid woman indeed! Isabella was a daughter of Alexander MacIver of Col, whose grandfather John MacIver had been a soldier in the Dutch East Indies in the early years of the Napoleonic Wars – so between them they had pretty well circled the world! One reason that she could not go to Canada at first was that she was expecting a daughter, Marion. As soon as Marion could be left with relatives, off Isabella went, and she and James Thomson – mac Alasdair Sheumais of No 15 Tunga – had four children in Canada, before returning home in 1889 and having a further six children.

Isabella Thomson's story also illustrates the extent to which Lewis men were involved in the Hudson's Bay Company.

In the late 1700s Orkney was the main source of employees for the Hudson's Bay Company, but in the early 1800s this changed to Steornabhagh. There were actually two rival companies recruiting there – the Hudson's Bay Company and the North-West Company, whose representatives competed and even came to blows in Steornabhagh harbour. In 1811 as many as one hundred and nine recruits sailed from Steornabhagh for a three-year tour of duty with the Company. Some returned with cash in their pockets, some, as we saw in Tolastadh, with wives and families, and others remained in Canada for the rest of their days. Little wonder that the north-west of Canada is full of Scottish descendants and Scottish place-names.

Tunga Farm was at one time the glebe of the church in Steornabhagh.

Rev. John Cameron found this less than convenient. He had to preach three Sundays in Stornoway, one in Knock and one in Back.

He was therefore frequently absent from his Stornoway pulpit. When the Hon. Mrs MacKenzie lodged a complaint, he gave her an account of some of the hardships he had to face due to the distance of his manse in Tong from the church in Stornoway. He explained how he often risked the lives of himself and his family by crossing the Tong sands to Stornoway, but in future he would only do this when tide was out and the sands dry. Many times he had gone to Stornoway on a winter's morning before dawn, and returned near midnight, having had to await the turn of the tide. Often the sea would be in the box of his cart, and if he preached hurriedly, this was to finish his sermon to catch the tide. He also suggested that if her Ladyship had seen the many poor creatures, male and female, wading through the Laxdale and Tong rivers, summer and winter, on their way to and from church, she would have made a road from Tong to Stornoway.

The glebe is eight acres arable in extent, with a little rugged wet, deep, mossy moor. The present glebe is an excambed one; the former glebe and manse were in Stornoway. The present glebe at Tong was designated in 1759; by that designation the grass glebe alone should support six cows coupled and their followers till four years old, with four horses, making at least thirty head of cattle and horses. But the glebe enjoyed by the present incumbent cannot support one-half of that number.[55]

Rev. John Cameron also tells how:

In shallow water on the sands of Tong, by the motion of my horse's feet, beautiful golden stars, of the size of half-a-crown, are made to float on the surface for a few seconds; these disappear and are succeeded by others, often to the terror of the animal. It is probable these appearances arise from the decaying particles of fish which float on the surface; and when the water is troubled, then escaping forms a globule, which emits a phosphorescent light before it bursts.[56]

In 1854 the glebe moved back to Steornabhagh, and the glebe in Tunga became a farm once again, leased first to an Alexander Grant and later to the Newalls of Tolastadh. Part of the farm was raided in the agitation after the First World War, and became the crofts of Pairc Thunga.

W Anderson Smith noted that:

Near the Pool of Tongue is the tract of Tussock Grass, acclimatised from the Falkland Isles, which seems to have found a congenial home.[57]

I found this fascinating, as although there was much commerce between Lewis and the Falklands in the 1890s and early 1900s, *Lewsiana* was published in 1875. What was the link between the Falklands and Lewis then?

I found the answer, in of all places a *Report on the Outer Hebrides by the Highland Relief Board* in 1849:

Tussack grass, which had lately been introduced into Great Britain from the Falkland Islands, through the enterprise of Dr. Hooker, and which seems to thrive best in mossy land, in a moist climate, and near the sea, was happily brought to this island for cultivation by Mr Smith of Deanston. Mr Mathieson has now got a large plot of it planted out, near the sea, in the bay of Stornoway, which gives every promise of success, and which, should it realise, it will greatly enhance the value of this extensive property; and not of this only, but of many large and unproductive tracts in the Western Islands.[58]

The only question left now is, who was Dr Hooker?

And then I found the answer to that too – he was a botanist on Ross's Antarctic Voyage with *Erebus* and *Terror* in 1839–43, before their fateful voyage into the Arctic with Franklin.

And as always when you have tracked down a problem to its source, it keeps cropping up:

> Proceeded to the Tussac Grass at Holm that transplanted last season seems to be doing very well. The old grass is now being cut and used in feeding the stock at Holm and is much relished – according to John Munro MacKenzie in his Diary 1851.[59]

Just to the east of Tunga is the Blackwater River, flowing through the Gleann Dubh, where there was a camp of Travellers. The Travellers were a community to themselves, with little link to the rest of the island people. It is sometimes claimed they were descended from families from Appin and Duror in Argyll, who, when the Campbells took over their territory, took to the travelling life. Certainly their most common names, Stewart and Drummond, could be linked to that area. They were good at training horses, and the men made much of their livelihood from ploughing for neighbouring crofters and farmers and from doing tinsmith work, which the women sold around the houses. The travelling women were the precursors of the later Pakistani pedlars, going around the houses with their *mailead* – shawls filled with a variety of little things useful for the house that would save the housewife from having to go to a shop. And if they were given to a bit of palm-reading, that only added a bit of fun to a day's work.

The travellers were hardy; they had to be to exist, as Professor Donald Macleod remembered from his youth in Lacasdal:

> We played football all day, every day. Even the tinkers played. Nothing remarkable about that, you might think, but there was; they had no boots. Many of us had horrendous boots, the soles covered in tacks or studs to prolong the life of the leather, and the toes and heels tipped with steel plates. They were probably designed for miners, but they would have done for divers. It was hazardous to be involved in any tackle involving such footware. To be involved barefoot would seem suicidal. But the tinkers thought nothing of it. They were brilliant and fearless footballers, and had a precociousness which always puzzled me because it never came to anything.[60]

Perhaps one reason for this was their constant travelling, making it difficult to have any continuity in their life, and it would not have been helped by the attitude of the authorities, who looked on the travellers as different – which they were – and inferior – which they were not. I remember noticing from the registers how many traveller couples were married in Harris compared with Lewis, to be told that it was because many of the Lewis ministers refused to marry them – and then complained that they had illegitimate children!

PART 2 – MU THIMCHEALL STEORNABHAIGH (AROUND STORNOWAY)

This is not so much an area in itself as one which does not fit in with anywhere else. Nowadays it is largely suburban, but nonetheless contains crofting communities. These were always different from the more rural areas in their proximity to markets and employment in Steornabhagh. The crofts are in general much smaller, and much less important to the economy of their tenants.

We begin in Lacasdal with its satellite townships, then head to the west of Steornabhagh itself, past the War Memorial on Cnoc nan Uan, so placed as to be within sight of parts of all four parishes in Lewis (and still not too far from Steornabhagh itself!).

Then we head through the suburbs of Maryhill and Marybank, along the edge of the Gearraidh Cruaidh – Castle Grounds – largely planted on imported soil by Sir James Matheson as policies for his Lews

36. The Lewis War Memorial

Castle, but allowed to decay for many years until recent work to undo the past neglect. Then we head west into the moors where the crofters of an Rubha had their summer grazings, on the boundary with Sgire nan Loch.

From there we go back to the shore and head east along the shore of Loch a Tuath to Mealabost and the Uidh.

Lacasdal (Laxdale area)

Lacasdal is like a spider sitting on the Lacasdal Bridge with legs running in all directions into the different townships. It is now primarily a suburb of Steornabhagh, which is only fitting since the townships there were formed as an early 'overspill' from the town. There were a few houses there in the early 1800s, but the major settlement there dates from the 1850s.

In the 1800s the Bayhead area to the north of Steornabhagh proper – the Manor Park area today – consisted of two main streets, Mill Street and Barvas Road. The occupiers of the houses were landless cottars, and although some were tradesmen, there were a great many paupers also. The area was pretty much a slum, as we will see when we come to look at the town and its history.

In the 1850s Sir James Matheson decided to do something about the slum. He was genuinely a benefactor, and besides he can hardly have relished a slum right beside his entrance to Lews Castle!

Up to 50 new crofts were made in 6 townships in the Lacasdal area – Beinn na Saighde, Giubhairsiadar, Lacasdal itself, Lacasdal Lane, Newvalley and Newmarket, and let to Bayhead tenants capable of stocking them (and paying the rent!). For some who could not afford a croft, a row of houses was built at Widows' Row.

Lacasdal area developed as crofts for tradesmen working in Steornabhagh. Masons and carters seem particularly to have thrived there. One family of masons had come from Bearnaraigh na Hearadh – Munros by name, though in Bearnaraigh they had been MacAndy, and in Lewis better known by the nickname of one of the family: the Pongos!

Newmarket township proper runs along the north side of the Lacasdal River, though the Newmarket croft numbers continue through Beinn na Saighde on the Barabhas Road, and along the Tunga Road. Thereafter the numbers were allocated according to the date of application, haphazard through the area – which must be a nightmare for a new postman.

Newvalley is on the southern side of Lacasdal River, and boasts its own archaeological site:

On the summit of the broad ridge Cnoc an t-Sagairt between Newvalley and the River, at an elevation of 200' above sea-level, and commanding an extensive prospect over the Eye Peninsula and the Minch to the east, are three prostrate pillar stones, the remains of a stone circle, which judging from the present position, must have had a diameter of about 50 yards.[61]

The problem with Cnoc an t-Sagairt and all the other pre-Iron Age sites in Lewis is that the change in climate in about 1000 BC, and the subsequent dampness, encouraged the growth of peat. Between five and six feet of peat were cut away from the Calanais stones to reach their original ground level, and who knows how many other early sites in Lewis are disguised or even completely hidden under the peat.

The Lacasdal River rises in the southern slopes of Beanntan Bharabhais and flows down past Hogaraid to the shore at Lacasdal. Only a dilapidated sheep-fank remains of the shepherds' stance at Hogaraid, and the whole area is in a disgraceful state of litter blown in from the nearby council dump. In its day Hogaraid was the northernmost stance of the common grazings for the district of an Rubha, though these are little used today.

From Hogaraid, the Lacasdal River flows east between Newmarket and Newvalley. Lacasdal is Norse for salmon valley, but it is a long time since there were many salmon there. In its day, however, it was a good source of lesser fish – especially for the local boys like Calum Smith:

> I would disturb the fish by thumping on the bank, and as the startled fish moved I watched where they went. I then waited patiently, giving them time to settle, before moving slowly and quietly into position, trying not to create any disturbing vibration of the bank. Lying prone on the bank the sleeve of my jersey would be rolled up to the shoulder, and the arm lowered silently into the water behind the fish. The hand was then brought into position over the tail and moved gently towards the gills (which were opening and closing rhythmically as the trout 'breathed'), with the thumb on one side and the fingers on the other, just, but only just, touching the fish. Then, timing the movement of the hand to the movement of the gills, the thumb and finger were inserted and with a flick of the wrist and a snatch of the elbow it was on the bank. I landed sea trout and brown trout by this method.[62]

In a pivotal position in Lacasdal are the school, the Community Hall, and the Lacasdal Bridge – a road bottleneck which the Comhairle have been trying to solve for many years, still without success.

Giubhairsiadar and Lacasdal Lane, and the old Widows' Row are to the east of the main road. On the side of the main road itself is Lacasdal Well, or Tobair an Righ – the King's Well – since King Edward VII had a drink of water from it on his way past in 1902, though judging from his reputation that must have been quite a change for him! On the other side of the road was the house of Alexander Morrison, better known as the Craggan, famous locally for the hard biscuits from his bakery.

On the hill behind Lacasdal was the old market stance, referred to in both Statistical Accounts:

> Near to Stornoway there is an annual tryst for cattle, where some hundreds are bought and exported, at from £1.10s to £3 a head. Beef is sold in Stornoway from 1½d to 3d per lb; mutton 5s and 6s per wedder; sheep 3s, 4s, and 4s 6d each; lambs, 1s 8d and 2s each; butter, 12s and 14s per stone; cheese, 4s and 5s per stone; veals, 2s 6d each, pork 2d per lib; fowls, 4d a cock and 6d a hen; ducks, 6d and 8d; geese, 1s 6d and 2s.[63]

> Near Stornoway there is a square mile of moor inclosed for an annual tryst or cattle market, where several thousand head of cattle are exposed for sale, and two thousand at least change owners, in two days. The prices and demand depend on the southern markets. From 20 to 30 drovers or cattle-dealers come from the mainland and some from England. The market or tryst is always held on the second Wednesday of July annually, by advertisement; and the packet waits to bring purchasers across the Minch.[64]

Murdo MacFarlane – Bard Mhealaboist – has a poem about his own memories of the Drobh:

> Air chomhnard Mhanitoba
> Gur bronach mis' an drasd,
> 'S gur 'n diugh Di-mairt na Drobh ac'
> An Steornabhagh mo ghraidh!
> B'e sud la mor ar solais
> An Leodhas thar gach la!
> 'N diugh 'g urachadh na h-oige
> Le goraich dhomhsa tha!

> Ged tha eadar mis' is i
> Tri mile mile 's corr,
> Gidheadh le m' inntinn chi mi
> Gach ni am Beinn-na-Drobh;
> Chluinn geum a' chruidh air thaodan,
> Am fonn tha sean is og,
> Is chi mi 'n drobhair cliceach
> Sior stri mu phris nam bo.

37. An Drobh – The Market

Nis cuin a dheannain d' fhagail-sa.
O arain chaileir chridh'.
'S nach molainn ann am dhan thu
'S nach molainn thu gun dith?
'S e leac dhiot rium a chordadh
Le d' uachdar milis min,
'S gur airidh thu 's gur h-iomchuidh
Air ait' aig bord an righ![65]

On the plains of Manitoba I am feeling sad, as this is Tuesday of
the drobh in my beloved Steornabhagh! That was the joyful day in
Leodhas over any other! Today reviving memories of youth for me.
Although there are three thousand miles between me and the drobh,
in my mind I can see every happening at Beinn na Droibh; I hear
the lowing of the cattle on their tethers, a tune both old and new,
and I can see the wily drover, haggling over the price of the cows.
How could I leave you out, O tasty gingerbread, and that I would
not praise you in my song and not praise you forever? I would love a
slice of you with your smooth sweet surface, and worthy are you of
a place at the King's table!

Aran-cridhe na droibh was a particularly sticky type of gingerbread,
whose recipe is strictly guarded by those fortunate enough to have it,
including my own Chris, handed down from her mother.

To the east of Lacasdal, almost on the shore, was the little township
of Gearraidh Sgoir. Little remains of it now – just a few ruins and a
clump of gorse bushes.

Marybank

South-west of Beinn na Droibh, and skirting the Castle Grounds, we come to the recent 'suburbs' of Maryhill and Marybank. In Marybank lived my great friend Angus Macleod – Ease – of Calbost, and in the years I lived in Steornabhagh, I wore a path through the Castle Grounds to his house, where he and I spent many a night working on our records of the families of South Lochs, many of which have been preserved in the Angus Macleod archive, now at Rubh' an Fhithich in Cearsiadar (Angus himself would never have called it Ravenspoint!). Angus and I could never agree on the politics of Island history, but we shared a determination that facts had to be ascertained first, and opinions could then follow later.

South again of Marybank the River Grioda runs on its way from the southern slopes of Beanntan Bharabhais to its mouth in the Steornabhagh Harbour. On its banks, just beside the present bridge on the main road to Harris, was the Lewis Chemical Works, another of the industrial experiments by which Sir James Matheson hoped to make an income from Lewis, and one which, like most of the others, failed through bad management.

A brief report on the Chemical Works was written by Donald Morison, production foreman at the works, and published by the Scottish History Society.

> The Distillation of Hydrocarbon oil from the Peat was first conceived by Henry Caunter, a gentleman of extensive Knowledge and sanguine temperment, possessed with an ardent desire to Therorise and experiment with the hope of Making a descovery hitherto unknown to the Arts and Sciences. Mr Caunter associated with him James McFaden, a Tinsmith then resideing at Stornoway, Who acted as Gas and Water Manager, Plumber and Fishing-Net Barker and clock repairer. They commenced operations by fitting up an apparatus for experimenting on the Distillation of Peat at the side of a Fish Pond in the Vicinity of the Lewis Castle, where soon the discovery was made that the Distillation of peat was deadly to Fish in the Pond.
>
> For about Two years various changes and alterations from time to time was done on the apparatus, when by patience and perseverance, about half a Ton of Peat Tar (Crude Hydrocarbon) was gathered from the Distilation of the Peat Gases. Mr Caunter could go no farther, That is to distill the Peat Tar into refined oils and Parifine. Which in the beginning of 1859 led Sir James Mathison to bring Dr B Hariot Paul, an eminent London Analyst and chemist to experiment and Analyze the Peat Tar.

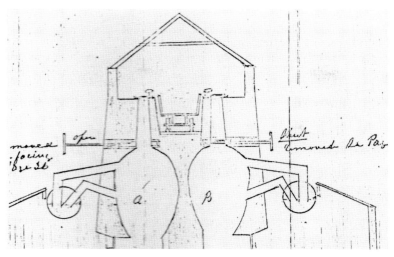

38. Diagram of Condensers at Paraffin Works

The results of Dr Paul's Analysis was so promising for the profitable Utilization of the Lewis Peat Bogs that Sir James Matheson commissioned Dr Paul to superintend the erection of Large Works for the Distilation of the Hydrocarbon oils etc. from Peats. In September 1860 All being ready the Kiln Furneces was kindled for first trial. The result of this Manner of Kindling the Furneces was, that an hour after Dr Paul left the works a Fearful Explosion took place.

The works lurched from crisis to crisis, and eventually a distillery was built – but in Garrabost, not at the works, and a light railway was built connecting them. When they were finally successful in distilling something commercial – Ligoulene or Lamp Oil – they found that the MacFaddens had been selling it on the quiet, and hardly any was left in the storage tanks.

In 1874 the LC Works ceased to exist both at Creed and refinery. When soon all the metal condencers, Pumps, Pans, Tanks etc. Was Broken up and sold as scrap Iron. As was the light Rails laid at Creed Works. The Iron rails of the refinery not sold as may be seen, off the Main Road, Striches of the Iron rails put up as fences by the Crofters.[66]

Donald Morrison allowed himself a rather catty end-note to his report:

Where a large quantity of peat cut, say from 3000 to 4000 tons as at the Lewis C Works, the loss in a wet season would be fully one third, as compared with a dry season, this and the various qualities of peat in the same district is quite overlooked by gentlemen of literary abilitys when writing learned essays on the utilization of peat.[67]

There is an interesting plaque in a lay-by near the Creed Bridge, pointing out the site of various parts of the works, but, other than that, virtually nothing remains, except the name of Rathad a' Pharaffin – with the accent on the last syllable.

Beinn a' Bhuna

Following the Grioda towards its source, we come to the area of moor where the people of an Rubha had their summer shielings. An Rubha has only limited land for summer gazings on the peninsula itself, and so was allocated extensive grazings on the moor west of Steornabhagh, between the road to Harris and the boundaries of Lochs Parish, on either side of the Pentland Road. Every year the sheep from the townships of an Rubha were driven through the town of Steornabhagh on their way to and from these grazings – a source of constant complaint from the townspeople, especially those with gardens!

The Rubhach grazings stretched from Hogaraid in the north to Beinn a' Bhuna, on the other side of the hill of Eitseal from Acha Mor. At the back of Maryhill is Loch Airigh na Lic, with the remains of a crannog in the loch and a massive landfill dump on its north shore. On the south side of the loch, a road runs out from the end of Marybank, eventually to split into the Pentland Road, to Carlabhagh area, and the Beinn a' Bhuna road to Acha Mor. At the junction was the old settlement of Airigh na Beist – oddly enough, I have never heard any story about what the beast was that gave it its name. A family of MacLeods and Nicolsons were the last to live there, but it has always struck me that the size of foundations in the area was too great to be just a single family.

Ian Stephen was less than happy with the present day Airigh na Beist:

You will not see the white hare
run on Airigh na Beist
and it is good that we are gone;
you will see, not mist,
but the smoke from the midden
at the edge of the town
to the close of the view
from Airigh na Beist.

and the television mast rises
but we see the plover and the lark

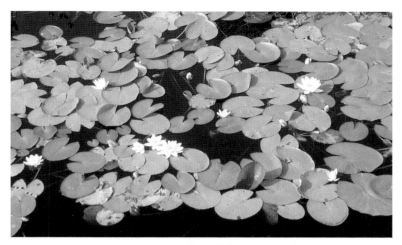

39. At Loch a' Chlachain

and white cotton by the reeds.
still, it may be good
that we are gone from here.[68]

Another little settlement of the same type was Airigh an Da Mhile –
the two-mile shieling – on a bend in the River Grioda.

On both sides of the Beinn a' Bhuna road were the summer shielings
of the Rubhaich, originally sod and stone bothies, which later diversified
into tin and timber shacks and even the odd decommissioned bus.
About a third of the way between the Pentland junction and Acha Mor
the road crosses the Grioda near the end of Loch a' Chlachain, and
it was here that my wife Chris's great-aunt Eiric and her cousin Janet
Montgomery – Seonaid Alasdair – were lost, drowned while gathering
water-lilies, in August of 1870.

Janet's sweetheart, Norman Murray from Pabail, was at sea when the
tragedy occurred, but on his return he gave to her mother the famous
song:

O'n dh'fhag thu mi 's mulad orm
'S duilich as do dheidh mi
An uair bha duil gu leanadh sinn
'S e dealachadh a b' fheudar.
O'n dh' fhag thu mi 's mulad orm.

Chan e 'n aois tha liathadh mo chiabhagan cho gle-gheal,
No siaban nan tonn fiadhaich no'n Cuan-a-Siar le bheucaich

Direadh staidhre Gharraboist bu shnasail thu 'na d' eideadh
An riobhadh bha 'nad ghruaidhean a' buaireadh mo cheile.

Ged a gheibhinn caileag, te cho beartach 's tha 'n Dun Eideann
Gum b'fhearr leam Seonaid Alasdair, 's cha chaillin air an fheill i.

O'n dh' fhag thu mi 's mulad orm.[69]

You have left me bereft, sad am I without you, when we expected
to be together we were forced to part. It is not age that leaves my
hair white nor the wild seas nor the Atlantic roar. Seeing you going
to church at Garrabost you were lovely in your finery, the colour in
your cheeks touched my spirit. Although I would get a lassie, as rich
as any in Edinburgh, I would prefer Seonaid Alasdair and I would
not give her up at the fair.

A strange sideline to this story is that Eiric's parents were away from
home at the time; her father was suffering from TB, and his wife had
taken him to 'take the waters' at Strathpeffer, and it was there that they
heard that their daughter had been drowned.

Cul-ri-Greine (Coulgrein)

Across the sands and the mouth of the River Lacasdal from Gearraidh
Sgoir is the township of Cul-ri-Greine, which is in two parts – Cul-ri-
Greine proper, or Sand Street, and the later crofts formed along the road
from the Lacasdal Road to Cnoc nan Gobhair, and in a flash of official
inspiration named Laxdale – Goathill Road, forming Cross Street and
the north side of Perceval Road. This had the awkward result of the
south side of the road being town and the other side country – and in
their day the two were very distinct!

40. Crossing the Sands

41. Cul-ri-Greine

Sand Street led down to the old ford across the sands to Tunga, and was the recognised thoroughfare from Steornabhagh north before the days of the road through Lacasdal.

Peter Clarke, a more recent wayfarer, has described the crossing of the ford:

> It is far shorter than the road. It seemed logical, therefore, that crofters drove their sheep and cattle across this ford. However, there seemed to be no memory of this route and local officials advised against it on the grounds of safety. Many fears raced before my eyes; being lost in sinking sands, being drowned by a rapidly rising tide, getting lost on the sands and wandering out to sea. I had no reason to doubt the stories of rapidly advancing tides. I reasoned that I would not lose my way if I could see Steornabhagh on the other side of the bay. I crossed the sands to the first channel of water. It was about eight metres wide. I crossed gingerly but the water did not rise above my ankles. A wide expanse of sand now stretched ahead. After all my anxieties, I quickly picked up a line of tractor tyre marks. I could see that a track came down to the foreshore from a road lined with houses and street lights. Before reaching it I had to cross another water-filled channel. This was about ten metres wide and half a metre deep. I crossed, reached the foreshore and eventually found myself in Sand Street.[70]

I am all in favour of taking due care, especially with water, but it is a strange comment on the times to embark with such trepidation on a crossing which was a daily occurrence not so long ago – and I can hardly believe that local people had forgotten the route, since it leads from Ford Terrace in Tunga to Sand Street.

My own connection with Sand Street was with the family of Calum

42. Sand Street

Chisholm, for many years coxswain of the Steornabhagh lifeboat. The connection was through Mrs Chisholm – Ciorstaidh Dhomhnaill Alasdair from Leumrabhagh – whose nephew Calum Louis and his wife Anita Dhomhnaill 'an Sheoic from Liurbost were friends from my student days at Glasgow. Calum and Ciorstaidh had at that time four daughters at home in Steornabhagh, all of whom smoked – a habit of which their father disapproved. I remember one occasion when the girls and I had been sitting round the fire, and Calum came in unexpectedly. Each of the daughters had the same thought, and placed her cigarette in my hands, so when Calum reached the room I had four cigarettes in between my fingers – and me the only non-smoker among them!

A rather odd thing occurred with me and the family, which makes you wonder about prescience. I had come up to the islands on the *Loch Seaforth* on my way to holiday in Harris – my Lewis friends used to tease me that my knowledge of Steornabhagh was limited to the distance between the *Loch Seaforth* and the Harris bus! Mrs Chisholm was by this time a widow, and I always made a point of calling there. This time I had planned to go to Harris first and call in at Sand Street on my way back home, and I was actually seated in the Harris bus when something made me change my mind, come off the bus and go to Sand Street first – in time to arrive for the old lady's funeral.

Calum Louis, Mrs Chisholm's nephew, worked at Woodilee Hospital outside Glasgow, and was an inveterate tease. He and Anita lived for a time in Bishopbriggs, where they took lodgers. One group was a party of Mormon missionaries, who bought Anita a budgie as a present. She called it 'Joey', which Calum extended first to 'Joey Smith' and then to 'Joey Smith's a Wee Free' – which meant that the budgie had to be hidden any time the boys' superiors called! On another occasion, when he had a young lass from South Uist as a trainee on the ward, he persuaded her to ask the patients whether they were Roman Catholic or Protestant, and, if the former, to give them only the aspirins with the 'Dettol Sword' trade-mark on the back!

Sand Street has changed since these days. Then it was mainly little cottages and working crofts behind them; now there are some beautiful modern houses and gardens. The whole place has become depressingly suburban, but surely they still remember the ford!

Steinis (Steinish)

There was a small township here since the 1820s, with only 14 crofts, but to me it was better known for its shore. The Teanga, or spit of sand from which Tunga takes it name, reaches its opposite end here, though there were deep enough channels in between to make it a rather dangerous choice for a ford, not to mention fast-running tides.

Peter Cunningham, in his excellent *The Castles of the Lews* – which covers much more territory than the name suggests – tells of the making of the first golf course:

> The Stornoway Golf Club had laid out an 18-hole links between Steinish and Melbost in 1890 on ground regarded by the crofters of the former township as their common grazings, leading to hazards not normally encountered in the game. One player found the shaft of one of his clubs sawn half-way through, and the greenkeeper was assaulted one day for cutting the grass on the fairways. But both organisations joined hands in the face of the common enemy, the aeroplane. The second fairway became the favourite landing place for exploratory flights, and when discussions began with the companies concerned, it was this area and the adjoining land which became Stornoway Aerodrome.[71]

We will refer to Peter again for the history of the airport when we come to Mealabost.

South of Steinis is Mossend, where there was at one time a Widows' Row, similar to the one in Lacasdal, and, later, a Fever Hospital. Widows' Row was just a few poor houses, but it almost had a link with the wilds of northern Canada and the fur-trappers of the Hudson's Bay Company. Among the files transferred in 1974 from the Company's offices to the University of Manitoba in Winnipeg was a collection of undelivered letters to Company employees. Several of them had been sent from Lewis, and Judith Beattie, who was supervising the cataloguing of the letters, asked us to try to identify the writers, which we were able to do.

43. Golf Course, Steinis

One of the letters was particularly tantalising, from lack of direct information. It was addressed to Allan MacIsac, Columbia River. Here is an extract:

1 october 1851

Dear allan I took the opportunity of writing you this few loins to let you know I am in good helth hopping this will find you the same . . . mind you and dond marry one that is out there.and I will not marry one that is here till you com. Mudena Campbell is a widow sinc you went . . . my mother sents her best respects to you and Donald my brother an Murdena Campbell and her mother and all my frends an Peggy macleod and mind whenever you get the letter mind and writ and Nil macKay sents his best respects to you an all his family is well and he is working with sapers. I have no more to say at present but your trew love till death.

Mary MacDonald[72]

Mary MacDonald in Stornoway was not much help in identifying the writer, but a Mary with a brother Donald and neighbours (presumably) Neil MacKay and a recently widowed Murdina Campbell gave a better chance of locating them in the census of 1851. We could not find a Mrs Murdina Campbell at that time, but we did find a Murdina Campbell who married a John Morrison in 1846, who must have died soon after, for she appears as a widow in 1851, living at Widows' Row. Checking the other houses there we indeed found a Mary MacDonald, with a brother Donald. We did not find a Neil MacKay there, but there was one on a croft in Sraid a Tuath, Cnoc Shanndabhaig, which backs on to Widows' Row. Was this our Mary MacDonald? – not absolute proof, but overwhelmingly probable.

We were able to trace Mary's later history – and despite her protestations, she didn't marry Allan MacIsaac. Or perhaps since the letter was never delivered to him, he may have thought she had given him up. However it came about, she married someone else in 1853 – a Donald Matheson from Grabhair.

South of Mossend are the houses of Sandwick Park – fishermen's holdings from the 1930s, those on the main road being better known as Leathad Oilibheir, from Captain Benjamin Oliver, the Customs Officer who is credited (?) with wiping out illicit distilling in Lewis.

Sanndabhaig (Sandwick)

Beyond this again lie the townships of Sannadabhaig – Mol Shanndabhaig towards the shore, and Cnoc Shanndabhaig along and above the main road, further subdivided into Sraid a Tuath and Sraid an Ear. Sanndabhaig was created as crofts for cottar families rehoused from the old Inacleit district of Steornabhagh when the slums there were cleared in the 1820s. At one time, Sraid a Tuath was known as Cnoc Dubhaig. In Sanndabhaig also is the main cemetery for the Steornabhagh area, with many interesting gravestones, which are being transcribed and indexed by Stornoway Historical Society – a work very much to their credit, and one which should be copied in many other island cemeteries where gravestones are being allowed to collapse, unrecorded.

There was a MacGregor family in Sraid a Tuath, one of whom, John – mac Iain Alasdair – became a Lieutenant-Colonel in the Indian Medical Service:

Eilean Leodhais, gur fada thriall mi
Bho d' bheanntan ard, ach cha d' rinn mi d' dhichuimhn'
Ged tha na h-Innseachan clith 'g am chrionadh,
Cha treig mi chaoidh thu, ged chlaoidh a' ghrian mi.[73]

The island of Leodhas, far have I travelled away from your high hills, but I did not forget you. Although the Indies have wasted me I will never forsake you, although the sun has weakened me.

Better-known, perhaps, is his *Tir nam Beann Ard:*

Togaibh fonn air an fhonn a bha calm' agus cruaidh,
Am fonn thar gach fonn feadh an t-saoghail thug buaidh,
'S do dhuthaich nam beann anns gach cruadal is cas,
Air cuan no air tir, bidh sinn dileas gu bas,
Tir nam Beann Ard.[74]

Raise a song on the tune that was brave and robust, the song above songs that was victorious all over the world, to the land of the hills in every battle and danger, on land or on sea, we will be faithful till death. Land of the high hills.

Lt.Col. John's other claim to fame is that he was the father of Alasdair Alpin MacGregor, the writer of many books of over-purpled prose about the islands, until he was asked to contribute a volume on the Western Isles in a definitive series, in which he castigated the island people for every vice he could think of – a vicious volume which I am surprised that the publishers accepted.

On a lighter note, he even dared to criticise Gaelic singers!

Sensitive people who find their way into the midst of such a large, carefree, uncritical party, can scarcely look at the human exhibits. The sight of them, added to the unmusical sounds they emit, is as much as the discerning concert-goer can endure. The favourite songster retains his place in the hearts of his audience by selecting for his encores well-known songs, in the chorus of which the audience can participate lustily. To this piece of simple psychology, our Highland and Island audiences always respond heartily, both with uplifted voice and with their beating feet.[75]

I am sure my cartoonist friend Calum would not agree with that.

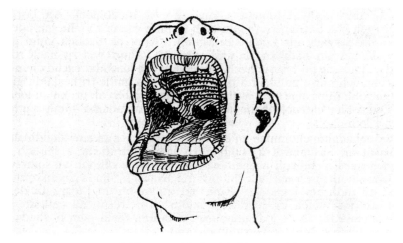

44. A Skyeman hitting his big toe with a
hammer or a Lewisman singing!

45. Etta MacDonald and Etta MacKenzie

Sanndabhaig was a halting place for people coming into town from an Rubha, and my mother-in-law remembered coming in from Seisiadar to Mol Shanndabhaig, then getting a lift from relatives in their boat across the bay to Steornabhagh. She used to go there on holiday to stay with MacLennan relatives – muinntir Iain Eoghainn. She remembered the old railway which used to run from the paraffin works to Garrabost; the section she remembered ran from the Braighe between the two cemeteries and on to the cannery. She used to take the MacLennan's cattle each day out to graze in a park beside where Sgoil Shanndabhaig is now and back again in the evening, and she got the fright of her life one day when a train came past! And she remembered that they used to go for water down to the end of Mol Shanndabhaig to a well down at the shore. There was a geo there and it was easy to walk down to it, so they went there twice a day when the tide was out. There was a hollow in the shingle and they would dig away there until they got to fresh water – and then the tide would come in and cover it again. The houses at the bottom end of Mol Shanndabhaig used to go there.[76]

One day that remained in her mind was when her sister Etta and her friend Eiric a' Phoidilidh (Etta MacKenzie) had been coming in from Seisiadar to school in Steornabhagh and they were caught in a heavy snowstorm. They decided to shelter against the wall of a house in Sanndabhaig, only to realise to their horror that their long hair had become frozen to the wall. Luckily their screams alerted the people in the house, but their hair had to be cropped short before they could be released. (And we think that the winter of 2010 was unprecedentedly severe!)

Tolm (Holm)

Behind Mol Shanndabhaig are Knockgarry and Stoneyfield farms and the village of Tolm. Tolm was originally at the shore opposite Eilean Thuilm, but was moved in 1868 to its present site, further east, to give more land for Knockgarry farm. In 1780 the tenant of Nether Holm was John Wylie, surveyor of Customs, and we shall meet his family again when we come to Marbhig in na Lochan.

Tolm itself has little in the way of history, but the offshore rocks of Biastan Thuilm – the Beasts of Holm – have only too much history, for it was on them that the *Iolaire* was wrecked on New Year's morning, 1919, with the loss of over 200 men returning from the war.

> They had lit up their windows for beacons, the women of Lewis,
> The peat-fires were glowing a welcome, the table was spread;
> The sea brought their sons back from war and the long years of tumult
> And cast them ashore on the cliffs of their boyhood – dead.

So wrote Neil Munro, in his rather incongruously named 'Prologue spoken by the Players' for a gathering in Glasgow to raise funds for

46. Cover of the book *Sea Sorrow*

Iolaire dependants. To me, Munro gets it just right – it was not just the appalling loss of life, but the fact that it came just as the island breathed a communal sigh of relief as its men had safely survived the war.

Much has been written about the loss of the *Iolaire,* most recently by John MacLeod in *When I Heard the Bell,* which is full of detail about all those lost, and those saved, including for once the few Harrismen who were on board, who are usually ignored.

But it is a token of how raw the wound of the *Iolaire* still is that quite a few people here felt that it was too soon for such a book to be written – there are still too many memories of the people whose lives were shattered by the tragedy.

The story begins at Kyle of Lochalsh on the evening of 31st December. A train-load of Royal Naval Reservists had arrived, all hoping to get back to Lewis for the New Year. Some had spent years at sea, others were youngsters, barely out of naval training – and there were far more of them than could be accommodated on the usual steamer, the *Sheila.* To try to get the others home, another vessel was used, called the *Iolaire,* though before the war her name had been *Amalthea.* Two hundred and sixty men were taken on board, far beyond the scope of the *Iolaire's* safety equipment. At 7.30 in the evening, she set sail, under the command of a crew who had never sailed into Steornabhagh before, certainly not in darkness.

She had been within sight of the lights of Steornabhagh when she took too close a course to the shore and hit the *Biastan.* She was only a few yards off the shore, but it was a dark winter night, with a heavy swell breaking on the rocky shore. Some of the men tried to swim ashore, but many were smashed on the rocks or swept away by the tide. John F MacLeod, from Port Nis, managed to get ashore with a line and others followed along it, some to safety and some to be swept off, until eventually the *Iolaire* sank, taking many more to their graves, although one man, Donald Morrison from Cnoc Ard, managed to cling to a mast until he was rescued.

It took time, perhaps too long, to mobilise a rescue team, but there was little they could have done. Over 200 were lost. Some of those who got to the shore made their way to Knockgarry farm, but others, soaking and exhausted, died above the shore. As the days went on, more and more bodies were discovered on the rocks and in the sea, but others were never found.

Nuair dh'fhuasgaileadh na ropan dhith, 's a sheol i as a' Chaol,
An Iolaire, 's i bu luaithe dh'aindheoin luasgeadh muir is gaoth;
'S iomadh oigear fuasgailte bha an uair sinn nach do shaoil
Cho goirid 's a bha chuairt ac' - beagan uairean anns an t-saogh'l.

Cha shaoilinn-sa cho bronach e nan ordaicht' e le Dia,
Gun tugaicht' suas an deo leoth' ri aghaidh comhstri dhion;
Nuair shaoil leotha a bhi sabhailte bho gach gabhadh agus pian,
'S ann ghoid a-staigh am bas orra, 's neo-bhaidheil a bha Bhiast.

Nis criochnaichidh mi 'n comhradh seo bhon 's sgoideach cainnt
　　mo bheul,
Cha bhard gu deanamh oran mi ged as coir dhomh dhol na
　　ghleus;
Ach innsidh na tha beo an-diugh dhan oigridh thig nan deidh
Mar dh'eirich dha na seoid ud bha air bord an Iolaire.[77]

When we untied the ropes and we sailed out of Kyle, the Iolaire was
fast despite the wild seas and the wind, Many an innocent youth
never imagined then how short his time was to be in this world. I
would not think it so sad if I thought if God had ordained it, that
they had died defending their country; when they thought they were
safe from danger and pain, death stole in on them, and the Biast had
no mercy. I will close the song now as my tongue is defective, but

47. *Iolaire* gravestone in Aiginis Cemetery

the youth who will come after us will now know what happened to the heroes on board the Iolaire.

The loss of the *Iolaire* receives much less attention than if it had happened anywhere on the UK mainland. Technically it was not a war-time loss, so the site is not regarded as a war-grave – indeed, with incredible insensitivity, the Admiralty tried almost immediately to sell her for scrap, even though there would almost certainly have still been bodies inside the submerged wreck.

Almost every township on the island had its losses, as can be seen on war memorials all over the island.

The losses of the First World War, and particularly those on the *Iolaire*, had a tremendous effect on Lewis. I can remember when I was coming to Lewis first that there was a whole generation of men missing; there were quite a few very old men, and plenty of middle-aged men, but very few in between. The number of unmarried women of that age was noticeable, and perhaps had its effect in religious revivals of that period. And no doubt they had their share in the decisions of many others to leave the island.

New Tolm is to the east of the old township, in an area which appears in old rentals as a separate unit under the name of Sildinis. Despite being under the flight path less than a mile from the end of the main runway of the airport, it seems to be a popular commuter area, with new houses being built.

Mealabost (Melbost)

At Tong, Coll, Gress and Melbost sands, in the Broad Bay, a great variety of shell-fish is found – clams, mussels, limpets, whelks, razor-fish and cockles. All these kinds are found on the Melbost sands, after a severe storm. The natives expect a bursting of the shell-fish banks, once in seven years; then immense masses are thrown up and found at low water; but this bursting happens oftener than once in seven years. The reporter has seen huge heaps thrown ashore twice during that period – which employed many carts and creels for several days, in carrying them away for food and manure.

The Broad-bay flounder is the finest in the world. The laithe far surpasses the whiting, in delicacy and sweetness. Hake is a strong, coarse fish, but when salted in spring is not disagreeable. The haddock is the general favourite, and is to be had, in all seasons, in the Broad-bay. There is a ready sale for it in Stornoway in spring, when the salt-beef becomes tough. Haddocks fetch 1s per dozen; at other seasons they are sold for half-pence a-piece. The country people

48. Bellag an Dotair and family

smoke them; and putting salt into their eyes, the brine runs down the bone, and keeps the fish from corrupting; it gives the fish a peculiar, but not unpleasant taste[78]

– so claimed Rev. Cameron in 1833.

Mealabost and Braigh na h-Uidhe, though their houses in places face each other across a street, are thought of as separate entities, especially by their inhabitants. I remember one Braigh na h-Uidhe lady assuring me that she had never slept a night in Mealabost – though it was only a few yards away from her own house! The two townships do have very different histories, so there was good reason for the distinction.

Mealabost was an old township, at one time much larger than today, before it lost land first to Gormacleit, or Mealabost Farm, and then to the airport.

Mrs Bella MacDonald – Bellag an Dotair – from Toronto, described the village of her youth:

Melbost was a large village, from Gob Srupair to Mossend – all that is on Melbost land. Before the war there were two roads that we could take to Steornabhagh. The south road was where the Point road is today, and the north road – well you can see part of it yet at the gate of the airport. It led up to Teedie's Park, or Gormacleit, and from there to North Street in Cnoc Shanndabhaig. Halfway out the north road was the Blue Gate, and there was a road going from there

49. Captain Fresson and the Lewis Girls

across to the Links and to the sands. It was known as the Lady's Road
– Sir James Matheson's wife used to drive out there in a gig.[79]

It was in 1933 that the first aeroplane landed in Lewis – but that was
an accident! Peter Cunningham takes up the story:

> The arrival the following week of a commercial aircraft belonging to
> the Midland and Scottish really heralded the beginnings of an air
> service to Lewis, for it made the first landing on what was to be the
> future aerodrome for Stornoway. The pilot circled the town a few
> times looking for a suitable site and decided on the second fairway
> of the golf course at Steinish, but on every approach a small boy ran
> out to meet him, and he had to abandon the attempt. He eventually
> came down on the adjacent beach, but when the plane began to
> sink into the sand had to take off again and land, this time without
> interruption, on the golf course.[80]

Was this the plane that my mother-in-law remembered? A friend of
hers, Mary MacAulay from an Cnoc, was among a party of fisher-girls
coming back from Orkney and they were offered the chance to come
to Stornoway on the plane. Mairi remembered going down to the golf
course to meet them, and always claimed they were on the first plane
to land in Steornabhagh.

In 1939 the lease of the ground for the airport was signed for the Stornoway Trust, and an airport was laid out to a plan by Captain E E Fresson, the pioneer of commercial aviation in northern Scotland, though it was later developed on a new plan by the RAF. It now has one of the longest runways in the UK and a good reputation for being fog-free, so it is little wonder that it was proposed as a major NATO base, which drew a lot of opposition at the time. A new terminal was added in the last few years, with a tea-room and a bar – a far cry from landing on the golf course.

Though one can appreciate the need for security in these days of international terrorism, it is rather incongruous to see a Lewis *cailleach* on her way to the hospital in Inverness being subjected to at least as rigorous a search as at any major international airport!

You do not think of Lewis as being directly affected by the war, but as Bellag an Dotair reminds us, Mealabost was just at the edge of the runways:

> It was scary living so close to an airport in war-time. You could see the planes flying out at night, and we counted all the planes as they left and we counted them coming back again in the morning. We always knew if some did not return. The noise of the engines was horrifying in the dark. One morning as we were getting ready to go to school, we heard a plane coming in really low. It was the autumn, because I remember that the corn was high and straight. The plane was touching the top of the corn – it came down where the terminal building is today. Another plane came down at the bottom of our croft, beside the Point road. It was in the morning that this one crashed too.[81]

There was a MacAulay family there too, who belonged to First Coast at Gruinard in Wester Ross. Duncan MacAulay and his wife had set off on an emigrant ship for Canada in 1827, but when they called into Steornabhagh for fresh water, his wife decided that, seeing how sea-sick she had been in the Minch, there was no way they were going to get her to cross the Atlantic. They got a croft in Mealabost, where they are still known as na Mor-Thirich – the mainlanders. A brother stayed behind in First Coast, and I had his great-great-grandson as a student when I was running the Land Economics course at Paisley College – the last I heard he was in real estate in New York, and doing rather well!

One family that certainly cannot be overlooked in Mealabost are the MacFarlanes. This is not a common name in Lewis, so where did they come from? The first reference we have to them is in 1811, when Donald MacFarlane had a child baptised in Mealabost. There were MacFarlanes also in Cuisiadar in Nis, and since Donald's wife was from Nis, he may well have come from that area also – but that merely shifts the question a stage further back. And just to complicate matters more, they were known in Gaelic as MacAindreas.

Whatever the doubts about the origin of the family, there is no doubt about the stature of Donald's great-great-grandson Murdo – Bard Mhealaboist. Murdo went off to Canada with so many other young Leodhasaich on the *Marloch* in 1924, but he was never cut out for life on the prairies, and one of his most famous songs is one of homesickness:

Faili, Faili, Faili ho ro
Faili, Faili, Faili ho ro
Faili, Faili, Faili ho ro
'S cian nan cian o'n dh'fhag mi Leodhas

'S fhada leam an oidhche gheamraidh,
'S fhada 's fhada 's fhada leam i.
'S, O, chan fhaic ach preiridh lom mi;
Cha chluinn tonn a' tigh'nn gu traigh mi.[82]

Faili, faili, faili ho ro, ages and ages since I left Leodhas, the winter night is long, ages long, I can only see an empty prairie and I cannot hear the sound of the sea coming in to the shore.

He returned to Mealabost to live and work on his brother Donald's croft:

Greas, thugainn do'n traigh
Tha barr a' bhraga ris
'S Langasgeir Mhor
Is Langasgeir Bheag tha ris.

MacRath is MacAnndaidh
Seall, sud seachad iad;
'S clann Mhurchaidh mhic Ainndreis
Chrom do'n chladach iad.

Greas, gearr, buain, gearr.
Luath sath do chorran innt'
'Se 'n fheamainn ni 'm barr,
'S e 'm barr ni 'n t-aran dhuinn.[83]

Hurry, let us go to the ebb, the top of the seaweed is showing, Langasgeir Mhor and Langasgeir Bheag are showing. MacRath and MacAnndaidh, look, they are passing, and the children of Murchadh Mac Ainndreis, they are on the shore. Hurry, cut, harvest, cut, fast cut with the corran, the seaweed will make the harvest and the harvest will make the bread for us.

50. Langasgeir

Murdo wrote love songs too, like the well-known *Mhorag leat shiubhlainn:*

> Cha leig mo luaidh-sa leas rosgan fuadain
> Neo snuadh na buthadh chur air a gruaidhean
> No dath a cheannach gu dath a cuailein
> 'S e mar an canach aig sgail nam fuar-bheann
> Mhorag, leat shiubhlainn gun churam gu cul na gealaich
> 'S milse leam do phogan gu mor na na cirean-meala.[84]

My love does not need false lashes or colour on her cheeks, she does not need to colour her hair, it is like the cotton-grass on the hillside. Morag, I would go with you to the back of the moon, your kisses are sweeter to me than honeycombs.

He was quite happy to make fun of local disputes in the church:

> 'S coma 's coma 's coma leam
> Rebel as no rebel ann
> 'Se mo cheisd an gille donn.
> Biodh an seisean, biodh a' chleir
> Biodh an sionadh thar a cheil'
> Cha chuir sud no ni fo'n ghrein
> Eadar mi 's mo Chailein fein.[85]

I do not care if he is a rebel, my desire is the brown-haired lad. The session and the presbytery and the rest can fall out, but that will not come between me and my Colin.

But he could have a dark side too, as in his poem about the dangers of nuclear war: *Leag iad am bom an raoir – They dropped the bomb last night.* There was hardly a topic but Bard Mhealaboist had made a song on it!

Braigh na h-Uidhe (Branahuie)

Braigh na h-Uidhe was a more recent township, mainly created for tenants evicted from Circeabost in Bearnaraigh, among them a group of MacMillans – clann a' Bhaird – some of whom moved on to the Eastern Townships of Quebec.

One of the earliest pioneers of the Lac Megantic area of the Eastern Townships was William MacLeod from Braigh na h-Uidhe. He had gone out with friends in an earlier settlement in 1842, but they were hearing word of good land on the shores of Lac Megantic, and decided to try there, as described by his grandson, Malcolm MacLeod:

> In the year 1852, William MacLeod, Rory MacIver and Murdo MacIver, all three of the Township of Lingwick, with the aid of a pocket compass, started eastward in search of government land. The township of Marston, where they finally located was not then surveyed, but these pioneers took their course through Winslow and Whitton until, after three days, they struck the shore of Lake Megantic at Black Point, where they made a raft and explored the shores of the lake as far south as Rocky Point.
>
> They spent a week in this vicinity and found fish and game very plentiful; then they retraced their steps, passing through Marston and Hampden. Early in the following spring they again sought the Lake Megantic region, carrying three bushels of potatoes. In the spring of 1854, when Marston was surveyed, each made a clearing on their respective lots. In addition to the necessary provisions to keep body and soul together each took a bushel of barley, which was sown, together with the potatoes they got from the acre planted the previous year.
>
> It was not, however, until the spring of 1856 that the families were moved and their long tedious journey through the forest began; children, cattle, furniture, provisions etc. being carried or driven to the new land. The writer well remembers the long weary days shoveling snow in the swamps to get cattle through, carrying a load of provisions or clothing ahead to some sheltered spot and returning for the cows and children in the rear and camping out at night. Everyone able to carry fifty pounds was up at daylight to start the next day's journey. Finally, at the end of six days. Lake Megantic was reached on May 20th 1856. Planting was late that year but the season was good and barley sown in the latter part of June ripened.

51. Uilleam Braigh na h-Uidhe and Raonaid

My memories of my grandfather, William MacLeod, are mostly those of childhood, although he lived to eighty seven. As children I think we rather feared the silent, rather stern-featured, indomitable veteran of the Hudson Bay wilderness, where he spent eight years of his youth, but we loved him too. Well did he deserve it for no kinder heart ever beat in a human breast, except perhaps in that of my grandmother, who accompanied him so cheerfully with her eight children in 1856. She was said to have been the first white woman who ever saw Lake Megantic.[86]

William was married to Rachel Finlayson, and it had puzzled me for years who she was. It must have been working away on my mind, for Chris tells me that I wakened her up one night, still sound asleep, and told her 'Uilleim Braigh na h-Uidhe was married to Raonaid Dhomhnaill 'ic Sheorais.Tell me that in the morning' – and promptly went back to sleep again!

Another letter in the Hudson Bay archive was from a John Morrison in Braigh na h-Uidhe to his son Alexander at Columbia River, thanking him for £4 sent through the Bank of Stornoway, and asking him to come home, as they were holding on to the land for him. He did indeed come home, and took up a croft at No 6 Braigh na h-Uidhe.

An unusual name found in Braigh na h-Uidhe is Montgomery. You might think that it is a recent name in the area, but there is a John Montgomery there in a rental of 1766. The name occurs only in an Rubha and Sgire nan Loch, and I have a feeling that, like sliochd a' Chaiptein in Tunga, they are refugees from the harassing of Raasay after the '45.

Loch Braigh na h-Uidhe occupies much of the western end of the isthmus between the village and an Rubha. It is a magnet for migrating wild-fowl, and a lot of the reports of odd strays in Lewis come from this loch.

The Braighe itself is a narrow isthmus, with a sandy beach on the north, and a shingle one to the south. Along it runs the only road to an Rubha district, and the whole road is so open to the weather that it is frequently closed in storms. My wife Chris remembers driving in to work from an Rubha one stormy morning and finding the road blocked by a cargo-boat, the *Atlantic Proctor,* which the storm had beached and heeled over right above the road. The crew were being taken off by breeches buoy, and the ship was eventually righted on the shore and towed away. That was a particularly bad storm, on New Year's Day 1975, but there is barely a year passed without the Braighe being closed by seaweed and shingle driven across it.

52. *Atlantic Proctor*

Chris's father remembered one occasion when the sea had broken across the Braighe, and the bus he was in had stalled in the middle. The seas were so fierce that some of the men in the bus had to brace themselves against the door to keep the waves out, while others carried the women passengers out the back door and through the graveyard. It was on this or another such occasion that Iain Mor was on the bus – called Iain Mor not only for his height but for his breadth and weight. Everyone else was taken off the bus except Iain Mor, but no-one was too willing to tackle the job of lifting him! 'Duff' from Seisiadar, as usual, had the answer – 'We'll just have to make two trips of him!'

At the east end of the Braighe is a large cemetery, mainly used by families from an Rubha. On a good day, it can be a beautiful site, but on a wild day it takes the full force of a storm, as I know from experience.

Some bodies were found buried on the shore below the graveyard a number of years ago, and, as I remember, there was a bag of coins, including a Dutch ritter, found beside one of the bodies. I think the generally accepted explanation was that they had been put ashore from a boat, having died of a plague of some type, and were buried so hastily that the bag of coins had been overlooked.

53. In the New Cemetery, am Braighe

It could be thought surprising that I have never heard any ghost stories from the Braighe, but as Chris's grandfather used to say, there were hundreds of occasions when he took empty coffins in his horse-cart to an Rubha in the darkness, past the graveyard on the Braighe, and if anyone should ever have seen a ghost, it should have been him!

PART 3 – AN RUBHA (POINT)

An Rubha has rather a different history from the rest of Lewis; Pabail and Garrabost are old townships, but both ends of the district were farms until the early 1800s, when they were broken into crofting townships, largely for tenants evicted from other areas, or coming to the burgeoning commercial fishery being set up in the area.

On the other hand, both the earliest church and the earliest clan castle in Lewis are in an Rubha, and some of the earliest (and oddest!) prehistoric relics have come from this area too. No doubt the apparent lack of historic traces in the area comes from the degree of cultivation and development there, which has obscured its earlier history.

Because it is out on a headland of its own, it is easy to forget that an Rubha is the closest part of Lewis to the mainland and so the area most open to mainland influences and families. The fishing banks of the Minch were also a link between the island and the mainland.

It is so easy to forget that the sea was the main means of transport until very recently. I remember being told of one crofter on an Rubha who, faced with a long wait for the use of mill at Garrabost, took his grain across to the mill in Lochinver to save time!

Aiginis (Aignish)

Immediately at the end of the Braighe lies the old church of the Uidh. Uidh – or if you want to be GOC-friendly (Gaelic Orthographic Convention), Aoidh – is the Gaelic word for an isthmus. It appears in old documents as Ui, and in English – in its usual phonetic perversion – as Eye, and an Rubha as the Eye peninsula. What is it about English monoglots that makes them insist that a Gaelic word must mean the same as its nearest phonetic equivalent in English?

54. Mainland from Point

55. Cabarfeidh Stone

It is said that there was an old chapel on the site, dedicated to St Catan, but the present ruin, which is thought to date from the fourteenth century, is dedicated to St Columba. The older part of the church, which is built mainly of local gneiss, is to the east, with a more recent, possibly fifteenth century, extension to the west, largely faced with local red sandstone. The west end of the church at least was slated, and was in occasional use in the 1820s, though the main church by that time was in Steornabhagh.

The old church is largely ruined, but in its day it was the chief church of Lewis and of the MacLeod chiefs. It is said that at one time the church was surrounded by a graveyard on all sides, but the sea of Loch a Tuath has long since carried away all that part of the graveyard which lay to the northwest of the church. William, 5th Earl of Seaforth, who died in 1740, is said to have been buried to the north of the church, and if so, it gives some idea of the speed of the erosion. Oddly enough, Lord Teignmouth, visiting Lewis in 1836, says that Seaforth lies 'beneath a flagstone on the pavement, undistinguished

56. At Uidh Church

by any description'[87] – but it seems very unlikely that Seaforth would have been buried in an unmarked grave. I wonder if Teignmouth's guide, on being asked where the Seaforth grave was, showed him a slab, rather than admit that there was no sign of it. But it does seem rather odd that we have no contemporary record of the funeral or the grave, or even a sketch of it.

There certainly are MacKenzie grave-slabs in the graveyard on the landward side of the church. I remember that Chris and I were there on one occasion, looking at grave-slabs, and we noticed a slab with some indecipherable carving on it. It was starting to drizzle, and we were going to give up, when we realised that the drizzle had brought up the carvings on the stone: a Cabarfeidh – stag's head – the family crest, and the standard symbols of mortality – coffin, skull, crossed-bones, funeral implements, hour-glass and a hand ringing a bell, emblems which are found on many tombstones of the seventeenth and early eighteenth centuries. Since then we have learned that the recommended method of 'lifting' the text on a stone is to spray it very lightly with water, for example from a perfume spray.

The initials KMK are carved below the Cabarfeidh, but it is hard to say whether they are of the same age as the main carving. Could this even be the original Seaforth stone, rescued from the sea and re-used?

My wife has a photograph of her brother Ian with friends, taken as recently as the late 1950s at the back of the church, beside an out-building of which there is no trace whatever now, the sea has come so

57. Uidh Church

quickly. The last time I was there, the sea had undercut part of the rear wall, and although this has now been infilled to prevent immediate danger of collapse, the whole building is now reckoned too dangerous to allow public access.

Over twenty years ago, my wife was involved in the local Comunn Eachdraidh in trying to get remedial work done, but the attempt became bogged down in bureaucratic detail. There have been other attempts since then, but they also have been unsuccessful, partly because of problems in identifying who actually owns the building. Apparently though Historic Scotland look after the building, they do not own it, and could do nothing without the owner's permission. I understand that that hurdle has now been overcome, but still they talk and still the building gets worse. Another group has been set up recently to try to have the building secured, but as yet nothing seems to have been achieved. My best wishes for success to them, but I have a horrible fear that by the time they get a plan agreed by all the parties, and find finance to carry it out, they will be preserving the base of the walls where the church used to be.

Inside the church, there are two inscribed grave-slabs, which at one time were, as was the custom, on the floor of the church, but were replaced on the walls for safety by Colonel Matheson in the 1920s. It will be rather a bitter irony if these walls themselves are now allowed to collapse, and the grave-slabs with them.

One of the slabs is reckoned to commemorate Roderick MacLeod, who died in 1498. The slab, whose relief has been badly worn away by the elements, shows a figure clad in mail armour, wearing a pommelled sword, and carrying a spear. The figure is not a representation of the particular chief buried, but a stylised figure of a warrior, almost identical

58. 'Roderick' Stone

to figures found on the Poltalloch stones in Kilmartin, Argyll, and on many other stones of the period. At the time of transfer of the slab to the wall, a stone was placed below it with the inscription:

Grave stone of one of the MacLeods of Lewis probably Roderick II, latter part of XVth century, father of Torquil IV & of Margaret MacFingone who was mother of John Last abbot of Iona.

Margaret, daughter of Roderick, is commemorated on the other slab. The pattern of the slab itself is very intricate, with interwoven patterns of foliage and animals within a Celtic design. Around the edges are traces of an inscription, now largely illegible, but luckily transcribed prior to the 1927 Report on Ancient and Historic Monuments as:

Hic jacet Margareta filia Roderici meic Leoyd de Leodhuis vidua Lachlanna meic Fingone obit m°v°iii – here lies Margaret daughter of Roderick MacLeod of Lewis, widow of Lachlan MacKinnon, died 1503.[88]

59. 'Margaret' Stone

The style of both stones is similar to many in Argyll, which suggests that the mason, if not from Argyll himself, was certainly familiar with their style. Until this time, Iona had been the place of choice for burial of clan chiefs, but as the Lordship of the Isles disintegrated, the chiefs began to construct burial places on their own lands. Despite this, Roderick's son Malcolm appears to have been buried on Iona, but then he had fallen out with his brother Torquil, the next chief, in the usual way of internecine strife among the MacLeods of Lewis.

When the MacLeods lost the island to the MacKenzies, they still wanted to retain their burial place at the Uidh. On one occasion, still remembered in oral tradition, it is said that a funeral party of MacLeods arrived at the Uidh, for the burial inside the church of a MacLeod whom they considered the representative of the MacLeods. A party of MacKenzies threatened to stop the burial, or even to disinter the corpse, and matters almost came to bloodshed. The danger was averted by John Morrison of Bragar, an ally of the MacKenzies, who, according to the version of the story published by Rev. William Matheson in *An Clarsair Dall*, proposed the compromise:

> Leodhas gu leir aig MacCoinnich
> Ach leud a dhrom' aig MacLeoid –
>
> Let MacKenzie have the whole of Lewis,
> but let MacLeod have the length of his back.

Although the official genealogies of the Clan MacLeod show that the nearest heir to the MacLeod chiefs of Lewis is in Tasmania, descended through the MacLeods of Raasay, it is well known in Lewis that there are heirs of the chiefs still in the Suardail area, though their descent is possibly through an illegitimate son of the last MacLeod chief of Lewis. In my *St Columba's Church at Aignish* I noted the inscriptions on a couple of MacLeod stones from the floor of the church, and also a Nicolson stone to which I will return when we get to Port nan Giuran.

After the construction of the new church at an Cnoc in 1828, the Uidh Church was allowed to fall into neglect. By 1875, the neglect was complete.

> Alongside the shore of Broad Bay, the waters of which have already carried away a portion of the ancient graveyard, strewing the beach with human bones, stands the ruined church of Knock. The graveyard is still in use, but is covered all over with the densest vegetation, breast high. There is no enclosure, and, although apparently the most aristocratic burial-place in the Lews, is utterly disregarded. There were monuments of beauty and value, but what desolation![89]

The part of the graveyard further from the shore was set out anew in the 1820s and different sections allocated to different villages in an Rubha. The last burial there was a young lad, Iain MacLeod – mac Sheonaidh Aonghais Uilleim – killed by a bus in Port Mholair in 1938, and later burials from an Rubha took place at the Braighe.

When the MacKenzies took Lewis from the MacLeods in the early 1600s, they gave most of the best tacks to their own relatives and supporters. By 1678 Aignis was held in tack by George MacKenzie of Kildun, brother of Kenneth, 3rd Earl of Seaforth. Among the tacksmen of Lewis, his was the only Roman Catholic family, and he was frequently in dispute with Rev. Kenneth Morrison of Stornoway – to the extent that it is said that Rev. Kenneth always armed himself when making his way across the sands from his manse in Tunga to his church in Steornabhagh.

MacKenzie once sent six strong men across to Tong to abduct Kenneth, who was so generous with liquid refreshment that his

60. Eaglais na h-Uidhe

would-be captors were rendered unconscious, and he was able to transport them, completely bound, across the water to Aignish, where he deposited them near the laird's door. When they were found in the morning, they were still stupefied and had no recollection of how they came to be there. MacKenzie congratulated them on their escape, saying that Black Kenneth must have been in a genial mood, as he might easily have left them below the low water mark.[90]

Kildun, as the only Roman Catholic tacksman, was an obvious host for a visit by the priest Cornelius Con in 1687. His journey there was not auspicious:

I was called by the uncle of the Earl of Seafort, my Lord of Kildune, to his Isle, where there had been no priest since the reformation. I crossed sixty miles of sea and as much by land; God was my consolation because in truth I am not capable of describing half of the misery I suffered during these three days, without anything to eat or drink except a little meal which my three guides had brought along for themselves. In the end, thanks be to God, I reached the isle of the said lord of Kildune. I heard the confessions of his whole family and of sixty other persons. The ministers of the Isle made to kill me. Having met three of them opposed to me we discussed informally the principal points of the faith, and they went away ashamed.[91]

I doubt if the ministers came to the same conclusion!

Con disgraced himself by fathering a child on one of Kildun's daughters. There are conflicting stories about whether Con became a Protestant in order to marry her, but in any case he was spirited away, probably on Seaforth's orders, and confined for years on various off-shore islands, including, it is thought, North Rona, forty miles north of Lewis. He is on record in 1699, asking for release from Edinburgh Castle, but thereafter disappears from history.

By 1718 Colin MacKenzie, son of George, was tacksman of Kildun, and had obtained the tack of Shulishader at the far end of an Rubha, as well as his own tack of Aiginis; shortly thereafter he obtained Airinis in na Lochan as well. In a rental of 1740 Airinis is tenanted by Lady Kildun, while 'Aignes etc' has passed to Murdo and Donald MacAulay, but in 1766 the tack was added to the vast tack of Gillanders, the factor.

The land around the church remained a farm until a hundred years ago, and was the scene of one of the land raids in the agitation following the Crofters Act of 1886, which gave security to crofters but did nothing for landless cottars.

The position before the riot can be judged from the evidence given to the Napier Commission, firstly by Rev. Murdo MacAskill:

There is the farm of Aignish, now under sheep, and it is by far the best arable land in the whole parish. On that farm rushes and ferns largely cover parks once yielding returns of every type of crop. That farm might accommodate some thirty families, and being contiguous to the sea, is admirably suited for the class of crofter fisher population that inhabit the district. And surely to make comfortable homesteads for some thirty families of the sturdy, hardy fishermen of the parish of Knock is of greater importance than the grazing of a few hundred sheep?[92]

Torquil MacLeod from Knock told the Napier Commission:

I remember the tack adjoining our township having been occupied by a crofting population. I could purchase a stone of meal from them when I required it, a barrel of potatoes, a bushel of oats and a pint of milk. I see nothing on that farm today except green grass, rushes and white sheep. It was a Mr Alexander that occupied it, and the farm was Aignish.[93]

MacLeod was wrong, in that Aiginis had never been a crofting township, but no doubt when Alexander had the lease of the farm, he also had sub-tenants on part of it, and this will be what MacLeod is referring to.

The tenant of Aiginis in 1888 was Samuel Newall, whom we met already at Tolastadh, and his evidence to the court in the trial of the rioters tells what occurred:

> On Saturday the 24th Day of December I was out with my gun on Aignish shooting rabbits, and about twelve o'clock I saw a number of people on the public road, which leads past my farm from Stornoway to Garrabost . . . A crowd of people, upwards of two hundred, crossed the fence by a gap in the wall near the gate, and marched to the farm steading where I reside. As the crowd was crossing the fence one of them said to me that I would have to quit the farm of Aignish with my whole stock within ten days or a fortnight as they were going to take possession of the farm and to commence to plough it.[94]

The would-be raiders met at Garrabost, and decided that:

> On the 9th January, all the able-bodied men of the parish should gather in the same place, and march as a body to the farms at Melbost and Aignish, driving the whole stock on these farms before them towards Stornoway and on to the Castle policies where they are to be left.

Hector Smith, police sergeant, tells of the day of the riot:

> On Monday the 9th January, I accompanied the rest of the Police Force to Aignish Farm arriving there before daylight . . . The people assembled about midday . . . As soon as they got on to the farm Sheriff Fraser proceeded to meet them; they were stretched in a long line almost across the farm and driving the sheep and cattle before them. I saw the Sheriff attempt to read something, and then I saw them break away. We all ran after them, but at this stage we had no orders to apprehend any, but shortly afterwards orders were given to make apprehensions. After that I took charge of the prisoners. We then proceeded until we came to an embankment near the road where we made a halt. During the halt near the roadside I heard Sheriff Fraser read the Riot Act. He then read it a second time and explained it in Gaelic. There were sticks and stones thrown by the crowd particularly at the police and I was struck on the helmet by a stick which was thrown at me. We kept the prisoners at the place mentioned for considerably over an hour until a detachment of the Royal Scots arrived and they were then marched away to Stornoway.[95]

61. Donald MacLeod (Am Boer) and his wife

The prisoners were sent to Edinburgh for trial on a charge of mobbing and rioting. Their defences were mainly on the question of whether those arrested had actually been involved, rather than on the merits of the case, but in the end they were almost all found guilty and sentenced to prison for periods ranging from 12 to 15 months.

It is interesting that almost all those arrested were from the Aird district at the far end of an Rubha from Aiginis. Donald MacLeod from Seisiadar, Chris's grandmother's brother, was one of those arrested. According to the family, Donald – better remembered as Am Boer – had not gone to take part in the Riot at all but was on his way to Steornabhagh for a message, along with his brother-in-law, when they stopped to watch what was going on. 'Let's carry on – this is not our quarrel,' said the brother-in-law, but Donald was stubborn and wanted to stay and watch, and of course got mixed in with the crowd – and the next thing he knew, he had been arrested and ended up in jail. When he was released, he was met on the pier in Steornabhagh by a piper, but that was at least partly in fun!

The result of the riot was inconclusive. Aiginis was eventually split up into 32 crofts, but that was not until nearly 20 years later, in 1905. There is still some crofting there, but a large part of the township has been given over to sites for housing for commuters, some of them rather

62. Cairn at Aiginis

over-ostentatious for a crofting area – I wonder what the rioters would think of the township today!

Opposite the church of the Uidh is a cairn, built to celebrate the Aiginis Riot; it was designed by the eminent Will MacLean and built by the mason Jim Crawford in 1995. But doesn't it tell you something about the powers that be on the island that money can be found to build monuments to the land-raids of the 1880s, but not to replace a priceless church?

Suardail and an Cnoc (Swordale & Knock)

The narrow crofts of Suardail and an Cnoc rise above the shore on the south side of the road opposite Aiginis.

Out on the headland south of Suardail are the ruins of another church:

> East of Chicken Head in a small enclosure on the left bank of a small rivulet, near the edge of a cliff which rises more than 100 feet out of the sea, are the foundations of a stone and mud building about 18 feet in length and 15 feet in breadth, orientated west-north-west and east-south-east.[96]

Etymologically, this raises a problem. Why is the headland called

Chicken Head (Ceann na Circ in Gaelic)? What have chickens to do with the headland? Was it really named after the old kirk, which got phoneticised into Gaelic as Circ, and then translated into English as Chicken? Who now knows?

The shore below Suardail was the site of a shipwreck in July 1821:

> A boat having been driven on shore below Swordale on Monday last by a gale which continued from Sunday till Monday night, the Custom House surveyor went down to examine her as a smuggler and found a large sum in dollars in the seamen's chests. The crew consisted of the mate and two sailors, natives of Britain and three foreigners, one of them a Maltese boy who took the opportunity of running off to the Custom House Surveyor, as he was leaving the boat and told him that the mate and the cook (a Frenchman) had murdered the captain and one of the crew at sea and seized the vessel and about 40,000 dollars which was on board; that the rest of the crew were compelled to join in sharing the money; two of them, Scots lads, were kept below for near 60 hours after the murder and were nearly smoked to death, but the attempt to smoke them to death having failed, they were allowed, on the intercession of the boy and another Italian sailor to get on deck after being sworn to secrecy. They meant to land in Scotland, came first to Barra, bought a boat there and came to the Broad Bay, when on Saturday night they scuttled their vessel (a schooner) and went into the boat, meaning to go to the mainland, but the gale put them on shore, and they hid most of the money in the sand.
>
> There has been got 31,000 dollars which are in the Custom House, and Captain Oliver takes the crew to Edinburgh to the charge of the Lord Advocate to whom we have consigned them.[97]

The schooner was the *Jane* of Gibraltar, and her story begins a day earlier, on the Sunday, when a wreck was seen off Tolastadh. The Tolastadh men had sent out a boat to her, and found her water-logged and crewless, and had tried to tow her ashore, but had to give up because of the weather. The story is told in full detail in James Shaw Grant's *The Gaelic Vikings*,[98] one of a series of books with a grand selection of tales from the Islands.

Evander MacIver of Griais remembered the occasion:

> But what I specially remember was the arrival at the Custom House of several carts loaded with silver dollars, and the turnout of the whole people of Stornoway, old and young, male and female, to see such a wonderful and rare sight as cartloads of silver in the streets of the town. It was currently reported afterwards that on the night in

which they had been deposited in Mrs Morrison's barn in Swordale, a considerable amount had been abstracted, but by whom or by what means never transpired. Certain it is that for a year or two silver dollars were current in the town and shops, and that when a pound note was changed, dollars formed part of the silver given for it. When I left Stornoway I carried with me several dollars for each of which I got 3s10d from a silversmith in the North Bridge, Edinburgh.[99]

There is a rental of 1766 for Suardail area in the Gillanders of Highfield Papers.[100] George Gillanders, the factor, held the lease of most of an Rubha, but sublet some of the townships in this area. The subtenants listed then are George Stewart, John Stewart, John Babie, Norman Bain, Donald McLeod, Archie McLeod in Suardail, and in an Cnoc, Torquil McLeod, Norman McNeil, Donald McNeil, John MacRonald, Norman Roy, Donald Bain, Murdo MacInnes, Donald Mcendhui, John macWilliam, John McCoil Oig, Norman McLeod, Donald MacLeod. Most of these are patronymics – so Norman McNeil is Norman son of Neil. The Stewarts are not indigenous to Lewis, so they have a surname, and the use of the surname by the MacLeods may represent a claim that they were *the* MacLeods – heirs of the clan chiefs. But who were the Babies? Today, they are MacKenzies, but it is suggested that they, like the Stewarts of Col, are descended from followers of Barbara Stewart, second wife of Roderick, the last MacLeod chief. I can understand how Babaich came from Barbara, but it is harder to understand why a family connected to the MacLeod chiefs would have eventually taken the surname of their successful adversary.

By the time of the *Jane* Suardail had become a farm again, tenanted by a family of Morrisons, two of whom reached fame in the navy: Lieutenant John Morrison, who fought at Trafalgar, died in 1827 and was buried in Aiginis, where there is an ornate, though rather badly weathered, stone; and James Morrison, who was one of the crew of the *Bounty*. James Shaw Grant has written at length of James Morrison and his connection to Suardail in his *Morrison of the Bounty*, and you can read the whole tale there, but I cannot refrain from quoting one marvellous more recent story. Apparently James had taken an elderly aunt, with Morrison connections, to see the film *Mutiny on the Bounty*; her reaction was that it proved there was a family connection, as the man in the film looked so like her people!

Many of the families of Suardail came there from Circeabost in Bearnaraigh when that township was cleared in the 1820s – MacMillans, MacDonalds, MacKays and MacLeods – while those of an Cnoc tended to have been living in the area before the crofts were made, possibly working on the farms there.

One family connected with an Cnoc are the Crichtons, who derive from a William Crichton, who was a mason on Aiginis Farm in the early 1800s. He is believed to have been a son of Colin Crichton, merchant in Steornabhagh, but since the Misses Crichton there are later described as the heirs of Colin Crichton, it may be that William was an illegitimate son, and so debarred from inheritance. Colin Crichton was married to Catherine MacKenzie of Ballone, but in one of the manuscripts he is named as Colin MacKnight! Certainly all the Crichtons in Lewis now are descended from William of Aiginis.

In 1823 legislation was passed in Parliament to authorise the expenditure of £50,000, in order to build thirty new churches in the Highlands, and rebuild another ten. Commissioners were appointed to be responsible for the location and building of the new churches, and they invited applications from local landowners, since they would be liable for part of the future upkeep of the buildings. Stewart-MacKenzie was one of the first applicants, with his application submitted the day after the first meeting of the Commissioners, for churches in an Rubha and Nis.

An Rubha was at this time without a church, except for occasional services in the Uidh Church. Rev. John Cameron, in the New Statistical Account of Scotland in 1833, notes that:

> The chapel at Ui has strong walls still standing. The south-west end of it is roofed and slated; the minister of Stornoway used to preach there, once in six weeks, before the Government Church was erected.[101]

The Commissioners appointed Thomas Telford as their Chief Surveyor, and the churches built to his plans and paid for by the Commissioners are generally known as Telford Churches, although the organisation of the work was done mainly by John Rickman, the Secretary to the Commissioners.

Sites were picked for the two Lewis churches in 1826, and work commenced the following spring. In March 1827, the Lewis Presbytery changed its mind about the site of the church, and wanted it moved to

63. Telford Church and Manse

Garrabost, then in June changed its mind again, in favour of a site in Pabail, but by this time the foundations had been laid at an Cnoc, and it was too late for any changes.

The Telford Church lost most of its congregation at the Disruption of 1843, when most of the families in an Rubha joined the new Free Church. The last minister there was Rev. Angus MacLeod – mac Choinnich Bhaird – from Suainebost. After this, the church was allowed to decay and was finally demolished in 1970.

Garrabost

At the west end of Garrabost is the Garrabost mill, one of the few still producing meal for sale. In the old rentals the reference is always to the Miln of Aignish, but this had long ceased to work, and the Estate Mill in Steornabhagh was the nearest place where crofters from an Rubha could have their grain milled. It was destroyed by fire in 1890, and an Rubha was without a mill for a few years. There had been an old 'Norse' mill on Allt na Muilne near the Garrabost churches, but this had long been out of commission. Unless you still had an old hand-quern, you had to go to Griais.

The present mill was built in 1895, and is noted by the architect Mary Miers in her book *The Western Seaboard:*

64. Garrabost Min-Eorna

65. Garrabost Mill

Mill building of locally quarried stone, with kiln and stables of Garrabost brick. The mill, which ceased full time operation in 1956 has an overshot wheel formerly powered by water from Allt nan Gall (no longer working) and what is believed to be the only surviving example of a Simplex Oil Engine, dating from 1908 and still operational. The meal-mill was restored to full working order in 1988–90 and produces barley flour used by the local bakery.[102]

The first miller was Malcolm MacIver from Bhataisgeir, but his family emigrated to Canada, and the mill passed to Angus Morrison from Tabost, Nis, whose family still run the mill.

The mill lade was fed from a reservoir on the moor above the main road, in an area where the travelling people used to camp. One night, after a particularly heavy storm, the dam burst and flooded the camp. The travellers fled, undressed for the night, down the stream and along the road towards Aiginis, where they caused a panic to folk who saw the naked figures running through the graveyard and reckoned it was *La an Ais-eirigh* – the Resurrection. James Shaw Grant tells this story also, in his *Surprise Island*, and ascribes it to Anderson Young, a salmon-curer at Sanndabhaig Cottage, of whom his wife said that his stories had just enough truth in them to hold the lies together.

There is a Gaelic saying *Mar a chaidh a maor troimh' Gharrabost* – as fast as the ground officer went through Garrabost. It is sometimes said that this was said of Donald Munro, the factor, because he was so hated by the crofter women that they pelted him with turf – and worse! – but this does not seem likely to me. Munro was a little tyrant, and I doubt whether anyone would have dared attack him openly. Rev. William

Matheson suggests that the saying is very much older, and belongs to the days of the tacksmen, who were always at loggerheads with the factor – though I must admit that the thought of Munro being chased by the *cailleachan* is much more appealing!

The tacksmen of Garrabost were a family of MacLeods. That in itself is strange, for most of the tacks in Lewis were given by MacKenzie to those who had supported him in his fight against the old MacLeod chiefs, but Norman MacLeod of Garrabost was married to a daughter of MacKenzie of Kildun, whom we shall meet later, in Airinis, and perhaps this connection made him more acceptable to the Seaforths. The MacKenzies of Kildun were one of the few Roman Catholic families in Lewis, and this presumably explains why two of Norman MacLeod's sons became Jesuit priests. Another son, Torquil, succeeded his father as tacksman of Garrabost. Though a committed Jacobite, he took no part in the '45 rebellion. Unfortunately, several years later he got into a drunken argument with Captain Barlow of the Buffs, who was in charge of an exploratory expedition to the Islands, and was heard to utter 'Treasonable expressions' for which he was arrested, and taken to London, from where he never returned.

He was succeeded by his brother George, and he was such a thorn in the flesh of the estate authorities as to suggest that it was he who gave rise to the saying about the *maor*. According to the Bannatyne manuscript 'he was bred to the Roman Catholic Church, was a scholar, an antiquary and one of the best genealogists in the Highlands'. Unfortunately, though he must have known the exact connection of his own MacLeods to the line of the old MacLeod chiefs, it has not been preserved.

George MacLeod's son Kenneth later moved to Leumrabhagh, and Kenneth's son John became famous in the story of the Hudson's Bay Company, as we shall see when we reach that township; but there was another, older, John MacLeod, also from Garrabost, who enlisted with the Hudson's Bay Company in 1811. Although he went out as a 'gentleman clerk', he soon found himself in the middle of the long-standing feud between the Hudson's Bay Company and the North-West Company:

> In summer 1815 after the Governor of the Colony was taken prisoner And all the Colonists & Company's servants were driven off the ground at Red River Settlement, and neither Mr Sutherland, Pritchard, Archd McDonald, the late Roderick McKenzie nor any other officers would remain in charge, I volunteered to Mr Sutherland to remain with 3 men, namely Archd Currie, Hugh McLean and James McIntosh, to look after both Company and Colony's. My opponent Alex McDonell of the N.W. Company had 70 men principally composed of Half Breeds with Cuthbert Grant

as his 2nd. After our people left me with only three men I collected all the property in the one House, but the following day McDonell sent Grant with 80 men and set fire to all the buildings. All I could do was to break open a window in the store the trading Goods were in and succeeded in safing the most part from the flames, for the Doors and the whole building were in flames before I could finish. Through Grant's lenity I safed the bulk of the trading Goods and after the enemy had dispersed I engaged the freemen & sent them to prepare timber to erect new buildings, got the crop secured, fences put up & had Fort Douglas erected before Mr Colin Robertson arrived with Brigade from Montreal.[103]

John MacLeod never returned to Lewis, but died at Hochega, now part of Montreal, in 1849.

On the western side of Garrabost is the area known as Buaile na Creadha – Claypark. There is a deposit of red clay here, and one of Sir James Matheson's ill-fated schemes was to build a brick and tile works here. The 1851 census lists a John Smith from Cumnock in Ayrshire as a 'tile manufacturer, employing 28 persons'.

The brickworks drew its raw materials from the clay found locally, and although demand for brick never really built up in the island, there were many houses with roofs made of Garrabost tiles – indeed the last example in Garrabost itself has only recently been demolished. Perhaps the brick and tile works by itself could have been a success, but unfortunately it was linked with the Lewis Chemical Works, a works for distilling paraffin and tar-products, which was set up near the River Creed, just outside the Stornoway Castle Grounds. By the time of the 1861 census, there was no longer a resident manager at the brickworks, but instead the house was let to Dr Benjamin Paul of the paraffin works, while the brickworks was being run by an Irish labourer, James MacFadden. He was then promoted to Chemical Manager at the paraffin works – with no qualification whatsoever – and his brother Hugh MacFadden took over in Garrabost until the failure of both projects in the 1870s.[104]

As we saw at the chemical works at Marybank, Matheson had a genius for picking the wrong people, and then leaving them unsupervised.

A gaunt red-brick building – an t-Seada Dhearg – still stands in Garrabost to mark the site of the brickworks, but there is nothing else apart from the name to tell that Buaile na Creadha was there.

Garrabost families include MacSweens, Montgomeries and MacLeods – Sliochd a' Chaiptein – all good Raasay names, which suggests that they were among the refugees from that island after its harrying by Government troops after the '45. An Rubha is after all the

66. An t-Seada Dhearg

first obvious landfall after coming round the north of Skye, and the MacLeod chiefs of Raasay always claimed a link with those of Lewis.

Of a different origin were the MacKays, the first of whom, Alexander MacKay, came from the Parish of Urray, near Dingwall, to the farm of Aignis in about 1800. He was married twice, with eight sons and three daughters, so it is little wonder that there are descendants all over an Rubha.

Garrabost is now the biggest township in an Rubha, with one line of crofts on a road running down to the shore, and another along the main road, the croft where they meet being known as 'Lot a' Chrossaich', from an Alexander Cross from Gairloch, who was the first tenant there.

One person in Garrabost who fascinates me, partly because of tales my late mother-in-law told, and partly because the story remains unfinished, is that of her grand-uncle Roderick MacDonald, son of Donald Og MacDonald of No 2 Garrabost. According to Mairi, he became a Professor of Greek in the Free Church, but fell out with them, and went to Greece, where he married. His entry in Ewing's *Annals of the Free Church of Scotland* is rather terse:

> Ordained as missionary to Madras, 1876. Married in the same year Rosa Traill. Translated 1878 to Calcutta from which he was removed in 1887.[105]

Rosa Traill was from Orkney, but she died and Roderick went to Greece to teach English, where he was married again, to a French lady remembered in Garrabost as 'Aphro'. We do not know when he died, but it is remembered that his widow used to send letters in French to

67. Garrabost

his brother Neil in Garrabost, who used to get a pupil in the Nicolson Institute to read them for him. However, despite requests to the Free Church headquarters, we have not been able to find out any more about him. Whatever the reason for his removal – I have heard that it was because he supported Darwin, but that is just hearsay – there must be a record of the decision and the reasons therefor in the Free Church records. The 'Professor' was an uncle of Dr Donald MacDonald – an Dotair Domhnallach – and John MacDonald, school inspector, in Steornabhagh.

There was a Murray family whose history was firmly rooted in Garrabost, though no doubt they would be derived from the Gobha Gorm whom we met in Part 1, coming ashore at Cunndal at Eorapaigh. The family can be traced back to Roderick Murray, who was born in about 1770, but our immediate interest is his grandson John – Iain Dhomhnaill 'ic Ruairidh. He had been on a couple of tours of duty with the Hudson's Bay Company, and was known as the Innseanach – the Indian – when he returned to Lewis. Eventually he married Kirsty MacAulay – ni'n Iain Duinn – from Seisiadar, and after a few years they decided to join the many Lewis families who were already in the Eastern Townships of Quebec. Most of the best arable land had already been taken up, and they settled along with some families from na Lochan in an area which they named Balallan. They had three children going out, and another in Quebec. They later moved to Manchester, New Hampshire, in the USA, where John had a box-making business. Just before the First World War, his son, Iain, came across to Lewis, and spent a holiday wandering the shores of Lewis and Harris. When war

68. John Murray (An t-Innseanach) and family

broke out, he returned to the USA, and the local people decided that he must have been a spy – who else would spend his time walking around the shore of the islands?

The Innseanach and his wife are buried in Riverview Cemetery in Scotstown, Quebec. Chris and I have visited their gravestone there, and have met their great-grandson Murray Higgins on several occasions here and in Canada.

In 1851 further crofts were made in the Newlands, on the moor side of the main road, but these caused many complaints from the existing tenants of the old crofts, who claimed that they spoiled the access to the common grazings.

Because of its position on the main road, Garrabost was the first village in an Rubha to have a post office, opened in 1855, with a weekly post, increased in 1873 to thrice weekly. In 1888, the post-run was extended to Port nan Giuran, and in 1901 to the lighthouse at Tiumpan, though Pabail had to wait until 1934 before they got a post-office, for which they had been agitating since 1889.[106]

69. Garrabost

Pabail (Bayble)

As far back as records exist, there seem to have been two separate tacks, of Pabail Uarach (Upper Bayble) and Pabail Iarach (Lower or Nether Bayble).

At the time of the Judicial Rental of 1754[107] Nether Bayble was a tack possessed by Murdo McKenzie, Thomas's son:

> Compeared Alexr.Morison, Tenant in Nether Bible, a married man aged about sixty . . . Depones that the town of Nether Bible consists of 3 pennies land and is possesst by Eleven Tenants and a half-farthing in the Tacksman's hand, Depones that each farthing land pays sixteen marks Scots money rent yearly, So that the whole Town pays one hounder and ninty two marks Scots money rent yearly, and that he has lived in Nether Bible upward of twenty years.

His evidence is corroborated by John Graham, 'a married man aged thirty years, who has lived in Nether Bible seven years past'.

Pabail Uarach was held in tack by George McLeod:

> Compeared John MacIntyre tenant in Upper Bible depones that the Town of Upper Bible consists of four pennies and a half, of which three pennies thereof is possest by Twelve tenants and the other pence and ½ by the tacksman. That each farthing thereof pays fifteen marks yearly money rent so that the whole town pays two hundred

and seventy marks money rent yearly, Depones they pay a weekly days service, a peck of meal, a cock and hen yearly, and that he has lived in Upper Bible twelve years . . .

again corroborated by 'Neil McCoul vic Conchie, who has lived in Upper Bible these six years past'. Neil McCoul vic Conchie would have been Neil son of Dougal son of Duncan, while John MacIntyre was most likely John mac an t-Saoir – John son of the carpenter.

A mark was ⅔ of a pound Scots, of which there were twelve to a pound sterling at that period.

Pabail took most of its income from fishing, but proper facilities were missing at the time of the Napier Commission in 1883, according to John Stewart:

> They say Cape Horn is a wild place. Now this place where I live is exposed to the winds that blow down upon the one side from Cape Wrath and upon the other from the Butt of Lewis – two places that are quite as wild as Cape Horn. Our shore is so exposed from these two quarters, that while we could work well enough at sea, we are not able to save our lives or our boats when we reach the land. For want of a place of refuge, I lost a boat that cost over £100. If we had a place of refuge there, since we can work well, we would be able to take our living out of the sea, as other people in Scotland are able to do.[108]

According to Mr Joseph Heathcote, chief officer of the Coastguard Station at Stornoway for the purpose of drilling the RNR men of the district, in 1885:

> Bayble have about 90 boats – from Bayble, Garrabost, Knock, Swordale produce a fishing population of from 600 to 700 men. Boats are from 10 to 20 tons each at an average cost for each of £350. Total population of these townships is from 1400–1500. A large proportion are RNR men, a fine, intelligent looking body of men.

Pabail is also famous for writers from the village. One of my wife Chris's treasures is an autographed first edition of Iain Crichton Smith's *The Long River*, which contains this short poem:

> Some days were running legs and joy
> and old men telling tomorrow would be
> a fine day surely; for sky was red
> at setting of sun between the hills.

> Some nights were parting at the gates
> with day's companions; and dew falling
> on heads clear of ambition except light
> returning and throwing stones at sticks.

70. Going to the Boats – Pabail

Some days were rain flooding forever the green
pasture; and horses turning to the wind
bare smooth backs. The toothed rocks rising
sharp and grey out of the ancient sea.

Some nights were shawling mirrors lest the lightning
strike with the eel's speed out of the storm.
Black the roman rooks came from the left squawking
And the evening flowed back around their wings.[109]

And of course there is also Derick Thomson – a bard in both Gaidhlig
and English:

Bagh Phabail fodham, is baile Phabail air faire
sluaisreadh siorraidh a' chuain, a lorg 's a shireadh
eadar clachan a' mhuil 's an eag nan sgeir,
is fo ghainmhich a' gheodha,
gluasad bithbhuan a' bhaile, am bas, 's an urtan,
an urnaigh 's an t-suirghe, is mile cridhe
ag at 's a' seacadh, is ann an seo
tha a' churracag a' ruith 's a' stad,
's a' ruith 's a' stad, 's a' ruith 's a' stad.[110]

Bayble bay below me, and the village on the skyline, the eternal action of the ocean, its seeking and searching between the pebble stones and in the rock crannies and under the sand of the cove; the everlasting movement of the village, death and christening, praying and courting, and a thousand hearts swelling and sinking, and here, the plover runs and stops, and runs and stops, and runs and stops.

and Chris has a special liking for his poem: 'Hol, air atharrachadh'

Is gann gu faca mi Hol am bliadhna,
bha e fas cho beag;
feumaidh gu robh 'n Cruthaighear trang
leis an tarbh-chrann
a' sgriobadh a' mhullaich dheth
a bha cho ard 's cho fionnar
's ga charadh aig a' bhonn,
a' toirt air falbh a chaisead,
agus is docha a mhaise
ga liomhadh gus a robh a chruth
air a chall.

Air a neo
's ann ormsa bha E 'g obair

'S mas ann
de eile rinn E orm?

I hardly noticed Hol this year,
it has become so small a hill;
the Creator must have been busy
with the bulldozer
scraping away its summit
that was so high and fresh
and depositing it at the foot,
robbing it of its steepness
and perhaps of its beauty,
smoothing it until its lines
were lost.

Alternatively
He was at work on me

And if so,
what else did He do to me?[111]

And we have more modern poets too, like Anna Frater:

Eilean Phabail

Mar thusa, tha mise
nam dhà leth;
a' seòladh air cuan
ach ceangailte ri creagan m' àraich
uaine agus flùran
a' sreap gu grian
agus nèamh;
creagan donn a' bàthadh
fo mhuir agus feamainn
agus dorchadas.

Like you, I am
divided.
floating on sea
but made fast
to my ground rock;
green and flowers
climbing to the sun
and heaven;
brown rocks drowning
under brine and tangle
in darkness.[112]

What a relief to be able to have poets' own translations, instead of
my own doggerel!

There is a well-known story about a murder which took place in
Pabail. Malcolm MacLeod, who had been a Gaelic school teacher in
Arnisdale, near Glenelg, had developed what today would have been
reckoned a religious mania, and killed his wife out of jealousy for her
position in the local church. An account of his trial occurs in Lord
Cockburn's *Circuit Journeys*, though he gives his name wrongly as
MacLean:

17th April 1838

On Saturday the 14th I was in Court until midnight. The only
curious case was that of Malcolm MacLean, a fisherman from Lewis,
who is doomed to die upon the 11th of May, for the murder of his
wife. He admitted that he killed her, and intentionally, but the
defence by his counsel was that he was mad at the time. There was
not the slightest foundation for this, for though he was often under
the influence of an odd mixture of wild religious speculation, and
of terrified superstition, he had no illusion, and in all the affairs of

life, including his own feelings and concerns, was always dealt with as a sound practical man.

This man's declaration, which told the whole truth with anxious candour, contained a curious and fearful description of the feelings of a man about to commit a deliberate murder. He is now low and resigned, and says he has not been so comfortable for years, because he has got the better of the Devil at last, and is sure of defying him on the 11th of May.[113]

Despite Cockburn's decision, local tradition said that MacLeod's sentence was commuted to transportation to Australia, as part of the celebrations of Queen Victoria's birthday, which seemed to me very unlikely.

However, just recently, a descendant has been in contact with us from Ottawa, and he had records to show that MacLeod, despite being sentenced to death, had obtained a commutation of his sentence to transportation, and had been shipped to Australia, where he died in 1858, after being for a spell on remote Norfolk Island.

Cockburn has an interesting comment on local culture:

One part of his pretended craziness was said to consist in his making machinery to achieve the perpetual motion, and his believing that he had succeeded. This shows that this famous problem is not in such vogue as it once was. But the thing that seemed to me oddest in the matter was the perfect familiarity with which the common Celts of Lewis talked and thought of the thing called the perpetual motion, whatever they fancied it. Their word for it, according to the common process of borrowing terms with ideas, was 'Perpetual Motion' pronounced and treated by them as a Gaelic expression.

THE BEACH, LOWER BAYBLE, STORNOWAY.

71. Pabail Iarach Beach

The words 'Perpetual Motion' were used in the middle of a Gaelic sentence without stop or surprise, exactly as we use any Angilified French term.[114]

Laurie Robinson, in his *Sea-Fishing in Scotland*, noted that:

Three or four miles off Bayble Island lies the first-class grounds where the local commercial fishermen shoot their great lines for cod, ling, conger and skate. The early months of the year are most productive on these grounds, though the weather is to be contended with at this time.[115]

South of Pabail Iarach lies a street of new crofts, known as Cnoc na h-Iolaire, but rendered into English as Eagleton. Now the road-signs say Baile na h-Iolaire, a straight translation from the English. I have no problem at all with Gaelic road-signs, but I do wish that they would get them right!

Siulaisiadar (Shulishader)

Siulaisiadar is now a fairly small township, but at one time it was a farm comprising the whole of an Rubha east of Garrabost and Pabail. There is quite a bit of confusion about the names of some of the townships in the area. In the Judicial Rental of 1754 there are two tacks – William MacKenzie at 'Sulishader or Point of Aird', and Alexander Morrison at 'Shather and Sheshaddir,' so it is clear that at this time, the name Shulishader referred not to the village now known by that name but to the farm of Aird, comprising the present townships of Port nan Giuran, Port Mholair and an Aird. In later years the farms of Shather and Shulishader were combined, and the name Siulaisiadar was eventually transferred to the old Shather village, two or more miles away from its original site!

In 1766 'Point of Aird' had been transferred to the huge tack held by George Gillanders, which included also 'Aignis, Knock, Swordale, Nether Bible and Branahaiy and Shildernish' – virtually all of an Rubha except Garrabost, Pabail Uarach and Siadar. In 1776 Garrabost also was added to Gillanders' tack, but Siadar and Seisiadar remained in the hands of Alexander Morrison.

Alexander Morrison probably died in 1780, for the lease of that year has his name cancelled out and John substituted. In the Sheriff Court Papers[116] for 1791, there is a set of 'warnings-away' at the instance of George Gillanders, tacksman, of Shader and Shulishader tacksmen – Ann MacIver, widow of Murdo MacKenzie and son Donald MacKenzie, John Morrison, and James Morrison, merchant in

Stornoway. The MacKenzies were at Point of Aird, while the Morrisons were at Shader.

There are copious letters from John Morrison in the Seaforth Papers, many of them urging Seaforth to do away with the tacksman system and let the land directly to crofter/fishermen. This may seem a rather strange point of view, as he had been a tacksman himself, but Morrison was also a fish-curer, who would stand to gain from the improvement in the commercial fishing industry.

Gillanders took the tack of Siulaisiadar into his own hands for a time, and was still tacksman there in 1814, but by 1825 it had been broken up; a small portion was held by Kenneth MacLeod, believed to have been a son of George MacLeod of Pabail and Garrabost, and the rest was shared between ten crofters who had been evicted from Circeabost on Bearnaraigh – MacMillans, MacKays, Buchanans and MacAulays.

In the late 1830s Kenneth MacLeod died, and his part of the township was made into a further seven crofts. A Donald MacKenzie from an Cnoc, but with an ancestry from an Aird, took one of them, and his son William MacKenzie – Uilleam Dhomhnaill 'ic Choinnich – wrote some of the most heart-rending poetry ever to come out of Lewis. He had been married to Mary MacKay – Mairi ni'n Alasdair – but she died in 1904 and left him heart-broken. By 1907 their surviving sons had emigrated to Canada, and now his daughter was keen to do so too:

Thug sinn fichead bliadhna posd'
Is bha sinn og ri leannanachd,
Is nuair a b' fhearr a bha ar doigh
Nach bronach rinn sinn dealachadh.

Tha an teaghlach is iad ri togail uam
Ri dol air chuan do Chanada
Bho chaidh am mathair do an uaigh
Is e sud thug fuachd do' n dachaidh orr'.

Is mi dheanadh deonach leo falbh,
Na' n cuirte marbh mi dhachadih as,
Is gun 'n cuirte laighe mi 's an uir,
Far bheil mo run is Alasdair

Cha do smaoinich sinn riamh 's i beo
Gu 'm biodh cuan mor 'gar dealachadh
Gu 'm biodh i adhlaichte air an Aoidh
Is mis' fo chraoibh an Canada.[117]

We were twenty years married
And sweethearts from our youth
Just when we were at our happiest
Sadly we had to part

The children are moving away from me
To cross the ocean to Canada
Since their mother went to the grave
There is a coldness in our home for them

I would willingly go with them
If my body could be sent home from there
So that I could be laid in the ground
Where lie my love and Alasdair

We never thought when she was alive
That the great ocean would divide us
That she would be buried at the Uidh
And I under the trees in Canada.

At length he decided to go, but left part of himself beside Mairi in Lewis – literally!

Cha bhi duil am tuilleadh tuille
Ma theid mi idir thar sal;
Tha falt mo chinn dhomh ag innseadh
Gu bheil mo thide gu bhi' n aird.

Chan fhaicear leam Eilean Leodhais,
'S cha 'n fhaic mi 'n t-Siumpan na h-Airde,
'S cha 'n fhaicear leam Cladh na h-Aoidhe,
Ged tha m'inntinn ann an sas.

Dh' fhag mi aon ann de m' fhiaclan
Thug mi as mo bheul le cradh,
'S e coltach gu 'm bi iomadh mile
Eadar i 's far 'n cuirear cach.[118]

I doubt if I will return again
If I once go across the sea;
The hairs of my head are telling me
That my time is almost up.

I won't see the Isle of Lewis
I won't see Tiumpan Point
I won't see the graveyard of Uidh
Even though my thoughts are there.

72. Uilleam's grandson, Ian MacKenzie,
at the bard's grave in Thunder Bay

> I left there one of my teeth
> That I pulled from my mouth with pain;
> Likely there will be many miles
> Between it and where the rest will lie.

And to hear these songs, sung in all their passion and pathos by the late Joan MacKenzie – Seonag Smiotch – is to understand the desperation of emigration for the elderly: for the young there was adventure and opportunity, but for the old there was only death in a strange land.

Chris and I paid a visit to her cousins in Thunder Bay a few years ago, where we made a visit to the grave of Uilleam Dhomhnaill 'ic Choinnich, and met four of his grandchildren. One of them expressed a wish to have a copy of the book of his poems – *Cnoc Chusbaig* – which is quite hard to get today. However Chris found one for sale on eBay – in Regina, Saskatchewan. We got it, and when we opened it, it was full of the smell of peat smoke. It had originally been sent to Canada by a lady from Tunga, and I reckon she had held it over an open peat fire before she parcelled it, to send an extra souvenir of Lewis along with the book!

73. Siulaisiadar Axe

Siulaisiadar also was the site of one the earliest archaeological artefacts found in Lewis – a Neolithic ritual stone axe-head with a hawthorn shaft, which has been carbon-dated to around 3150BC. It was found at the bottom of a peat-bank – another example of the spread of peat over the landscape of the Hebrides.

Seisiadar (Sheshader)

The crofting history of the village only goes back to the 1820s, but unlike most of the other townships of the area, it seems to have been settled mainly by people who were already in an Rubha, probably working on the farm of an Aird. But the area has a much older history than that, and peat-cutters frequently find old walls, pottery, etc. under the cover of peat.

The oldest – and oddest – thing found in Seisiadar is just that: the 'Seisiadar Thing'!

It consists of a pad of compressed cattle hairs attached to several cords, some of twisted wool and some of horse hair, dating to 1200–950 BC.[119]

It has been assigned to the Bronze Age, but nobody seems to have a clue about what on earth it was. It has obviously been manufactured, but why?

Seisiadar is my wife Chris's own home village, and she has a great many stories from the old people there, some of which we published in *Sgeulachdan a Seisiadar*.

From the days when the tack was taken over by George Gillanders in 1791, there is still a place-name Bathaichean Gillanders – Gillanders' barns – out behind the post-war allotments to the west of the township, and known as Hiort because they were so far out, nearer the main road.

74. Feannagan – Rigs

Kenneth Nicolson – Coinneach Fhionnlaidh – at No 6 Seisiadar remembered his granny telling about her granny:

> ag innseadh dhi gu robh cuimhn' aice air corc a bhi fas aig na feannagan anns a Bhaile Shuas agus i ri tighinn tarsuinn na mointich

– telling how she remembered the corn growing on the rigs in the Baile Shuas when she was coming across the moor from Pabail to Seisiadar.

Seisiadar appears in the report of the Board for Congested Districts in 1902:

> On 31st August 1901, we received an application from the Landward Committee of the Stornoway Parish Council for grants in aid of the construction of two public ways – one of which was a footpath 5 feet wide from the village of Sheshader to the Aird School. They stated that the want of this path is keenly felt, as there are about 90 children of school age in the village. The length of the path was given as 1200 yards and the estimated cost as £80. We consulted the Scottish Education Department, and were informed that the proposed footpath is urgently needed in the interests of education in Sheshader village. In wet weather the children suffer greatly from the effects of spending the day in school with wet feet. Our Engineer reported favourably to us, and we accordingly informed the Landward Committee that we were prepared to make a grant of £60 on the usual conditions.[120]

75. Chris's Mother and Granny Outside their Shop

In Chris's day there were less than 30 children going to Aird School
from Seisiadar, and they had a bus going to school, but on a good day
they still went home along the Rathad Beag.

On a recent visit to Thunder Bay, Chris and I met Nan Anderson
and her sister Etta Hancock. Since the 1890s people from an Rubha had
been going to Fort William and Port Arthur, now joined as Thunder
Bay, to work on Lake Superior and in the grain elevators – little wonder
it was known as 'Point on the Lake'. They had lived in rooms above
Mac's Imperial Bar in Steornabhagh, then her father had gone to Fort
William, and they went to live with their grandfather Murchadh Alasdair
Dhuinn in Seisiadar. Etta remembered a big white ship going past in
the Minch – the biggest ship she had ever seen – and her granny crying.
When she asked why, she was told it was because all the young men were
going away on the ship – the *Metagama*. She remembered going across
the Rathad Beag to school in an Aird, and stopping at 'Cilidh's' shop
to buy a *Brisgeid Chruaidh* – the hard biscuits that Craggan in Lacasdal
made – to take to eat in school, though very often they ate them first.
She remembered seeing her friend Chrissie MacMillan going past the
school, and asked her mother when she got home why Chrissie had not
been in school, to be told that it was because she had been going round
the houses saying goodbye before leaving for Canada. 'And when are
we going to Canada?' asked Etta 'In August, when the school closes'
she was told, and off they went on the *Marloch*.

When they got to Fort William, they went to a friend's house in
Syndicate Avenue for a meal, then her father said they were going home.
Etta got quite upset, as she thought he meant all the way back to Lewis,

76. Grain Elevator at Thunder Bay

but her father explained that he had a house ready for them on Mary Street in Fort William and that was where they were going to stay.

Etta also remembered her first day in school in Canada, when the teacher took her out of her first class to see the head-teacher. Poor Etta thought she was in trouble, but it was only that her Lewis education was far ahead of that of her age group in Fort William, and she had to start school some classes further on.

Chris's cousin Jessie MacKenzie – better known as Sweet – was a great collector of Gaelic songs, and many of her recordings are still in the School of Scottish Studies, including *Cuir a Chinn Dilis*:

Cuir, a chinn dìlis, dìlis, dìlis,
Cuir, a chinn dìlis tharam do làmh,
Do ghormshùilean meallach a mhealladh na mìltean
B' amaideach mi nuair thug mi dhut gràdh.

Rinn deisead do phearsa, nach fhacas a thuairmeas,
'G imeachd fon chuach-chùl chamagach thlàth;
Rinn deàlradh do mhaise is lasadh do ghruaidhean
Mise ghrad-bhualadh thairis gu làr.[121]

Oh faithful one put your arm around me,
Your witching blue eyes, which might bewitch thousands,
Foolish was I when I fell in love with you.

77. Jessie MacKenzie, 'Sweet', 2nd from left, and friends

The perfection of your figure, with which none can compare,
Topped by ringleted, curled, soft hair –
The shine of your beauty and the brightness of your complexion
Struck me down suddenly to the floor.

Seisiadar always had a reputation for stories, like the story of Seumas
an t-Soithich – James of the Ship – which Chris heard from Murdo
Donn's grand-daughter Katie-Ann 'Leitch' – Mrs Fairchild, now in
Australia.

Murdo Donn MacAulay of Seisiadar was of a family who came
originally from Uig. He had for six months sheltered a boy called James
who had deserted from a naval vessel in Stornoway. Murdo's house
was surrounded one night and in spite of the boy's cries he was taken
away. On being told he had broken the law Murdo replied that he
obeyed only one law – the Law of God which ordered him to entertain
strangers – but he was still fined five shillings.

A great number of Chris's own family, like many others in an Rubha,
went to Canada – one went over and did well, and sent for the next,
and so on. We had visited cousins in St Catharines and in Thunder
Bay and other parts of Canada, but there was one group of cousins she
knew of, but could not trace. Their name was Pawsey and they had
come home to Lewis in 1923 on a holiday, and Chris had a photograph
of them then, but they had gone off to Jamaica and all trace was lost.

78. Pawsey family at 11 Seisiadar

All that was remembered was the name of one of the daughters – Mary
Mabel Magdalene!

When we began to use the Internet, or rather Chris did – I am
a real technophobe – Chris thought that she might be able to find
out something about them, so she posted a message on a Jamaican
genealogy message board. Nothing happened. Then over a year later,
there was a reply from a grand-niece of Mary Mabel Magdalene, who
was actually still living in Jamaica, at a very advanced age. So contact
has now been made with these cousins also, after all these years.

Chris has a friend from her nursing days in Glasgow who now lives
in Hamilton, Ontario, though she originally came from Jamaica, so she
wrote to tell her what had happened. She wrote back, to say that she
knew the family very well, as she had been at school with two of them.
So the information about them could have been available all the time,
but Chris had never thought to ask her about them!

Chris would not forgive me if I omitted one of her favourite songs,
by Donald MacKay from No 22 Seisiadar – *Domhnall Chaluim
Chailein*:

> Bha'n didig aoibhneach os mo chionn air maduinn shamraidh
>   bhaigheil
> Cho ceolmhor binn is i ri seinn am fonn le maise Naduir;
> Bha 'n seilean mile luchdaicht trom is srann aige dha 'm fhagail
> 'S bha dealt mar reultan air gach tom 'cur loinn air Cnoc a'
>   Charnain.

79. Taigh Amhlaidh, 9 Seisiadar

Chi mi 'n gleann aig Cnoc an Eich 's ceo gheal na h-oidhch' 'na
   tamh ann
Is chi mi ait' 's 'm bu tric mo chuairt – a' bhuaile bh' aig a'
   Bhanach;
Chi mi 'n Grianan 's an Dun Dubh, an Tiumpan 's Rudh' na
   h-Airde
Is chi mi 'n Sithean-Mor ri m' thaobh 's mi sinnt air Cnoc a'
   Charnain.

Chi mi Seisiadar mo ghraidh, an t-ait' 's an d'fhuair mi m'arach
Is chi mi Buim 's an t-Eilean Glas, ait' neadachaidh nan Stearnag;
Chi mi beallaich 's aillidh dreach, 's an canach geal fo bhlath orr'
Is chi mi cuan nan iomadh snuadh 's mi cuairt aig Cnoc a'
   Charnain.[122]

The joyful lark was above me on a lovely summer's morning, so
tuneful and melodious was the song she sang to the glories of Nature;
the honey bee was full and heavy, humming as it moved away, and
the dew lay like stars on each hummock, adding to the beauty of
Cnoc a' Charnain.

   I see the glen at Cnoc an Eich clothed with the mantle of the
night's white mist, and I see the place that oft I walked to – the park
of the Banaich; I see the Grianan and the Dun Dubh, Tiumpan and
the point of Aird. And I see the Sithean Mor beside me as I lay on
Cnoc a' Charnain.

   I see my beloved Seisiadar, the place where I was reared, I see the
Buim and the Eilean Glas, nesting place of the terns, I see lovely hill
passes, clothed in cotton grass blossom, I see the ocean of varied hue
as I walk on Cnoc a' Charnain.

An Aird (Aird)

As we saw earlier, the name Shulishader used to apply to the whole of the far end of an Rubha – Port nan Giuran and Port Mholair, as well as the present township of an Aird.

The rental of 1766 shows 'Sulishader or Point of Aird' as let to a William MacKenzie, who appears in a romantic tale, told in a letter of 1782 from Rev. John Downie of Steornabhagh. This was drawn to my attention by Mrs Rhoda MacLeod of Seaview, an Cnoc, but originally from Siulaisiadar, who in turn had it from Rev. William Matheson of Edinburgh University:

> You want the history of the heiress of Tympanhead. My wife's cousin came on his Addresses there without my participation or knowledge until the matter was all over, when it was out of my power to give him any assistance. He brought Ballone to the country with him, whom he thought an irresistible orator. Having made Stornoway their headquarters, they opened a Correspondence with the young lady, at the same time her father was on his deathbed, which came to the old man's knowledge, at which he was not a little irritated & made his son write them a smart letter a few days before his death. They thought however they were sure of the main chance having obtained two Epistles from the young lady, which tho they contained nothing particular, showed no aversion to the proposal. On this they returned to the mainland, after burying the father. The young man returned after the interval of a Packet, squired by the most wrong-headed fellow in the kingdom – John Ross at Poolewe – but armed with full powers from his father to make a settlement, imagining that he had no more to do but to go thro the ceremony. But he reckoned before his host. A woful change of sentiments had taken place. They had been guilty of two capital oversights. They had consulted neither Carn or Murdo Dell, who were both affronted at the neglect. And what was worst of all they had exposed the ladies letters to so many people at Stornoway & in the Packet that they became the common subject of conversation on both side the water. The next morning after the young man landed in Stornoway in great glee, he & his squire set off by daylight for Tympanhead. Murdo Dell happening to be in town he and Carn immediately assembled and sent off an Express with a letter informing of the use they had made of the letters etc., with perhaps the stormiest day of this stormy season. The question was which would arrive the soonest; the wooer or the Express. By the influence of some evil stars, the Express tho he left Stornoway the latest arrived the soonest. Nay the young man and

squire lost their way in the snow and fell in on George Macleod where they were obliged to lodge for the night. George knowing their errand did them the favour to escort them the next day to their Journey's End – when to his unspeakable mortification the young man met with a stern absolute rebuff, but by George's mediation got his share of a Cane bottle of spirits to soften his grief. An end of the matter. I hear she declares against entering into any engagement till she sees her brother settled.[123]

William MacKenzie was still subtenant of 'Shulishader' in 1771, but probably died fairly soon thereafter. His son Murdo must have died quite young, for he was unmarried at the time of the story, yet in 1791 the farm was held by Ann MacIver, widow of Murdo MacKenzie, and son Donald MacKenzie. So the story must date from quite a few years before Rev. Downie's telling of it in 1792.

In 1791 the MacKenzies had five sub-tenants in 'Shulishader' – John McCoil vic Ean vic Conachie (John son of Donald son of John son of Duncan), his brother Kenneth, John macNeill Roy (John son of Red Neil), Malcolm Porter, Murdo Donn and Norman macEan vic Hormod Bhain (Norman son of John son of Fair Norman).

Gillanders still had the tack in his own hands in 1814, but by 1825 the township of an Aird was divided between ten crofters, many of whom appear to have been working there previously. As well as the crofting township, an Aird has straggled along and across the main road and around the shores of Loch an Duin, which, as the name would suggest, has the remains of an old island broch or dun on it, though but little remains to be seen of it today.

'S an cois Loch an Duin a chunnaic mo shuilean an la
Druim-Oidealair dluth 's Allt Diobadal lubadh mu shail;
Cnoc h-Ealair ri m' thaobh 'san sealladh a chi thu bho barr
Thar muir agus tir chan iarradh tu chaochladh gu brath.

'S Eilean beag Leodhais sior aite-comhnuidh nan sonn
Is maighdeannan stolda nas boidhch' cha do choisich air fonn;
Am briodal no 'n ceol, an coimeas no 'n seors' chan 'eil ann
Ag eisdeachd ri'n orain chromadh an smeorach a ceann.

Bheir tacan de thim dol troimh 'n a' Chuan Sgith anns an luing
Beinn Bharbhais gu Urnabhaigh, 's Muirneag gu lag Braigh na
    h-Uidh
An Rudh' air a stiuir-a-bord 's Steornabhagh dluthachadh ruinn.
'San taobh bhios mo shuil, cha chuir mi mo chul ris a chaoidh.[124]

It was by Loch an Duin that my eyes first saw the light of day, close by Druim Oidealair with Allt Diobadal flowing by, Cnoc h-Ealair

80. Class of 1912, Sgoil na h-Airde

81. Class of 1953, Sgoil na h-Airde

beside me and the sights you see from the top, on sea or land you would not see better.

Eilean Leodhais is the place of heroes, and the quiet maidens are as lovely as any that walked the earth, in their speech and song, and in comparison none can equal them, listening to their song even the lark would bow his head.

Take some time to go through the Cuan Sgith in the ship, Beinn Bharabhais on Urnabhaigh and Muirneag on Lag Bhraigh na h-

Uidh, An Rubha to starboard and Steornabhagh drawing close, my eye will be towards you, I will never forsake you.

So wrote Iain Ruadh Campbell of an Aird – and incidentally, the *comharradh*, or marks he gives, would indeed take you to the fishing bank we already mentioned off the coast of Pabail.

His niece, Anna Sheumais – Annie MacKenzie – from an Aird was a music teacher in the Nicolson Institute. Her book *Amhrain Anna Sheumais* contains many songs for children, like *Is guirme do shuil na 'n dearcag fo' n driuchd:*

Is guirme do shuil na 'n dearcag fo 'n driuchd
No 'n guirmean tha 'm buth nan ceannaichean.

Is gile do bhian na sneachd air an t-sliabh
No ite fo sgiath nan ealaichean

Bha thu cho grinn gu siubhal na h'oidhch'
'S nach fhaicinn ri soillse gealaich thu

Bha thu cho meanbh 's nach fhaicinn do dhealbh
Ged thug thu le cealg mo char asam.[125]

Your eye is more blue than the dewy crowberry or the indigo in the merchants' shops. Your skin is whiter than the snow on the plain or the down under the swan's wing. You moved so neatly at night that I could not see you in the light of the moon. You were so slim that I could not see your likeness but with your deceit you cheated on me.

The school in an Aird served all of an Rubha east of Garrabost, but is now closed due to falling school rolls and centralisation.

Port nan Giuran (Portnagiuran)

Port nan Giuran was in its day the main fishing port in an Rubha, but the area has a much earlier importance in the history of Lewis:

A mile or so west of the township, on a gentle slope about 50 yards from, and 25 feet above the high-water on the northern side of the Eye Peninsula, is an irregular heap of stones known as Caisteal Mhic Reacail.[126]

Although the Commission report suggests that the site was a chambered cairn, oral tradition has a different story. MacReacail translates as MacNicol or Nicolson, and the Nicolsons are known to have been the lords of Lewis before the MacLeods. Was this their castle? After the Battle of Largs in 1264, the Hebrides had become a part of

82. Port nan Giuran

Scotland once again, and Lewid had passed to the Nicolsons, themselves descendants of the Viking rulers. Torquil Nicolson's daughter and heiress had married a son of MacLeod of Harris and Dunvegan. The two parties were sailing back to Lewis when they were caught in a dense fog in the Minch. Suddenly the fog parted and MacLeod realised that he was in danger of ramming the Nicolsons' boat. 'That is all that lies between our son and Lewis' said his wife, so he carried on, sank the Nicolsons' boat, drowning them all, and claimed Lewis for himself.

It is easy to dismiss these old tales as fantasy, but remember that we saw that one of the last burials in the MacLeod church at the Uidh was that of a Nicolson.

Port nan Giuran is thought to appear in another important step in the history of Lewis. When the Earl of Huntly invaded Lewis in 1506, to counter Chief Torquil MacLeod's support for Donald Dubh, claimant to the Lordship of the Isles, it is thought that Port nan Giuran was his army's landing place, on the way to the battle at Allt an Torcan, as we shall see when we come to Acha Mor.

Port nan Giuran seems to have been the main base for the fishery industry in the days of the tacksmen in an Rubha, and when it was first broken into eight crofts in 1825, the new settlers were mainly from the west-side of Lewis.

According to Heathcote in 1885, Port nan Giuran had:

about 150 boats; fishing population 900 men. The most law abiding people on the island and provided the largest number of RNR men who are also considered the most intelligent of that body of men. Need of small harbours for both Bayble and Portnagiuran. He can't understand how they can land their fish in heavy weather in Portnagiuran and how they haul their boats up. With the exception of one small space, the whole shore is a mass of rocks.

83. Port nan Giuran

A pier was recommended in the 1880s, but not built until nearly eighty years later, by which time there were only a few boats there, and the pier was not long enough to reach the sea at low-tide!

In 1856 six crofts were made along the road between Port nan Giuran and Port Mholair, and were given the name of Brocair. In 1871 a Newlands was added to Port nan Giuran, with two crofts out on the Ceann Beag, and the rest on the west of the township, in the area now known as na Fleisirin, to which a large number of feus and other sites have been added since.

Another couple we met in Thunder Bay were Chrissie Coombs and her sister Cathy, whose father, Donald Smith, came from Port nan Giuran. He had done well in school and hoped to go to the Nicolson, but the minister's son got precedence and Donald was so disappointed he decided to go to Canada, though he was only 16. In the war he enlisted with the 43rd Battalion Cameron Highlanders of Canada, came back to Lewis on leave, met their mother-to-be Catherine Martin from am Bac, then went back to Canada again. When he had made enough money, he sent for Catherine to come to marry him – and they married the day after she arrived!

Catherine's parents were left in Lewis, and in time her father died. Catherine decided that she was not going to leave her mother alone, but was going to bring her to Canada. So off she set, across the Atlantic, along with her two children, aged 4 and 2, to fetch Granny. Back they came across the Atlantic again, only to meet trouble when they got to Montreal. Granny had no papers – and no English – and they refused to let her into Canada, saying she would have to go back to Scotland. Chrissie's mother wasn't having that; she parked her children on a trunk, with Granny and herself and all their luggage beside them, and announced that none of them were moving until Granny was allowed

84. Chrissie Coombs and sister Cathy

to stay. The officials argued and argued, and inisisted and insisted, but she stuck to her guns – and her seat – until by the following morning they accepted that there was only one way they were ever going to get rid of them, and waved Granny through! And that is how Granny got to Canada – and after all that, she hated it!

From na Fleisirin, I always liked the story of . . . well, perhaps I had better not name him. He had an unusually big mouth, and on one occasion in the pub with his mates, he was offered a drink. 'Gabhaidh mi balagam' he said – literally, I'll have a mouthful. 'You'll make do with a pint like everyone else!' was the reply. But he had his good points, too. During the war his ship, HMS *Wren*, was torpedoed, and he and his mates were left swimming in the sea. 'Toisich a' slugadh agus chan fhada gus am bi sinn air tir' – 'Just you take a few good swallows, and we'll soon be aground' – was his mate's suggestion. It is almost a shame to have to admit that they were rescued by another ship!

Port Mholair (Portvoller)

Port Mholair was another part of the tack of 'Shulishader or Point of Aird' until 1825, when eight crofts were made there, again mainly for

85. Port Mholair

86. Zorra Church

fishermen from the West-side of Lewis. The exception to this was a Kenneth MacKenzie who came from the Parish of Lochs – though that could have been the detached part of the Parish around Carlabhagh and Siabost. Anyway, MacKenzie did not stay there long, but emigrated in the 1850s to Zorra West Township, near Woodstock in Ontario – one of the very first Lewismen to go to that part of Canada.

There was a post-office in Port Mholair, as remembered by Calum Ferguson in his *Children of the Black House*:

Of course in those days, there wasn't any radio or television to keep the people informed about the war. News reached us through newspaper reports that were, usually, a few weeks old. More up to date news came by telegrams which were exhibited on the windows of the post office. On the way home from school after four o' clock, we always stopped at the post office and try to understand what the telegrams said so that we could report the news as soon as we reached home. Another kind of telegram also used to arrive at the local Post Office. Those were personal black-edged telegrams from the War Office which weren't stuck up on the post office windows but were delivered by the Church Elders to those to whom they were addressed. It was a frightening thing to see the Church Elders walking down the street dressed in their black clothes. Whenever they appeared, everybody stopped work and watched them apprehensively, never sure whose house they were going to visit.[127]

Chris's mother remembered their postman shouting and laughing from a distance any time he had a good telegram, just to assure them that it was not bad news.

Beyond the village of Port Mholair a road leads around Loch an Tiumpan to Tiumpan Head Lighthouse. There had been argument about the need for a light at that point on the coast, and it appears that when it was finally approved in 1879 it was as much in order to keep an eye on illegal fishing in the area as for the safety of sea-traffic. The lighthouse was designed by the Stevenson brothers, who were responsible for the design of so many lighthouses around the coast of Scotland, and became operational in 1900.

Now like so many of the Island lighthouses it is automatic, and the buildings have been converted to a boarding kennel and cattery. Like most lighthouse sites, Tiumpan is very stormy, but I hope that the story of the terrier that blew away in a gale is apocryphal!

The other Brian Wilson, in his kayak-trip round Scotland, got a bit of a fright below Tiumpan:

Tiumpan Head was a déjà-vu experience of high cliffs, light-house crowned and turbulent below. But this time a sabre-fin rose about twenty metres from me, three feet high, followed by a broad, smooth black back, and disappeared with a smart rolling tail-flick. An electrical ripple twitched my nerves, but I paddled on, scanning the water on both sides and behind. It appeared again, only this time I saw the thin edge of the fin. It was moving towards me fast! Another killer!

I stopped paddling, wondering if it was aware of my paddle splashes, or even my hull, and this time I did feel frightened. Again

87. Tiumpan Head Lighthouse

88. At Tiumpan
Head Lighthouse

it surfaced and I saw another fin cut the surface to my right, two more on my left were cruising at speed together. This was no playful display; I had blundered into the middle of a hunting pack of killer whales fishing the rich waters below the headland. But it was fascinating to be among them, almost one of the pack, and before long the rolling fins seemed to move more to my left and I breathed easy as they headed for the deeper waters of the Minch.[128]

Wilson heads for the Minch, and we can head south to na Lochan – the Parish of Lochs.

PART 4 – SGIRE NAN LOCH (LOCHS PARISH)

Sgire nan Loch extends from the outskirts of Steornabhagh to the border with Harris. The northern area, around the villages of Liurbost and Ranais, was sufficiently close to the town to be influenced in its development by the economics of trade there, while the central area, Ceann a' Loch, was on the main route to Harris.

The third area, am Pairc, was in most of its history a preserved deer-park, and although it seems to have been settled around its coasts, these settlements appear to have been deserted in the early 1800s, to be replaced by refugees from the deer-forest of North Harris. Most of these were in their turn cleared out in the late 1820s and early 1830s when the deer farm was converted to sheep-farms, only to revert to deer-forest later.

In most of na Lochan the soil is poor, but there are extensive moors, rising to substantial hills nearer to the Harris boundary. One of the dominant hill-scapes of the area is that of Sithean an Airgiod – the Sleeping Princess – where the silhouette of the hill from some directions can be seen to resemble the outline of a prone female figure. A whole prehistoric religious scene has been built around this figure, especially in relation to the stone circles of Calanais, but I am afraid that I have never been convinced that the interpretation does not owe as much to late Victorian 'Celtic Twilight' as to prehistoric man.

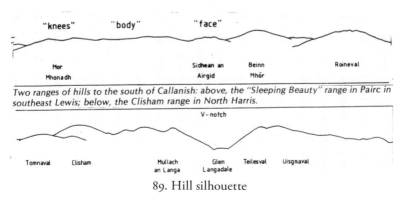

Two ranges of hills to the south of Callanish: above, the "Sleeping Beauty" range in Pairc in southeast Lewis; below, the Clisham range in North Harris.

89. Hill silhouette

Airinis (Arnish)

We saw at Aiginis how the MacKenzies of Kildun obtained Airinis and moved there, taking the name of Kildun with them. Mr Colin

MacKenzie was the tacksman in 1726, but by 1754 the lease was held by Lady Kildun, presumably his widow. She had her moment of history in 1746, when Prince Charlie, fleeing after the defeat of Culloden, tried to obtain a ship in Steornabhagh, to take him back to France.

> Donald MacLeod was dispatched by the Prince to Stornway in the island of Lewis in order to hire a vessel under the pretence of sailing to the Orkneys to take in meal for the Isle of Sky, as Donald used to deal in that way formerly.
>
> He sailed for Stornway, where he remained some time without making out the design on which he was sent. But at last he succeeded and then dispatched an express to the Prince in Scalpay to inform him that he had got a vessel to his mind.
>
> The Prince set out on foot for Stornway. In coming from Harris to the Lewis they fell under night, and a very stormy and rainy night it was, which fatigued them very much. When in sight of Stornway the Prince sent the guide to Donald MacLeod to inform him that he and the two captains were at such a place, desiring withall that he would forthwith send them a bottle of brandy and some bread and cheese, for that they stood much in need of a little refreshment. Donald immediately obeyed the summons and came to the Prince, bringing with him the demanded provisions. He found the Prince and his two attendants upon a muir all wet to the skin, and wearied enough with such a long journey through the worst of roads in the world. Donald told the Prince that he knew of a faithful and true friend to take care of him till things should be got ready for the intended voyage. This was the Lady Kildun at Arynish, to whose Donald conducted the Prince and his two attendants.
>
> When they were in Lady Kildun's house they had killed a cow, for which the Prince desired payment to be made; but the landlady refused to accept of it. However, Donald said, before they left the house he obliged her to take the price of the cow 'For' said Donald 'so long as there was any money among us, I was positive that deel a man or woman should have it to say that the Prince ate their meat for nought'.[129]

The plan to get a ship in Steornabhagh fell through, as we shall see when we reach the story of the town, and the Prince and his party had to return to Uibhist.

Lady Kildun lost Airinis in 1766, when it was added to the huge tack of Gillanders the factor, from whom it passed to his successor as factor, James Chapman, along with Aiginis. A Philip MacRae from Kintail had Airinis as a sheep-farm in the 1840s, but thereafter it fell into the hands of Sir James Matheson himself.

90. Prince Charlie's Lake, Airinis

More recently Airinis became the centre of industrial development in Lewis, as a construction site for oil-rigs, but that era has now passed, and although various attempts have been made to establish the yard as a base for wind-power constructions, their success so far has been limited.

Griomsiadar (Grimshader)

Griomsiadar was a part of the tack of Airinis until 1835, when two new townships were made – Griomsiadar and Ceann Thurnabhagh – though they were later joined as the crofting township of Griomsiadar. In our *Croft History of Griomsiadar,* we included an interview with Donald Morrison – Domhnall Chalaidh – who had spent part of his youth on the whalers at South Georgia:

> The blue whales were really big. I saw one that was ninety feet long. There was a ton in weight to every foot in length. We went up the Weddell Sea and then up the Ross Sea. You had to keep an eye on the weather – if there was any change at all – get out of there! It wasn't really too cold, so long as your hands weren't wet and you didn't touch iron. You cut them in two places near the tail. You didn't cut right through. The weight of the beast itself pulled the skin off and you had to run for your life then. You had leather boots with spikes, to give you a grip on the deck. We would strip all the flesh from the whales and leave nothing but the bone. The meat was good with onions, but most of it was going to Liverpool for fish-meal.
>
> I was at the opposite end of the world too on a boat – in the Arctic. We were running between there and Mexico, and there was one man on the boat who got frostbite and sunstroke on the same trip![130]

In 1964, near the junction of the Griomsiadar road and the main road to Harris, two Crosbost men, Donald MacLeod of No 26 and his cousin John Duncan MacLeod, were cutting peat, when they came across the remains of a body about 2 feet down in the peat-bank.

> The skeleton was in a poor state of preservation, the bones being reduced to the consistency of rubbery seaweed; in contrast, the woollen clothes were well preserved. The man had been wearing a much-mended thigh-length jacket over a shirt reaching the knees and a ragged undershirt of similar length; cloth stockings, patched and wrapped around the feet with rags, were gartered below the knee with strips of cloth, and there was a knitted bonnet on his head. In the clothing were found a small striped woollen bag containing a wooden comb and a small block of oak, a horn spoon, two quills, and three clews of wool. The back of the skull proved to have been damaged before burial; the position of this fracture would be consistent with a blow with a weapon wielded by a right-handed assailant attacking his victim from the rear.[131]

The most probable date given by researchers for the burial was early eighteenth century. Only woollen clothing had been preserved – the stockings had been worn through, and new toe pieces fitted, but the right stocking had a hole under the foot, patched with a piece of rag tied over the foot, so presumably he had been wearing shoes, but the leather must have all rotted away in the bog.

91. Domhnall Chalaidh on *Moraldie*

What makes this find so fascinating is that there was a tradition, recorded by Hely-Hutchinson in 1873, of two youths, coming from school, quarrelling, and one being killed by the other, who then fled the islands. Hely-Hutchison adds details, such as the youth returning home, being recognised and eventually being hanged on Gallows Hill in Steornabhagh, but, stripped of such accretions, the original story fits so well that there can be little doubt that this was the body in the peat!

For the benefit of the ladies:

> The bonnet was knitted in stocking stitch, worked in the round. Beginning with the inside of the headband, 85 stitches were cast on and gradually increased to 200 at the maximum width of the crown; as the work proceeded towards the centre of the crown the stitches were decreased until 12 were left, these being pulled together at the centre. The bonnet was apparently made large and then considerably shrunk by milling, to make it waterproof. It was dyed with indigo, and was finished by the turning in of part of the fabric to form a double headband, decorated every two stitches with knots of red wool.[132]

I am told, on reliable authority, that this is enough to allow a knitter to make a replica bonnet – though bearing in mind the source I am not sure that I would want to wear it!

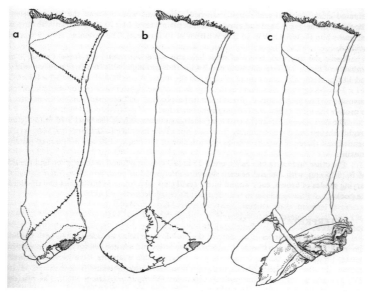

92. 'Griomsiadar Stocking'

Laurie Robinson, in his *Sea-Fishing in Scotland*, waxes lyrical over what he terms the Carronoch Reef, opposite the mouth of Loch Griomsiadar:

> A legendary 'humdinger' of a spot, rather difficult to locate unless you have an echo sounder aboard, though the locals never fail to find it. This is a reef about a mile long and some quarter of a mile wide in about 29 fathoms, and it falls away on all sides to 40 to 50 fathoms. It abounds with huge cod, ling, conger and wrasse, and the fishing will satisfy even the expert sea angler. I fished this reef last year for 45 minutes, time did not allow any longer, with amazing results. Local knowledge is essential, as unless you are right on top of the reef, the returns will be poor.[133]

Ranais (Ranish)

One of the families to come to Lewis with the MacKenzies was Clann Mhurchaidh Riabhaich. John MacKenzie of this family held the tack of Ranais in the early 1600s, but he was murdered there in 1616 by a group led by one of the many illegitimate grandsons of Roderick MacLeod, the last chief. There is reason to think that this was not an isolated killing but an organised attempt to drive out the incomers.

There is a verse of poetry:

> Is ann an Ranais nan Loch
> A nithear a' chreach nach gann;
> Ann an sgailte nan creagan
> Bithear a' sgoltadh nan ceann.

At Ranish in Lochs they will spoil and devour at the foot of the crags, and will split heads by the score

– one of the 'prophecies' of the Brahan Seer which in fact tell of past happenings, not future. Martin Martin refers to the church of St Pharaer in 'Kaerness', which is almost certainly a misprint for Raerness – and the site of the *teampull* is still to be seen there. Very often the incoming tacksmen built houses in or near a recognised religious site, so that they could claim sanctuary there from their enemies – but that was not enough to save Iain Og mac Iain Mhurchaidh Riabhaich.

Later generations of these MacKenzies seem to have moved to Liurbost, for the next tacksman on record in Ranais, though still a MacKenzie, is of quite a different family, descended from Colin Ruadh of Baile Ailein.

John MacKenzie is on record as tacksman of Ranais in 1726, and was succeeded by 1754 by his son Allan. According to Rev. William Matheson:

There is mention of him as one of the guests at evening dinner at Seaforth Lodge one Sunday in September 1778. He was looked upon with favour by the powers that were as a progressive farmer, and seems to have been a man of outstanding personal qualities. We find him referred to as Honest Allan and an allusion in another letter is as follows – Allan himself recovering slowly from one of his three month fevers, but his affairs are carried on with great propriety. He even had an orchard at Raanish. There is a letter of his to the Chamberlain, dated at Raanish, 5th November, 1770, in which he writes that with the letter he is sending a present of some of his crop of apples.[134]

Allan had a daughter Anna, who has been referred to as the Grace Darling of Lewis:

On 1st December 1778, William Crichton, merchant in Stornoway, his son Murdo and three young lads who formed their crew, were drowned off Rarnish Point. The Crichtons left Stornoway in what is described as their 'barge' in order to visit lands of which they held a tack in Park. They landed a man on Rarnish Point but five minutes later the vessel was overset by a squall, and immediately disappeared. Allan MacKenzie, we are told, was looking at her from the Gavell of his house; he, with all the speed he could, launched a boat and he, his son John, his daughter Anna and a servant rowed to the place at the hazard of their lives in hope of saving some of the people, but did not succeed.[135]

Allan may have been popular with the estate, but his son Murdo was not, and he was forced to give up the lease and retire to Steornabhagh. The tack passed to Donald MacAulay of Linsiadar, notorious for attempting to clear the sub-tenants off his farms, but the estate opposed him and his lease ran out before the clearances could be effected, and Ranais was broken into crofts in 1828.

In her introduction to our *Croft History of Lewis, Vol 6 – Ranais*, Chrissie MacLean tells us of the later history of the *teampall*:

The cemetery is enclosed by a drystone wall, believed to have been built late in the nineteenth century, as it was not shown on the first Ordnance Survey map published in 1852, but did appear on the second one in 1898. There are ruins of two small buildings within this enclosure. One is believed to have been a mausoleum, measuring approximately 6 metres by 3.5 metres in size. Local tradition states that it was a man known as an Diuc who built it. Little is known of this man, other than that he had worked as a butler for a Duke on the mainland for some time, before building a house and settling in

93. *Teampall* at Ranais

Liurbost. Apparently at this time the wall around the graveyard had fallen into a state of neglect, so an Diuc paid someone to rebuild the wall, and also to construct a mausoleum for himself. Some people believe that it was a Murdo MacAulay from Bearnaraigh, Uig, who built it. He settled initially at Croft No 9 Ranais in 1827, but moved to Griomsiadar in 1841. It is possible that both versions could be right. It could indeed have been Murdo who built the mausoleum, but that he was the man paid by an Diuc to do so, and that it is an Diuc himself who is interred there.[136]

When Norman MacDonald – an Diuc – died in 1901, he was described as a 'retired coachman', but, as we will see at Torosdadh, where he lived for a time before coming to Liurbost, he laid claim to much wider interests.[137]

Crosbost (Crossbost)

The first mention of Crosbost in the Seaforth Rentals is in 1780, when it is let along with Ranais, and probably that had been the case for some time previously. Allan MacKenzie had it, and it then passed to Dr MacAulay. After him, there were a few non-resident farmers, then in 1843 it was broken into 27 crofts for tenants evicted from Leumrabhagh and Orasaigh in Pairc.

Mrs Mary MacLean, in an interview for our *Croft History of Crosbost*, told us:

My grandfather was from Loch Sealg. He and his family were put out of the land they had there and they came to the middle of Crosbost. They brought the roof-timbers of the house with them on their backs. They brought the cow too. There was an old woman in the house beside us, and she remembered coming behind the cow from the time that they left Stiomrabhagh, and they rested now and again. They came round the head of the loch.[138]

Mary also told us of the women's dress and work in her young day:

The women wore a 'polka-tidy', a shaped jacket made of thin linen, with buttoning down the front. You started wearing this when you left school. If you had long hair you had to gather it up on top of your head then. Below this the women wore a striped shirt made of cotton, and it buttoned at the back. After you married you always covered your head with a Currac. Everybody had Sunday shoes and weekday shoes – Seven Tacks for during the week and lacing shoes for Sunday.

They knitted at home all the time – the women never stopped knitting. I remember making stockings with the Indian Corn pattern; Prince of Wales' Feather was another. It was the girls who made these, decreasing six, making a stitch and increasing six. Then you made the opposite.[139]

I am hoping that some of our lady readers know what she was talking about!

Mary's family had the post-office in Crosbost. This was set up in 1874, but became much more important ten years later

when a service was inaugurated by rowing boat across the mouth of Loch Erisort to Cromore and thence southward through Gravir to Leumrava.[140]

The ferry run was only discontinued in the early 1930s, when a motor mailvan from Steornabhagh was introduced, on the completion of the new road.

Liurbost (Leurbost)

One of the first tacksmen of Liurbost was John MacKenzie, son of Colin Ruadh of Baile Ailein, but it soon passed to the tacksmen of Ranais and remained with them until it was broken into crofts in 1828. Today the crofts of the township straggle along the village road from the Crosbost boundary to the Baile Ur beside the main road, making it vie with Baile Ailein for the title of the longest township in Lewis.

Murdo MacLeod of Liurbost was a *ceisdear*, or catechist, in the local church, and his son Murdo – Murchadh a' Cheisdeir – wrote one the best known of Lewis songs – *Eilean an Fhraoich*:

A chiall nach mise bha 'n Eilean an Fhraoich,
Nam fiadh, nam bradan, nam feadan, 's nan naosg,
Nan lochan, nan oban, nan osan 's nan caol
Eilean innis nam bo, 's aite-comhnuidh nan laoch.

Tha Leodhas beag riabhach 'bha riamh 's an taobh Tuath
Muir traghaidh is lionaidh 'ga iathadh m'un cuairt;
Nuair dhearrsas a' ghrian air le riaghladh o shuas
Bheir i fas air gach siol airson biadh don an t-sluagh.

Chan fhacas air thalamh leam sealladh as boidhch'
Na ghrian a' dol sios air Taobh Siar Eilean Leodhais,
'N crodh-laoigh anns an luachair, 's am buachaill 'n an toir,
'G an tional gu airigh le al de laoigh og.[141]

O that I was in the the isle of heather, the deer, the salmon, the plovers and the snipe, the lochs, the bays, the rivermouths and the kyles, the isle of cattle grazing and where the heroes dwell.

Little speckled Lewis, isle of the north, the ebb and flow of the sea that surrounds it, when the sun shines on it from above, it will make seed grow to feed the people.

I have never seen a more beautiful sight than the sun setting in the west of Leodhas, the cows in the rushes, the shepherd herding them, and gathering them to the shieling with their calves.

Some years ago we were asked to research a Malcolm MacLean who was born in about 1852 but left Lewis in his teens to enrol with the Hudson's Bay Company. We were able to trace him to a family in Liurbost as mac Alasdair Iain 'ic Ruairidh, of the MacLeans who traced their origin back to the Iain Dubh from Mull whom we met in Mangurstadh in Part 1. We also discovered that he fell out with the Company, having neglected the absolutely basic rule of getting home first, and was left in the North-west River area of Labrador – a remote area even for that remote land.

They had obviously had a visit from a trader selling a bolt of cloth! We thought that that would be the end of the story, until last year Chris was reading a book, *Northern Nurse* by Elliott Merrick, about Kate Austen and her experiences as a nurse in Labrador, and who turned up in it but Malcolm MacLean!

Old Scotsman Malcolm MacLean, taciturn and hawk-eyed, his square white beard waving in the wind, supervised the loading; sons as well as grandsons obeyed a mere nod of his head, or a flick of his eye. He was eighty-four years old, and still absolute boss. Now married to his third wife, his twenty-third child had just been born. He was the patriarch, the tribal leader. At nineteen Malcolm had come here

94. Malcolm MacLean and family

from Scotland to be a 'servant' of the Hudson's Bay company in the fur trade. After some years, with no choice except Indian or Eskimo, he took an Eskimo woman, and began the Kenemich settlement as a trapper, hunter and fisher, supplying himself from the land with all the necessities he could, and trading furs and fish to the Company for those he couldn't. If he needed a boat, he built one; if he needed a house, he built that too; when he needed food, he shot it or raised it if he could. For a while he took to raising sheep, and thirty years after leaving Scotland, he made from memory a spinning wheel, a carder and a loom for weaving homespun.

That union of Scotch and Eskimo culture, with Indian skills that Malcolm had learned in the bush thrown in for good measure, was the basis of present-day Hamilton Inlet charm and uniqueness. Malcolm came in for a moment, tall, straight, a man made strong by the years. He bowed to me slightly, a grave, proud gesture filled with traditions and obligations for guest as well as host. The only fitting return would have been a deep, deep curtsy to the floor.[142]

It is strange, the things that stick in one's memory, and for me, Liurbost always calls to mind – green eggs! Liurbost was the first village I ever stayed in in the Islands, in a house called Esperanza.

95. 'Esperanza'

There lived Donald MacLeod – Domhnall 'an Sheoc – and his wife Anna. I was working in a surveyor's office in Glasgow as part of my first year in the University Law Course – which then had classes first thing in the morning and last thing in the afternoon – a test of physical stamina as much as of intelligence. In the day the students worked in offices and I, being awkward even then, had ended up in a surveyor's office rather than a lawyer's.

I often say that my living in the Islands was caused by my height of 6'3" (when I had hair). My parents used to tour in Wester Ross in their car in the summer, but I never really fitted into the cars of the time, so I decided to have a break by sailing from Kyle to Steornabhagh on the Loch Seaforth. A lady who was working in the office offered to write to her cousins to get somewhere for me to stay – and the rest, as they say, is history!

Donald and Anna had been among the many families who went from Lewis to work on the sheep ranches in Patagonia in the early 1900s. Single men and families went there, particularly from na Lochan, as you can read in my friend Greta Mackenzie's recently published *Return to Patagonia*. Their daughter Anita, who with her husband Calum were to become great friends of mine in my Glasgow days, was born and spent her early years there, and had a habit of lapsing into Spanish when she was excited, which could be quite a problem for me as a Gaelic-learner. They came back to Liurbost and built a house there – hence Esperanza. Anna also brought back hens from Patagonia, small dark birds with

96. Taigh Chaluim Bhig

green legs, which laid green eggs. I understand now that lots of people in Lewis had these hens, but they were a novelty to me!

I enjoyed the 'different'-ness of Liurbost: the thatched houses, the smell of peat smoke, and piles of tweed at the roadside, waiting to go to the mill for finishing, and everywhere the clickety-clack of the looms. A young lad from a neighbouring house was detailed to show me around (and no doubt to keep an eye on me) and I remember particularly wandering out to Rubha Ranais, and watching the boats going up and down the Minch. That little boy became Director of Education for Comhairle nan Eilean Siar, and has now retired, which makes me feel my age to think of it!

One particular house I remember, a thatched house which always seemed full of peat-smoke, even though it did have a chimney of sorts. There lived Calum Beag and his mother, and there we used to meet another lad, Eachainn, who later worked in the Met Office at the airport in Steornabhagh. Sadly Eachainn died fairly young, but for years he had contributed a column for the *West Highland Free Press* – *Aimsir Eachainn* – full of sly comments on the happenings of the day, and the people involved.

He would have had something to say about the road-signs in Liurbost (or as some of them say, Luirbost). It is surely not beyond the ability of Comhairle nan Eilean Siar, when erecting Gaelic road-signs, to make sure they are spelled correctly, or at least consistently.

And I remember lifting peats beside Loch Sranndabhat – by the time I was there they would be ready for bringing home, and I remember the tractors taking the peats to the roadside, for loading onto the lorries to take them home. I remember throwing the peats up to the catchers on the top of the lorry – my aim was none too good even then – and I remember being hit by an errant hard black peat (at least I hope it was errant), which has left a slight scar on my nose even today.

But, most of all, I remember seeing, for the first time, the hills of Harris.

Crothaigearraidh (Croigarry)

This little farm at the head of Loch Liurbost also had its moment of fame in 1746, for it is said that Prince Charlie was given a cup of tea there on his way to Airinis. At that time Crothaigearraidh was a part of the tack of Liurbost, and probably occupied by a shepherd, but for a time later it was a tack on its own, let in 1780 to 'Mrs Annabella Mackenzie, relict of the deceased Murdoch Mackenzie, sometime merchant in Steornabhagh'. Much later it was the farm of a family of Gillieses from Uig, who had been shepherds in Harris.

Across the Harris road from Crothaigearraidh is the hill of Nisreabhal – the site of an infuriating puzzle to me!

There is an entry in the Old Parochial Register of Lochs for 21st March 1840, when Mary MacIver of 'Nisraval' marries John MacKay of Uig Parish. There is nothing to be seen on Nisreabhal now but *airighean* – summer shielings – but as my friend Margaret MacInnes from Liurbost pointed out, they would hardly have been at the *airigh* in March! So was she the daughter of a shepherd, otherwise unknown to records? Who now can tell?

97. Crothaigearraidh

Acha Mor (Achmore)

A few miles along a road leading west from Liurbost to Uig and Carlabhagh is the village of Acha Mor – an anomaly in Lewis villages, as it is not on the shore. It was first created in the 1820s for families evicted from Peinnthindelein, opposite Bearnaraigh in Uig, though they were later joined by families for Circeabost and from Sildinis in na Lochan.

Long before the village was settled, the stream of Allt an Torcan, at the east end of the village, had its place in history. There is a 'prophecy', ascribed as usual to Coinneach Odhar, the Brahan Seer, that tells of destruction at Allt an Torcan:

'S ann latha Allt an Torcan
Nithear olc air mnathan Leodhuis;
Eadar Eidseal 's Ard a' Chaolais
Theid na faobhair a bhualadh.
Thig, thig, chan fhada gun tig
Iad air tir am Port nan Giuran
Chuireas an duthaich fo chuis bhig
H-uile gin de Chlann Mhic Amhlaidh
Theid a cheann a sgaladh mu lic
'S marbhar i fhein cuide ris.[143]

It will be on the day of Allt an Torcan that evil will come to the women of Leodhas; between Eidseal and Ard a' Chaolais, the swords will be struck. Come, come, soon they will come ashore in Port nan Giuran and the land will be laid low, each one of Clann MhicAmhlaidh will have his head broken against a flagstone and she will be killed with him.

Rev. William Matheson points out that this, like many other of the prophecies, is in fact a re-telling of earlier events.

The escape of Donald Dubh from Inchconnel Castle about 1502 to claim the Lordship of the Isles was the signal for open insurrection. Donald put himself under the protection of Torquil MacLeod of Lewis, whose wife was his mother's sister, and the Lewis chief became his leading supporter. Before the rebellion was finally quelled it was necessary to send an expedition to Lewis under the command of the Earl of Huntly. Huntly's invasion took place in 1506, and was for the MacLeods a calamity of the first magnitude. The castle of Stornoway was taken, the island was reduced to obedience and Torquil MacLeod was brought to ruin.[144]

98. Tree at Cleasgro

The MacAulays had been the main supporters of Torquil MacLeod, and would certainly have shared in his downfall. The 'prophecy', since it comes from Uig, took their loss as its main theme – and ignored the main victims, the MacLeods.

At the east end of Ach Mor is Cleasgro. Sir James Matheson had planted trees between there and the Acha Mor road end, and appointed a forester to look after them. Sadly they were destroyed in a fire, and there is only one tree left today – and even it does not look very alive!

As we saw in Liurbost, many men from na Lochan went to work on the sheep ranches in Patagonia in the early 1900s. Another of these was Malcolm Smith, grandson of a forester at Cleasgro, and father of my friend Mrs Greta Mackenzie from Ceos.

From our house, my father went over and then his brother Alec. My father went over in 1921, and they learnt Spanish quite quickly and that opened up opportunities for them, and if you were a good worker, you could be a manager in a short time. My father stayed for eight years. He returned home to marry and I know that he expected to return. He had started to build a house for himself and his wife was going to return with him. My father came home in December 1928 and married in Acha Mor, but Anna would not go when she started to understand the kind of life they would have, how far away the place was, and how lonely and difficult a life it would be.[145]

Greta's own book *Why Patagonia?*,[146] published in 1995, gives a vivid picture of life in Patagonia, and her own visits there. An extended version is now available (*Return to Patagonia*).

This poem on Patagonia by Garbhan MacAoidh was published in *Gairm*, along with the accompanying picture by E Castells Capurro.

Ach 'sann am Patagonia farsaing, fuar,
A fhuair a' mhor-chuid de na Gaidheil beo
Is anns an fhasach sin fhuair moran bas;
Ciobairean, aoghairean, fir aonarach,
Fad' air an aineol ann an duthaich lom
Feadh Innseanach, Chileanach is Basques.
Rinn iad tir ur, neartmhor, foghainteach,
Am malairt Tir nam Beann a dh'araich iad.
Chaill iad am fearann, canain is an coir,
Ach thog iad saoghal eile anns an Iar.
Chruthaich iad, chunnaic iad gun robh e maith,
Ach loisg an cridhe-san le cianalas,
Fo reultan fuar na fasaich iongantaich.[147]

It was in wide and cold Patagonia that many Gaels made a living and in that desolation many died; shepherds, herdsmen, lonely men, long time on their own in a barren country, amongst Indians, Chileans and Basques. They built a new land, strong and bold, trading in their own land, they lost the land, language and their rights, but they built a new world in the west. They created, they saw it was good, but their hearts burnt with homesickness, under the stars of this strange wilderness.

99. 'On the Trail' in Patagonia

Beyond Acha Mor, the road leads west to Loch a' Ghainmhich and Uig, and the first part of my *Lewis in History and Legend*.

Sobhal (Soval)

The road south from Liurbost runs along the shore of Loch Sobhal, passing a rock-face called Creag a' Bhodaich, on which the light of car head-lights showed a shape resembling that of a soldier. Plenty of superstitious stories arose from it, until, I am told, an over-zealous minister took it upon himself to obtain some dynamite and blast away the offending rock-face, resulting in a charge against himself for unauthorised use of explosives!

I am not sure whether to believe the story, as I think that it was told to me by the late DHM MacIver, who was himself brought up at Sobhal, and whose stories always had at least a foundation of fact – but not always very much else!

DHM's father had been a keeper at Sobhal Lodge, which was the base from which Rev. Hely Hutchinson wrote his *Twenty Years Wild Sport in the Hebrides* under the pen-name of 'Sixty-One'.[148]

Ceos (Keose)

Ceos itself is a long-established township, though it is poorly represented in written records. The tenant in 1718 was Kenneth MacIver, but by 1740 the tack had become the glebe for the parish of na Lochan, with the manse at Suardail, on the southern shore of Loch Liurbost. This seems a very unhandy place for a manse and glebe, far from any roads, but at that time there were no roads anywhere in the parish, and most transport was by sea. The church at Suardail appears in a traditional story, dated to 1808, when a naval ship anchored off Loch Liurbost and sent a press gang ashore to take away thirty young men who were at the service. It is claimed that Rev. Alexander Simpson, the minister of the time, if not actually complicit in the deed, did nothing to prevent it.

Rev. Simpson in the Statistical Account of Lochs in 1797 tells that a new manse was built in the previous year. By the time of the New Statistical Account in 1833, Rev. Robert Finlayson could report that:

> There is a stinted scraggy copsewood of birch of small extent in a point of this parish called Swordle, near the spot on which the first manse in this parish stood. The (present) manse of Lochs stands on an eminence, on the north side of Loch Erisort. It is a commodious house, but very much exposed to the inclemency of the weather. It was built upwards of thirty years ago, and is, with the exception of

100. Ceos

the farm house of Valimas, the only house in the Parish of Lochs which is built of stone and lime.[149]

The new manse was in the township of Ceos itself, though Suardail was still retained as a glebe.

The parish church is a new building, sufficient to accommodate 700 sitters. Public worship is well attended, excepting when the violence of the weather detains such of the parishioners as must have recourse to boating, in coming to church.[150]

Rev. Finlayson was married to Lily MacAulay of Linsiadar, whose sister was married to Alexander Stronach, innkeeper at Garbh. Stronach's son, always known by the patronymic Mac an t-Sronaich, was for years an outlaw wandering the hills of Lewis and Harris. The story of his first murder is told in Part I of my *Lewis in History and Legend*, but thereafter he was a figure to cause fear all over the islands, not least because he was too well connected to be dealt with by the authorities in Steornabhagh. There are many stories connecting him with the manse in Ceos, where his aunt used to provide him with food.

The ministers would certainly have had sub-tenants in the township of Ceos, but it does not appear to have been crofted, in the sense of let directly from the Estate, until the 1830s. In the 1930s, the land around the Manse was broken into crofts under the name of Glib Cheois.

In the after-war years there was a flourishing seaweed industry based on Ceos. Cutters were employed all over Lewis and Harris, and I remember helping cutting weed at Cuithdinis in the Bays of Harris,

101. Sea-weeding at Ceos

to be loaded on a lorry belonging to a contractor in Lingreabhagh, for hauling by road over the Cliseam and on to Ceos. Alginate Industries had the factory then, housed in the old church, but they gave up when, as usual here, it proved cheaper to import from elsewhere than to transport from Lewis. A local co-operative then took the business over, but the factory is now closed, though seaweed is still processed at Airinis.

Lacasaigh (Laxay)

This township, between Ceos and Baile Ailein, was let in 1718 to Murdo MacKenzie, then to his widow. When Seaforth was in exile after taking part in the Jacobite Rising of 1719, Murdo MacKenzie had the task of taking the collected rents of Lewis to him. He found Seaforth cutting peat; 'Bha latha eile aig fear na monach' said Murdo – it is a changed day for the man at the peat – and got the response 'Chaneil fear gun da latha ach fear gun latha idir' – there is no man without two different days, except the man with no days at all.

By 1740 the tacksman was Kenneth MacKenzie, later joined in the tack by his son Murdo, who may have died young, for by 1780 Kenneth shared the tack with two Smith nephews. It being

> declared and settled that in the event of the said Kenneth MacKenzie's decease during the currency of the lease the said Malcolm and Murdoch Smith are to succeed him in his half of the said tack.

Kenneth must by this time have been elderly, and puts his initials to the lease in a very shaky hand, but he was still alive at the time of the rental of 1787. A list of kelp-makers in 1819 shows John Smith and Donald Smith, each as part-tacksman, and ten other kelp-makers, presumably subtenants. There is a family of Smiths now in neighbouring Ceos, whose by-name is Tuathanach – farmer – who claim descent from Murdo Smith, the joint-tacksman.

Murdo Smith entered into a contract with Seaforth on 5th November 1767 to manufacture kelp on the shores of Lochs, and his successive tenants must have kept up the trade, for there is a note by the factor in about 1820 of where tenants in Lochs would go if removed from their present lands:

> The tenants of Lacksay are all up to the manufacturing of kelp and those not determined would have named or fixed on some lands they would take, only that they were expecting to be continued at Lacksay; they would much rather be continued at Lacksay.[151]

Lacasaidh derives its name from the Norse for salmon island, and the fishings of the river of Lacasaigh are still famous. According to Rev. Finlayson in 1833:

> The only river in the parish of Lochs which produces salmon is the river of Laxay. The river Creed, which separates the parish of Lochs from the parish of Stornoway, produces a few salmon also; but they are not so abundant nor so good in quality as in the River of Laxay. The proper season for fishing this river commences in November and continues until July. The fish taken in the early part of the season are always the best. The river runs out of Loch Triallivall, which loch is fed by Loch Adigo in the parish of Uig. The water of Loch Triallivall is more transparent than that of any other lake in the parish. This lake has a sandy bottom; but almost all the rest are mossy in their bottom, which darkens their water.[152]

Marion MacLeod – Mor Thorcaill – from Lacasaidh was married in Acha Mor, but was never happy there:

> Chuir iad mise gu Loch an Acha
> 'S beag mo thlachd a dhol ann a chomhnuidh;
> Cha chluinn mi iomradh air lion no bat' ann,
> Cha chluinn mi cail ach an crodh 's na h-oisgean.
>
> Tha cuibhl' an fhortain a' cur nan car dhith;
> 'S ann dhomhsa thachair sin ged a b' og mi;
> Am fear a b' fhearr leam a bha 'san aite
> An diugh gur grain leis mi dhol 'na chomhradh.[153]

102. Loch Bhaltois

They sent me to Loch an Acha, little was my desire to go there to live;
I will not hear of nets and boats there, all I will hear are the cattle
and the lambs. The wheel of fortune is turning, it happened to me
young as I was; the one I preferred more than any, today he does not
want to speak to me.

Baile Ailein (Balallan)

Traditionally the first tacksman at Baile Ailein was Colin MacKenzie –
Cailean Ruadh, the Chamberlain of Lewis – but the earliest written
references to the tack of Baile Ailein show it tenanted by Alexander
MacKenzie, his wife Isabella MacLennan and their son John. By
1740 it was in the hands of Murdo MacKenzie of Achilty, who had a
widespread business in Lewis as a cattle drover. In 1754 it was let to Mr
Daniel MacLeod, a merchant and shipmaster in Steornabhagh, and
a leading organiser of the emigration from Lewis to Carolina in the
1780s. His father's patronymic was Domhnall mac Iain mhic Thorcaill,
and, as mentioned in Part I, there is a family in Carolina whose family
name 'MacForth' is almost certainly a mis-transcription of 'MacTorkle'.
Daniel's brother John was a plantation owner at Colbecks in Jamaica,
and in 1762 he matriculated arms as chief of the MacLeods, though
there is great dubiety about whether this claim was justified.

    By 1771 Baile Ailein was in the hands of joint-tenants – Donald
MacIver and 20 more, according to the rental, and it remained in joint-
tenancy until the beginning of crofting in the early 1800s, when it was
set out as 26 crofts, 11 of which were sub-divided, to give 37 tenants,
including the brothers Malcolm and Murdo MacLeod, who, it is noted,

103. Feill at Baile Ailein

'require to be separated because of bad behaviour'! By 1851 there were 65 crofts and there are now many more feus and allotments, especially on the moor side of the main road.

An unusual name, recorded in Baile Ailein in 1780, is Montgomery. The Gaelic version is MacGumraid, but this may be only an attempt to phoneticise the English name. The name is found on Raasay, so could this be another family who left that island after its harassing after the 1745 rebellion? There is an interesting entry among the Burial Lists of the Old Parochial Register of Urquhart in Moray for

> Alexander Montgomery, Parishoner of Lochs in Lewis Island, sailor, who was washed from on board a vessel belonging to the West isles which vessel was stranded opposite to the town of Mathmill on Wednesday morning November seventeenth day 1756 & his body being found upon the shore was buried in this Churchyard Monday December twentieth day.

We mentioned this death in our *Lewis Families and How to Trace Them – Lochs*,[154] but closer examination of the original entry allows us to revise the wording slightly.

The phrasing 'parishoner of' is rather strange – we would have expected 'native of' – so perhaps this lends a little weight to the suggestion that the Montgomeries were recent arrivals in Lewis. Wherever they came from, they are to be found now in an Rubha, and Ranais area as well as around Baile Ailein.

The first postal service to Harris ran through Baile Ailein – literally so! Although a road was completed in 1854, it was a road only in name, and the post office employed one foot-runner to take the mails as far as

104. Baile Ailein in Snow

Baile Ailein, and another to take them on to Harris. A year or two later a horse service was added, and in 1859 a gig, but these did not pay, and in 1866 the service returned to a foot-runner. In 1880 K D Henderson in Steornabhagh started a mail cart again, but the whole service to Harris was abandoned in 1887, and Harris mail routed through Portree in Skye.

Baile Ailein did not get its own post office until 1878, and in 1880 a twice-weekly foot-post to Isginn was started, but only in the fishing season. As better roads were made, the Baile Ailein service got its own 'mail car', though not until the 1920s was this a motor-car.

Several years ago, during research on a family in Cape Breton, we were sent a copy of a letter of 1868 from a lady in Baile Ailein to her sister in Cape Breton, who had emigrated from Ath Linne some 40 years before:

> Dear sister, I thank goodness that I have heard from you, & indeed it gives me great satisfaction to hear from you & now I may tell you of my condition as follows, I got 2 children since you left this place, & I am with the youngest of them, his name is John, he is married to an Uig woman, he got 9 of a family, and four of them are not. We are in the very spot where you left us but all the rest of the children, that is my children, are married and Murdo my husband died since 7 years & I am very light-sighted now, but I am able to move about as yet . . .

She continues with details of all the children and grandchildren – just like one *cailleach* comparing family notes with another. If the style

105. Looking north from Roineabhal

of language seems rather unlikely for an old *cailleach*, the explanation is on the last page:

> Now the one writes this is a son of Christine, the second of her family, and I send this to you and to Donald your son and would be glad to hear from Donald. My age is 19 years, and I am in school ever since I could. I have been 3 years in a shop in Stornoway but I left, and since a year I am in school just now and I intend going to College to Edinburgh in a month or so, and I would be glad to write to Donald or to any other of your sons that would kindly write to me, I may give you my address as
> Murdo Morrison Jr
> Teacher
> Laxay Lochs
> By Stornoway, Lewis
> N Britain

Baile Ailein, like Liurbost, is a long village with crofts running below the road to the shores of Loch Eireasort, and from about halfway up the village, there is a magnificent view along the length of the loch to its mouth, between Ceos and Eilean Chaluim Chille at Cro Beag.

West of Baile Ailein, the landscape is dominated by the hill of Roineabhal. I remember climbing it on a fine summer's day, and being amazed by the sheer number of lochs that lay below me on all sides. To the west and south, the long stretch of Loch Langabhat running away

106. Loch Langabhat from Roineabhal

right to the Harris boundary; to the north, Loch Airigh na h-Airde and the chain of lochs leading to Griomarstadh in Uig; and at my feet the double loch of 'Fadagoa' – which appears in Gaelic on the OS map as Loch Fad a' Ghobha, but I am not convinced!

Sildinis & Cleitir (Shildenish & Cliatair)

Just beyond the head of the loch, on the south shore, are the joint villages of Sildinis and Cleitir. When the townships further south in the Pairc were being cleared, Cleitir was frequently a temporary stopping place. John Smith of Baile Ailein gave evidence to the Napier Commission in 1883. The questions and answers can be summarised as follows:

> I was born in a place called Eesgin of Park and I left there when I was about fifteen. My father was one of those sent away from the place. He came to another portion of Park called Cleater, over upon the other side of the loch from Balallan. He had Cleater for himself for nine years, and then another man was put in who got two-thirds of it, and my father for five years had one third. He was fourteen years there altogether. He was one of the sixteen who were removed to Balallan when Mr Scott became tenant of Park (1838).[155]

John Smith was a son of Malcolm Smith – Calum Taillear – who is thought to have been a son of Angus Smith, tacksman of Sildinis in 1770, and later tacksman of Tabost and Cleitir.

Tabost (Habost)

Many of the Tabost men were fishermen as well as crofters, travelling around the north and east of Scotland following the fishing. One group were in Wick in August 1859 and were involved in what became known as the Wick Riot – though it seems more to have been a running skirmish over a few days. It is one of those stories from oral tradition which unfortunately has gone wrong in the details, although the gist of the tale is correct. According to the usual version, the main actor in the story was Malcolm MacLeod – Calum Alasdair Iain – the 14-year-old son of Alexander MacLeod of No 2 Tabost. Some say he stole an apple, and some say he was fighting over it with a local boy, but either way he was arrested and jailed. His father's friends rallied round and broke down the door of the jail with the mast of their fishing boat to let him out, the ensuing fracas lasting for a few days. The problem is that Calum Alasdair at this date was more than forty years of age, and was living in Baile Ailein, though he did move a few years later to Tabost. It must have been one of his sons who stole the apple – and he did have a son Calum.

I have fought for years to have oral tradition recognised as a valid historical source, but the Wick story shows why it always has to be checked. To the story-teller, it did not matter whether it was Calum or Calum Chaluim, nor whether it was before or after his move to Tabost – these were both peripheral to the main story. But before it can be accepted as detailed history, it has to be checked, and, as in this case, slightly corrected if necessary.

Tabost appears in the 1718 and 1726 rentals as let to an Alexander MacKenzie, then in 1780 to Angus Smith, who remains as tacksman until 1807. Angus Smith was married to Barbara MacLeod, a sister of John MacLeod of Colbecks and of Daniel MacLeod of Baile Ailein. There is the ruin of a house in Tabost said to have belonged to 'Lady Habost', and this name appears in a list of tenants in Baile Ailein in 1808, to which she had removed as a widow.

The tack passed to Allan Morrison, who was succeeded by Neil Morrison, probably his son, and there is a complaint in the Seaforth Papers from him in 1827, alleging poinding of his cattle by Alexander Stewart, tacksman of the Farm of Pairc. The note adds that Neil is 'living on the conquest money of his wife, who is illiterate' – conquest being the legal term then for money inherited by a wife in her own right.

From Morrison, the tack passed to Duncan MacLellan, formerly tacksman of Eansaidh in Harris, who brought several shepherds and farm-workers from Harris, whose families are still represented in the area. Duncan MacLellan was not a successful farmer, and parts were gradually taken from the farm and given to crofters, until by 1851 there were eight crofts in the township, and the farm consisted only of the western third of Tabost, and by 1860 this also had been divided into five crofts, one of them reserved for the MacLellans.

One of the families to come to Tabost with MacLellan was a Duncan MacAskill from Aird Asaig in Harris, whose wife Kirsty Morrison was a sister of MacLellan's wife, but when MacLellan lost the tack, MacAskill returned to Aird Asaig, where his descendants remain.

Cearsiadar (Kershader)

A note in the rental of 1780 shows that Cearsiadar was formerly held by Colin Crichton, merchant in Steornabhagh, who had also held the neighbouring tack of Gearraidh Bhaird, but as we saw in Ranais, he had been drowned with his son there in 1777, despite the attempts to save him by Allan MacKenzie and his daughter Anna. Crichton had been one of many merchants in Steornabhagh to take on a tack in na Lochan for the sake of the fishing and kelp there.

After Crichton, the tenancy passed to Alexander MacIver, also merchant in Steornabhagh, and in 1791 to Norman Morrison, shipmaster

107. Cearsiadar

in Steornabhagh, who held it until 1807, when the township was divided among four former sub-tenants.

John MacLeod of Cearsiadar was a witness to the Napier Commission in 1883, and his main complaint was the lack of a road to South Lochs. His evidence is again summarised:

> We are about 14 miles from the high road, going round the loch; the ferry will shorten it with us, but not with the rest of the district. There are several townships all round where there is not an inch of road, nor is there a post office on the south side, nor any civil benefit whatever. The post office is in Balallan, the most inconvenient place for the parish that can be. Letters for Kershader would be dropped with some person on the road, and I must send for them, or pay extra to the man who would go for them.[156]

Another tenant in Cearsiadar was Malcolm MacLeod, known as Calum Rubh' an Fhithich from the headland below his croft. There now are the headquarters of Co-Chomunn na Pairc, and the Angus Macleod Archive of papers from the collection of my friend Ease, whom we met in Marybank.

Gearraidh Bhaird (Garyvard)

Gearraidh Bhaird was generally let along with Cearsiadar until it was divided into five shares in 1807. Among the tenants then was Malcolm MacLeod – Calum Buachaille – of the Maidsearan MacLeods from Scapraid in Uig.

CROFTERS STACKYARD, LOCH ERISORT, LEWIS.

108. Loch Eireasort

Another tenant there was a John MacDonald – Iain mac Alasdair – who had a son with the unusual name of Thomas, taken from his mother's MacKenzie family. Thomas emigrated with his family to the Eastern Townships of Quebec in 1863, and I remember meeting his grand-daughter in Scotstown there. The Gaels there used the same type of patronymic as here, so she was Harria Dan T, named after a friend of her father called Harry Bender. She was married to Kenneth MacLeod – Kenny Gabhsann – as they had lived in Galson in Quebec, though by the time I knew them they were living in a Seniors' Home in Scotstown. Harria knew little about the family in Lewis except that John MacDonald had two brothers who went to Cape Breton – Murdo and Dougal, who was 7' 4" in height!

Cabharstadh & Torosdadh (Caversta & Torasta)

These townships were originally a part of the tack of Cro Beag, until the 1870s, when three crofts were made in Cabharstadh, to the west, entering from the road beyond Gearraidh Bhaird, and two in Torosdadh, to the east, entering from Cro Mor.

The 1871 census of Torosdadh includes a Norman MacDonald, who lists himself as a 'retired gardener and student of Latin, French and Geology'! He later appears in Liurbost in the census of 1891, when his birthplace is given as Caolas Scalpaigh in Harris. Locally he had the nickname ''an Diuc' because he had been in service with the Duke of Sutherland.

Cro Beag & Eilean Chaluim Chille (Crobeg & St Colm's Isle)

Eilean Chaluim Chille in the mouth of Loch Eireasort, opposite Cro Beag, appears in Dean Monro's *Description of the Western Isles* in 1549:

Within the Lochis foirsaid lyis Ellan Cholmkle callit in Inglish St Colmis Isle. Within the Ile Mccloyd of the Leozus hes ane fair Orcheard, and he that is Gardiner hes that Ile frie.[157]

It appears in the early rentals as a separate tack, let first to Alexander MacKenzie, then to Chamberlain George Gillanders, as part of his tack of Aiginis. In 1796 it passed, to Donald MacAulay of Linsiadar, 'with necessary access through the farm of Cro Beag'. MacAulay still possessed the island in 1822, though it soon thereafter became a part of the farm of Cro Beag.

According to the New Statistical Account of 1833:

There is a ruin on the island of St Colm, in the entrance of Loch Erisort, which was once a religious edifice. The ground surrounding this ruin is the only place of interment in the parish of Lochs. St Colm is the place on which the first factor sent to the Lewis by the MacKenzies, then of Kintail, resided. It is the general opinion that the said ruin on the island of St Colm is the ruin of a place of worship erected in the days of 'Mac Mhic Mhoruchi', which was the patronymic of the first factor sent to this island by the MacKenzies.[158]

Most likely MacKenzie would have followed the usual pattern of taking advantage of an established site of sanctuary, so although he may well have built that particular church, it was almost certainly on the site of an earlier one. When John Sands called there in June 1876 on his way to St Kilda, he found the graveyard sorely in need of maintenance:

On the 12th I made a trip on board of the Vigilant to Loch Erisort, a few miles to the south of Stornoway. We anchored near the mouth of the Loch, and Captain McDonald took me in his gig to see a churchyard situated on an island called St Colme. It is quite close to the water, and is about sixty feet square. It might have been originally large enough for the district, but now the accommodation is shockingly insufficient. Although there seems plenty of suitable ground outside, the people persist in interring the dead within the ancient limits. Nay, not interring, but piling the coffins one on top of the other, until they have risen to a height of ten feet above the surface. The coffins are not even covered with earth, but are only wrapped in turf. In some places they look like the steps of a stair covered with a carpet. One can count the tiers. As Captain McDonald stepped before me I expected to see his nautical, square-built figure sink, like the ghost in Hamlet, through the hollow turf. I myself felt as if I were walking on thin ice, which might give way any moment and bury me in corruption, I was surprised that no foul smell pervaded this charnel pit, until the Captain pointed out that there were two holes made in every coffin by the rats, and that a body was no sooner left than it was devoured. He poked with his cane, like a tide-waiter, into a new coffin, and nothing but bones. The place swarmed with rats. We could hear them in the still evening air squeaking and fighting over their horrible banquet under our feet.[159]

Cro Beag, with Cro Mor and the surrounding area, appears in 1780 as part of the tack of Bhalamus. From Alexander Gillanders it passed to his father Chamberlain George, then in 1796 was added to the Rosses' tack of Cro Mor. In the 1830s Cro Beag, with Eilean Chaluim Chille passed to John MacDonald from Applecross, probably through his marriage to Mary MacIver, daughter of Mary Ross. This Mary MacIver was known as Mairi Laghach and her husband is said to have made a song for her:

> Ho, mo Mhairi laghach,
> 'S tu mo Mhairi bhinn.
> Ho, mo Mhairi laghach,
> 'S tu mo Mhairi ghrinn.
> Ho, mo Mhairi laghach,
> 'S tu mo Mhairi bhinn.
> Mhairi Bhoidheach lurach
> Rugadh anns na glinn'[160]

My lovely Mairi, you are my sweet Mairi, my lovely Mairi, you are my elegant Mairi. Lovely, lively, Mairi, born in the glens.

Cro Beag passed to his son Donald, who in the 1870s removed to Dun Charlabhaigh, and the farm then passed to Roderick Martin, Baile Ailein, along with the tack of Orasaigh. More recently it passed to Charles Menendez MacLeod – you could guess that his father had been in Patagonia – better known as Charlie Barley, though I believe that his family are giving the farm up now.

Cro Mor (Cromore)

In 1780 Cro Mor was part of the tack of Bhalamus, but in 1787 it passed to Roderick Ross, who was married to a daughter of Allan MacKenzie of Ranais. At the same date, Stiomrabhagh was let to John Ross, merchant in Steornabhagh, who was no doubt of the same family, perhaps Roderick's father. Roderick Ross had at least three sons – Allan in Maryhill, Crosbost; Kenneth in Ceos and latterly in Carlabhagh; and Donald, who went to Canada with the Hudson's Bay Company. He became chief clerk at Norway House in Manitoba, where he kept extensive records of the local weather, over a period of 27 years:

20 May 1832 Weather cloudy; wind northerly light airs; 28/40 The spring advancing but slowly – not the smallest appearance as yet of any vegetation and the little open water there was last week is covered in ice.

26 October 1834 Snowing all day; wind NW fresh breeze 28/29 There is now more snow on the ground than we had last year in the month of January.

19 August 1835 Wind SE with a good breeze and cloudy weather 32/46 A heavy dew with frost during the night which I

109. Norway House

fear has destroyed our potatoes, the tops being perfectly black this morning.[161]

Writing this in December of 2010, he has my sympathy!

Roderick Ross must have died before 1814, for in the rental of that year, Cro Mor and Cro Beag are let to Mrs Ross and son. A list of tenants in about 1820 lists 17 tenants, one of them being a Bell Ross, with a note:

the Cromore tenants are well up to fishing and are excellent kelp manufacturers; they are all willing to remain at Cromore as fishermen.

By the 1830s the township was divided into 25 crofts and there are now several feus and allotments in the Caros area to the west of the main township.

On an islet about 50 yards from the end of a promontory on the west side of Loch Cromore, and springing direct from the water's edge, is the ruin of Dun Cromore, sometimes called Dun Ban; a broch occupying the south-eastern part, with the remainder to the north-west forming an outer ward enclosed with a low broken wall about 4'6" thick and 28' at its most distant from the broch. It has been connected to the mainland from the ward by a causeway still visible under water. Captain Thomas mentions that within the gallery at the time of his visit a stair of seventeen steps led up to a third gallery, and underneath them a smaller stair led down from a second but with no exit. Though the gallery walls still remain as shown on his plan, there is now nothing to suggest that stairs ever existed here. [162]

110. An Dun, Cro Mor

An unusual surname which appears first in Cro Mor is Chisholm. There is Kenneth Chisholm there in 1810, and tradition claims that he came first to Cro Beag as a *balach laoigh* – the direct translation 'cowboy' conjures up a rather different picture! Kenneth appears to have had three sons, Murdo, John and Angus, and they were the progenitors of all the Chisholms now in South Lochs, mainly Grabhair and Leumrabhagh – and my friend whom we met in Cul-ri-Greine.

More recently, my wife's aunt Etta MacDonald was a schoolteacher in Cro Mor in the 1930s, and my mother-in-law remembered going by boat to visit her there.

Marbhig (Mariveg)

Another part of the tack of Bhalamus in 1780, Marbhig was held with Cro Beag until 1796, when it was shared between six joint-tenants. By 1814 there were twelve crofts in the township, two of them leased to MacFarlanes. This is a most unusual name for na Lochan, though there is a Donald MacFarlane in Isginn in a list of persons eligible for militia service in 1797.

Norman MacFarlane in Marbhig, son of Donald, was married to Margaret Wylie, daughter of Alexander Wylie, Surveyor of Customs in Steornabhagh. It is said that her family were so upset by the mesalliance that they disowned her, only relenting when she died, when they allowed her to be buried in their family plot in Sanndabhaig. Oral tradition seems fairly hard on this family, for it is also said that Norman's sister Kirsty 'was twice deported for theft' – perhaps my source had had a row with one of the family!

Much more recently Marbhig was the home of Murdanie Kennedy – Murdanie Mast – author of many local songs, including *Oran na Beart*. Listen to it sung by the Lochies, and I defy you to keep your feet still.

'S i bheairt a rinn mo sharachadh;
'S i bheairt a rinn mo sharachadh;

III. Etta MacDonald and pupils at Cro Mor School

Nuair a chuir mi innte spal
Bhrist ise h-uile snath a bh' ann.
'S i bheairt a rinn mo sharachadh.

Ged nach eil mi eolach oirr',
Tha eagal orm nach cord i rium;
Tha na h-iomallan innte cho dluth
Agus chan eil suil far 'm bu choir dhi bhith.
'S i bheairt a rinn mo sharachadh.[163]

The loom exhausted me; when I put the shuttle in, it broke all the threads. Although I am not used to her, I am afraid I will not like her; the heddles are so tight and there is no eye where there ought to be one.

Calbost

Calbost today is a ghost village, but in its day it was a thriving fishing township. At one time it was tenanted by a Robert Weir, who is best known in formal records for having gone bankrupt in 1818, when the Seaforth Papers record all the furnishings and plenishings of his farm and house in a roup. The village was then let to seven fishermen (who had probably been Weir's subtenants up till then). One of these was Coinnich Mor (Kenneth MacLeod) who according to tradition was from Carlabhagh, where his mother was lost over a cliff while attempting to catch a cow, when Coinneach was carried across the moor in a creel to Calbost, to be brought up by her sister Mrs Marion MacKenzie.

Both Calbost and Grabhair had an influx of families from Carlabhagh about this time, caused partly by the introduction of commercial fishing to the area, and possibly also by the period of bad harvests we already noted, following the eruption of Hecla in 1765, and the accompanying increase in fish stocks.

Calbost prospered with the fishing, and the original seven crofts were subdivided and by 1891 supported 200 of a population in 35 households. Crofting in Calbost was marginal at best, and as the fishing declined, largely due to overfishing, there were far too many households for the land to support, and families began to move to new housing being built in Steornabhagh, until by the late 1990s, Calbost was empty.

One of the best known sons of Calbost was my good friend Angus Macleod, better known as Ease. Angus was both a champion of crofters' rights and an avid collector of things historical – both physical objects and information. In an old house in Calbost he collected a museum of household and agricultural articles, working on the basis, as he often said to me:

> People may think it is out-dated rubbish, but the time will come soon enough when this is all that is left to show life in our parents' and grandparents' time.

A dish, a chair, a lamp, a home-made cradle, a plough, parts of a horse's harness – all sorts of things were gathered together in Ease's museum, now housed in Museum nan Eilean in Stornoway.

Ease also gathered a mass of information, both written and from oral tradition, and this is now the basis of the Angus Macleod Archive, held at Ravenspoint in Cearsiadar.

I used to hear Ease telling the romantic story of Matilda MacLeod – Maiglin Chaluim Bhain – of Cro Mor. She had a boyfriend Norman MacKenzie – Tormod Og Thormoid Bhuidhe – from Calbost, who was a fisherman. Maiglin's parents reckoned that they could find a better husband for their daughter, and fixed on John MacLeod – Iain mac Iain Oig – from Cro Mor.

Tormod was away at sea, and they persuaded Maiglin that she and Iain Og should go to Ceos to marry. As this was a formal occasion, they went by gig along the road through Baile Ailein. While they were on their way, Tormod returned, and, when he heard what had happened,

112. Mr and Mrs Angus MacLeod

took his boat straight across the loch to Ceos. He arrived as the minister was asking if there was any objection to the marriage, so he objected on the grounds that he wanted to marry her himself. The minister, no doubt rather non-plussed at the turn of events, asked Maiglin who she wanted to marry. '*B' fhearr leam fear nam botannan mora*' – I would rather have the one in the big boots – for Tormod was still wearing his sea-boots! So the minister married Maiglin to Tormod, much to the chagrin of Iain Og, left at the altar.

One could have sympathy for Iain Og, but when we check the records, we find that Tormod and Maiglin were married on 11th February 1839, and Iain Og got married a fortnight later, on 25th February, to Kirsty Smith, also of Cro Mor – perhaps having made all the arrangements for the *banais*, he felt that there was no point in wasting them!

Grabhair (Gravir)

A narrow road winds its way south from Calbost to Grabhair, though there is a more direct route from Gearraidh Bhaird. The township comprises three sections – Tom an Fhuadan, on a plateau above the south shore of the loch; Gleann Ghrabhair, a more recent settlement, running west along the glen leading from Grabhair to Loch Sgiobacleit and Ceann Shiophoirt; and the township of Grabhair itself, along the north shore of the loch. There was also a settlement to the east of the main village, called Lite Sithein, but nothing now remains of this except the name, and the marks of cultivation on the ground.

According to MacBain's *Place-names of the Hebrides,*[164] Grabhair is derived from the old Norse *grof* – a ravine – and this certainly describes the village, rising sharply from the shores of Loch Odhairn. The crofts rise steeply from the shore, many of them marked with lines of piled stone, taken from the surface of the ground in the process of cultivation. Whatever else may be said of Grabhair, the people there must have developed strong legs!

The first friends I knew in Grabhair were the Campbells at No 13: Roderick Campbell – Ruairidh Dhomhnaill Ruairidh – and his wife Kate MacMillan – Ceit Chaluim a' Bhaird. Ruairidh was well-versed in the history of his own family, and from his own grandfather could go back a further two generations to an Alexander Campbell, who came from Harris. According to Ruairidh, Alexander Campbell had settled first at Ceann a' Mhuire on Loch Siophoirt, then had moved to another Ceann a' Mhuire, east beyond Tom an Fhuadain, at the mouth of Loch Odhairn. From there the family moved across to Lite Sithein, and then to Grabhair itself. Alexander's son John – Iain mac Alasdair – appears in the Old Parochial Register of Barvas Parish on 25th July 1811, when he married Elizabeth Moire of Barabhas Uarach. Ruairidh did not remember much about Betsy, as she was known in Grabhair, though she probably had been in service in the manse in Barabhas Uarach, but he did remember that she had a sister Ann, and that a little bay below their house was known as Port Anna Mhuir, but he was not sure whether it was because she used to fish there, or whether she had been drowned there. It was just this sort of traditional family knowledge which was so important to that generation, and has generally been lost by their descendants.

Ruairidh's own grandfather, and his brother Alasdair with another four men from the area, were drowned off Ranais in 1873, on their way back from Steornabhagh.

We mentioned Chisholms in Cro Mor, and there was a branch of the family in Grabhair, including Norman – Tormod Aonghais – whose daughter, Mairi, Chris and I have met several times in Canada. Mairi was married to Malcolm MacCrimmon, a piper who was in his day the hereditary piper to Dame Flora MacLeod of Dunvegan – a position now held by his son Iain. Malcolm's ancestors were from Glenelg, and came from there across to Ontario. Malcolm's grandfather, also Malcolm, was

113. Malcolm and Mairi MacCrimmon

a railway engineer, and it was he who planned the railroad through the Kicking Horse Pass in the Rockies between Banff and Kamloops. The last link in the railroad was at a place which the Canadians insist in calling 'Craiglockie', but should really be Craigellachie, and Malcolm MacCrimmon senior is in the souvenir picture of the driving of the last spike, but as usual the engineers are hidden well behind the dignitaries in the front line!

We paid a memorable visit to Banff in Alberta with Mairi and Malcolm, including a visit to Lake Louise on a frosty autumn morning. Malcolm of course had his pipes with him, to the great delight of some young Japanese ladies, but the cold had affected the reed of the pipes and he could not play properly. I wonder whether, like Baron Munchausen's, his music emerged later, as the air warmed!

Another Grabhair name was Carmichael; the first of the family was probably Hector Carmichael, who is said to have been brought to Lochs as a *balach-laoigh* – calf-boy – on one of the farms. Some say it was Cro Beag, but others say Ceos, though by 1810 he was in Grabhair, where he appears in a list of kelp-workers. Hector had at least five sons – Archie, Robert, Donald, John and Neil, of whom the first three emigrated to Cape Breton in the 1820s. John settled for a time in Leumrabhagh, then moved with a few of his neighbours in 1843 to Gleann Tholastaidh, leaving Neil in Grabhair as the sole member of the family in Sgire nan

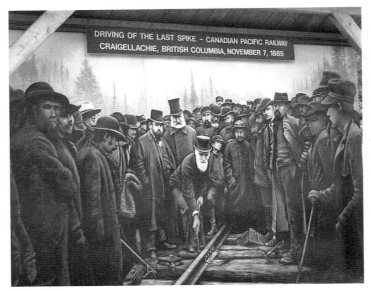

114. 'Driving the Last Spike' at Craigellachie

Loch, where his descendants, known as na Piobairean – the Pipers – are now mainly in Leumrabhagh.

Another old Grabhair family are the Mathesons, who originally came to Lewis with the MacKenzies and settled in Uig. An Andrew Matheson came across to Grabhair and his descendants – clann Iain 'ic Aindreis – are numerous there, the most famous no doubt being Murdo Matheson, who used to cause great hilarity in the 1960s with his comedy sketches of 'Cailleach an Deacoin' – the deacon's old woman. Strangely enough, his grandmother was the Mary MacDonald in Widows' Row who was writing a love letter to her first boyfriend in Hudson's Bay.

Almost all the old families of the Pairc had representatives in Grabhair – Nicolson, MacInnes, MacMillan, MacLean and Smith, along with a few who had come across from Carlabhagh area in the heyday of the fishing.

One of those who came from Carlabhagh was John MacPhail, and it was his great-grandson Donald – Domhnall Choinnich Dhomhnaill Iain 'ic Phail – who wrote the well-known song of the First World War *Smuaintean Saighdeir an deidh Blar Mons* –Thoughts of a Soldier after the Battle of Mons – much better known from one of its verses as *Isein Bhoidhich*:

Isein bhoidhich tha ri siubhal
Null gud nead an tir an fhraoich,

115. Malcolm MacCrimmon

Ma thadhlas tu an Eilean Leodhais
Thoir mo shoraidh gu mo ghaol.

Thoir mo shoraidh gu mo mhathair
'S gu mo chairdean baidheil ciuin;
Innis dhaibh gu bheil mo smaoin orr'
'S m' aghaidh air a' bhlar 's an raon.

'S truagh nach b' urrainn mi leat amharc
Null tre mhonaidhean 's tre chaoil
Dh'fhaicinn sealladh air Gleann Ghrabhair
Far na dhealaich mi rim ghaol.[165]

Lovely bird, flying back to your nest in the land of the heather, if
you reach Eilean Leodhais, bring my blessings to my love. Give my
blessings to my mother and to my loving, gentle friends, tell them
my thoughts are with them, as I face the battle on the plain. I wish
I could go with you over moors and seas, to get a glimpse of Gleann
Grabhair, where I parted from my love.

Leumrabhagh (Lemreway)

Norman MacLeod, nephew of George MacLeod, tacksman of Garrabost,
was a merchant in Steornabhagh, and like many of the merchants there,
obtained a tack in na Lochan, to take advantage of the incipient fishing
industry there.

According to a rental of 1780:

116. Leumrabhagh

Norman McLeod Merct in Stornoway agrees to accept of his present possession of Lemmiry and Isle Ewart lying in the Parish of Lochs for seven years from Whitsunday next for payment of the sum of Twenty Four Pounds Fifteen Shillings of yearly rent.[166]

Although he is noted as a merchant in Steornabhagh, he clearly resided at Leumrabhagh for at least part of the year – which he probably regretted! Rev. William Matheson tells us that:

in the summer of 1780, a French privateer, the *Sans Peur* of Dunkirk, under the command of an Irishman named Luke Ryan, put into Loch Shell, made the tacksman of Lemreway prisoner and held him up to ransom.[167]

In 1796 Kenneth MacLeod of Pabail Uarach, cousin of Norman MacLeod, took on the lease of Leumrabhagh. The Chamberlain reckoned that:

Kenneth is still a better tenant for Lemreway, as he would live on it, and improve it both in fishing and lands, and would set an example much wanted in Loch Shell.

Kenneth MacLeod of Leumrabhagh was married to a daughter of Kenneth Campbell of Scalpaigh, and their son John – Seoc Choinnich Sheorais – is well-known to history, both in Canada and in Lewis.

By 1827 he was based at Fort Simpson on the eastern slopes of the Rockies, where, for the time at least, he seems to have been none too happy, as he wrote in a letter of 1827 to John MacLeod of Red River, whom we met in Garrabost:

Pray when do you expect to go and pay a visit to our Calf Country, or have you relinquished the idea entirely; you will perhaps ask me the same question; well, let me tell you, that if my purse could have afforded me so doing, I would have surprised some of them before now, but alas my means cannot gratify what my inclinations wishes

117. Leumrabhagh in 1934

much to accomplish. I must not, however, dispair, and hope for the
day to come that I will, if not to my Calf country, steer my course
to some other part of the world and bid adieu for ever to this savage
part of the globe.[168]

By 1831 he is happier, and looking forward to a voyage of exploration
in the Rockies:

I am to take my departure in a couple of days on a Surveying voyage
by the west branch of the River Liard, a stream as yet unknown
only from Indian report to any of us in this quarter. We expect to
be able to cross the West of the Mountains by the present intended
route, which if found practicable will soon augment the Returns
of this quarter. How the voyage may terminate time can only
determine.[169]

Fort Simpson is on the MacKenzie River, to the west of the Great
Slave Lake in the Northwest Territories of Canada, and the route he was
hoping to take would lead him far into the present Yukon, through the
northern spurs of the Rocky Mountains. However it still did not provide
the viable route to the Pacific that so many explorers, from Alexander
MacKenzie on, had been hoping to find.

He must have done well from this trip and the consequent trading,
for in 1841 he left Canada and came to Steornabhagh to marry Barbara

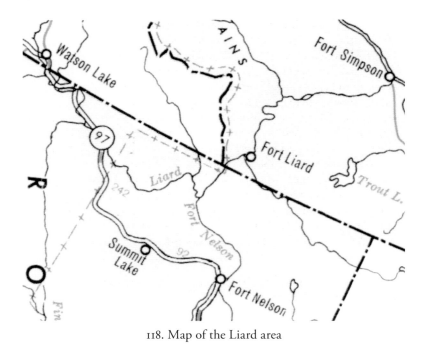

118. Map of the Liard area

Morrison. They lived for a few years in Liverpool, then came back to Steornabhagh, where they settled on Kenneth Street, where he started a shipping business. In this, according to local tradition, he soon lost all the money he had brought back from Canada.

Eilean Iubhard

Off-shore from Leumrabhagh, in the mouth of Loch Sealg, lies Eilean Iubhard. According to Dean Monro in 1549:

> ane Ile callit Ellan Iffurt, sum manurit land, with gude pasture and scheling of store, with fair hunting of Ottiris out of thair bowris.[170]

It was never inhabited, but did at least once have a distinguished visitor! Prince Charles Edward, after failing to get a boat in Steornabhagh:

> sailed for Island Euirn, twelve miles from Stornoway, and landed safely. This Euirn is a desert island round which the people of the Lewis use to go a fishing, and upon which they frequently land to spread their fish upon the rocks of it for drying. Upon the desert island they found plenty of good dry fish, of which they were resolved to make the best fare they could without any butter.

Upon this uninhabited island they remained four days and four nights in a low, pitiful hut, which the fishers had made up for themselves; but it was so ill-roofed that they were obliged to spread the sail of the boat over the top of it. They found heath and turf enough to make a fire of; but had nothing but the bare ground to lie along upon when disposed to take a nap, without any covering upon them at all. When they were consulting about taking their departure from this barren island, the Prince ordered two dozen of the fish to be put on board whatever might happen with them, and said that he would leave money for them, placing the cash upon the fish, that so the people, when they missed of the number of their fish might find the value of what they wanted. But O'Sullivan and O'Neill told him it was needless to leave any money, lest vagrants should happen to land upon the island and take the money which did not belong to them. These prevailed upon him to allow the money to be taken up again.[171]

From Eilean Iubhard the Prince and his party sailed for Harris, and out of this book.

Orasaigh (Orinsay)

With Orasaigh we come to a township which is still occupied, but with many changes along the way! In 1776 Orasaigh was let to 'John MacEiver, merchant in Stornoway', then passed to his son Major MacIver and then to his daughters Christian and Annabella, along with their farms of Aignis and Airinis. The MacIvers had sub-tenants, as we have a list of seven kelp-workers there in about 1810. By 1841 there were twenty-five households in Orasaigh, with a population of 147. In 1843 the township was cleared, and many of its tenants resettled in Crosbost, or in Cape Breton.

Angus Macleod of Calbost, among the voluminous papers he collected on the history of the Pairc, notes an article from the *Inverness Courier* of 15th June 1842, on the attempted eviction by the Lewis Seaforth Estate of the total crofter population of Orinsay and Lemreway.

Another of these painful scenes which lately have been too prevalent, connected with the removal of Highland crofters, took place on 2nd June at Loch Shell, Parish of Lochs, in the County of Ross and Cromarty. The Sheriff, Procurator Fiscal and Factor, with a party of ground officers, constables and others proceeded to the spot, and commenced throwing down the houses. A number of women then rushed upon the party and drove them off the field, without committing any bodily injury except a little rough handling to one of the officers. The people told the Sheriff that they could not leave their homes with ruined characters, as one cause for removing them was given as that they 'had stolen a number of sheep from the adjoining farm, whereas, in reality, not a single act of theft had ever been proven against any of them. They were not in arrears of rent and they numbered from three to four hundred souls'.[172]

Ease used to say that the women, unwilling to offer direct violence, threatened to cut the Sheriff's Officers' braces. The thought of being left with their trousers round their ankles was too much, and they retreated from the field.

As in all such cases at that time, the Establishment's first thought was to call in the military in order to enforce the policy of the Estate. On reflection, however, the Trustees of the Lewis Estate concluded that an attempt to remove the recalcitrant Loch Sealg crofters by means of military force at that time, when the Lewis Estate was on the market, might injure the sale. In the circumstances, the 65 families, consisting of 178 persons in Lemreway and 145 persons in Orinsay were given one year's grace and they were expected to leave voluntarily before the end of that period.

Among those who went to Crosbost was Alexander MacInnes, whose father was Murdo MacInnes – Murchadh nan Luachrach – who came from the old township of Luachair at the head of Loch Reusort, one of the many Harrismen who came to Pairc in the early 1800s.

Another tenant in Orasaigh was Donald Gillies, of Raasay origin. He is said to have come ashore at Bhalamus, some say from a shipwreck, and others say hotly pursued! He had several daughters, all married in the area, but only one son, Roderick, who married Rachel Cunningham from Scalpaigh.

There was an unsuccessful land raid in 1891, but after a further period of raiding in 1920–21, the township was resettled in 1922 as 14 crofts, mainly for cottars from Leumrabhagh.

Probably the best-known of all the people from Orasaigh was the singer Calum Kennedy. After winning a Gold Medal at the Mod in 1955, he went on to become one of the best-loved and instantly recognisable voices in Gaelic song. Especially in some of the earlier recordings such as *A' Pheigi a' Graidh,* he had a clarity of sound and timbre of voice that few could rival.

Stiomrabhagh (Stimreway)

Stiomrabhagh is a mile or so to the west of Leumrabhagh, to which it is linked in many of the old rentals. Later, it was split off into a separate unit, leased to the Nicolson brothers, Louis and Neil, previously tenants

119. Stiomrabhagh

at Isgein. Nicolson is not a Pairc name, apart from this group of families, and most of the Nicolsons of Lewis today derive from Uig roots. It may be relevant that the tenant of Leumrabhagh in 1817 is noted as 'Angus Nicolson, merchant in Stornoway' – could the Stiomrabhagh Nicolsons have come to Pairc with him?

Whatever their source, they were in Stiomrabhagh in 1834 as joint tacksmen, with seven sub-tenants. In 1841 there were still seven sub-tenants, but all seven had come into Stiomrabhagh from other townships since 1835 – so what had happened to the earlier subtenants they replaced? The answer may lie in a note from the estate factor to Seaforth in 1834:

> Archibald Stewart's accusations against the Nicolsons I do not believe a word of, neither does William MacGregor (tacksman of Gabhsann) nay more, he says that he does not believe that they, the Stewarts, had the smallest real grounds of complaint of sheep-stealing against one of the small tenants they have been the means of removing . . . The object they strive for is not so much getting rid of the Nicolsons as bad neighbours as to get possession of the farm of Stiomrabhagh for themselves.[173]

The Stewarts were not successful, as the Nicolsons retained the tack until 1857, by which time the Stewarts had gone, but in 1857

Stiomrabhagh was cleared for their successors in the Pairc Farm, and the Nicolsons and their sub-tenants were given crofts in Leumrabhagh. One of the old subtenants in Stiomrabhagh was Angus MacMillan, son of Norman Bard of Eisgein. The late Murdo MacMillan – Murchadh Fhionnlaidh Mhurchaidh an t-Saighdeir – of Leumrabhagh told his great-grandfather's story in our *Croft History of Lewis, Volume 14 – am Pairc*:

> He was taken away by the Press Gang when he was thirteen and a half, and his parents did not know if he was dead or alive until he turned up seven years later. They had named another child Angus. He had a commission when he came back – he was an officer. Ease had a story about the Saighdear. He went across the loch and he was staying in Crosbost. When he left the house the woman had a child in a cradle, and he said to look after her well as he was going to marry her! He did marry her – and he was twenty-three or twenty-four years older than her.[174]

Pairc Deer Forest

West of Stiomrabhagh we come into the deer forest of am Pairc, which merits a section of its own, before we look at the individual townships. When Dean Monro wrote his description of Lewis in 1594 he noted:

> In this cuntrie of Haray north-wart, betwixt it and the Leozus are mony forests, mony deir but not great of Quantitie, very fair hunting games without any woods, with infinite slaughteris of Otteris and Martrikis.[175]

In 1628 Colin, Earl of Seaforth, John MacLeod of Dunvegan and other island landlords entered into an agreement to prevent poaching in their Deer Forests:

> It is heirby speciallie condiscendit with consent of the saidis honorabill pairties abone written that nane or ather of thair cuntriemen or people shall tak thair courss be boatis ather to the lochs or harboreis with the forrestis of Lewis and Hereiss exceptand the Loches of Herisole in Lewis pertaining to the said noble erle; the loche of Tarbet in Hereis . . . incais thay be not dung and distrest be stress of weather. And incais thay be dung and distrest be storme of weather in ony uther loches within the Ilandis of Lewis and Heriss, it is heirby condescendit that the kippage of everie bote that salhappin to cum in with thair boittes on ony of the lochs abonewrittin with hagbuttis, bowis nor dog, sall not pass nor travel fra their boittis

ane pair of buttis. And gif ony beis fund with gun, bow or dog to exceed the saidis boundis, heirby sall be holdin as ane offender and contempnar of this present contract and condescending, and to be punished and fyned.[176]

No doubt the MacLeod chiefs had had Pairc as a deer-forest also, but at least some of the land was in use as summer grazings for tacksmen in Uig, as is suggested by the place-name Airidh Dhomhnaill Chaim, commemorating the shielings used by the MacAulay chiefs. Even this seasonal use would seem to have been stopped by the Seaforths, who isolated it by a wall built at Ceann Shiophoirt, and in their day the Pairc was probably inhabited only by a few keepers at strategic points along the shore.

Martin Martin in 1703 tells us:

> there are abundance of Deer in the Chase of Oservaul, which is 15 miles in compass, consisting of mountains, and Valleys between them; this affords good pasturage for the Deer, black Cattle and Sheep. This Forest, for so they call it, is surrounded by the sea, except about one mile on the west side; the Deer are forced to feed on Sea-ware, when the Snow and Frost continue long, having no wood to shelter in, and so are exposed to the Rigour of the Season.[177]

The Pairc seems to have remained as Seaforth's deer-forest for more than a century, until the development of sheep-farming suggested a more commercial use for the land. In 1740 'The Forrest' was held by Colin MacKenzie, the Lews Baillie, but by 1755 Pairc was let to Donald MacNeill, a sheep-farmer from Ardmeanish in Argyll. A rental of 1766 lists the lands in his personal possession as:

> St. Columb's Island with all the islands thereto belonging, Crowbeg, low Caros and his other tack there Crowmore, Marvick, Callypost and all the islands belonging to these tacks; his possession in the hills and forest – Vallimus, Keanchrinaig, Skelladal, Carishal, Island Ewart.

In a rental of 1780

> John McLeod Tacksman of Seaforth, agrees to accept of his present Possession of the Towns and Lands of Seaforth, Brinigil, Stromos, Baremseva and the half of Island Seaforth, as the same is possessed by himself, and the possession of Skelladale as the same is possessed by Colin Crichton and his subtenants.[178]

So it would appear that the shores of Loch Siophoirt were not included in MacNeill's tack. Is this the same John MacLeod whom we met in the first volume of *Lewis in History and Legend*, in the township of Giosla, as the forester of Uig?

As commercial fishing prospered, we find parts of the tack being leased to Steornabhagh merchants who no doubt had the fishermen as subtenants. By 1800 fishing in Pairc seems to have ceased to be such a good investment, and many of the merchants' tacks were given up and added back to the farm. For a time kelp-cutting and burning became the main industry of the islands, and kelp-workers were settled in many places around the shores of the Pairc, not this time as sub-tenants but as crofters holding directly of the Seaforth Estate. But the kelp boom was short-lived and many of these crofting townships were cleared once again in the 1820s, and added back into the farm.

But the problem arises that almost all the new kelping families came from Harris, so what happened to their predecessors? It is always assumed that they were cleared by the landlords, but why would a landlord clear them in order to replace them with Hearaich? It doesn't make sense.

It occurs to me that at the same time as these people disappear from Lochs there was a major settlement of families from Lochs on the Gulf Shore of Nova Scotia, between Wallace and Pugwash. The settlement was in the 1800s – so early that there are very few detailed records apart from the inscriptions on their gravestones, such as 'Allan MacKenzie who departed this life July 1850 aged 64 years born in Parish of Loch, Lewis, Scotland' or 'Alexander Ross died March 24 1872 aged 79 years Native of Lewis Island Scotland'. Could these be the same people? If so, far from being driven out of Lochs, they seem to have arrived in Nova Scotia in fairly prosperous circumstances, at a time of high travel costs, and acquired good land there. If they are the same people, it will require a major review of the history of the Pairc.

A rather controversial suggestion, but one which would at least seem to merit further research.

The Crofters Act of 1885 gave security and Fair Rents to crofters, but did not address the problem of landless cottars, of whom there were many in the townships of Lochs Parish. The Pairc Deer Farm had become a focus of their attention, and petitions had been sent in 1882 to Lady Matheson asking for parts of the previous sheep-farm to be given to crofters. The petitions had not been granted, and had been repeated, together with an unfortunate reference to the hope 'that they would not be led, reluctantly, to take such steps as many of their unfortunate countrymen were forced to adopt'. This was construed as a reference to the tenant unrest in Ireland, and had the effect of confirming the estate in the policy of trying to maintain the integrity of the farm.

Donald MacRae, schoolmaster at Baile Ailein, began to organise the cottars, and in November 1882, a party of them, over a hundred in number, gathered at Ceann Siophoirt, with the avowed intention in

120. Gulf Shore Cemetery

invading the forest and driving away and killing the deer. A base was set up at Sromos, and the first group of deer to be killed were brought there, cooked and enjoyed. Platt, the shooting tenant, was away from the island at the time, so Mrs Platt went to meet and remonstrate with the raiders, only to be met with the answer of 'No English, my lady!' On the following day, more deer were killed, but Sheriff Fraser had arrived from Steornabhagh, and formally read the Riot Act to them, and between that and the miserable weather that had blown up, many of the raiders began to drift back home.

The sequel is recounted by I M M MacPhail in his *The Crofters' War*, a book much undervalued today, possibly because of its approach of impartiality in dealing with so emotive a subject:

> The Sheriff's party was accosted on their return journey by a young man carrying a gun and a stag's head, which he was taking home as a trophy of the chase. He was Donald MacKinnon of Balallan, a keen member of the Highland Land League. MacKinnon foolishly challenged the strangers, who he failed to recognise in the dark, and threatened to shoot if they moved. When the Superintendent declared his identity, MacKinnon realised the enormity of his offence and fled, reaching Balallan in a distressed condition. There he met with Donald MacRae, the schoolmaster, who advised him to disappear for a while; but MacKinnon, still distraught, did not take the advice and set off for Stornoway, where he surrendered to the police. He was interviewed by William Ross, the Procurator Fiscal,

who seems to have persuaded MacKinnon to give evidence for the Crown and regain his freedom. With the help of MacKinnon, the Procurator Fiscal drew up a list of men to be arrested.

Only 6 were brought to trial in the High Court of Edinburgh. Lord Shaw acted as defence counsel, and in his address to the jury, he attacked the chief witnesses for the Crown, ringleaders in the raid and now witnesses against their fellow-raiders 'If Donald MacKinnon had not been here, there would have been no case'. The jury took less than half an hour to return to the court with a verdict of Not Guilty on all charges.[179]

The Pairc Deer-Raid in itself did not achieve much (apart from the filling of many hungry bellies with venison!) but the acquittal of the prisoners encouraged groups all over Lewis, and the other islands, to take matters in to their own hands, as we saw at Aignis.

Isgein (Eishken)

The township of Isgein was on the north shore of Loch Sealg, about halfway along the loch. The access today is by road from Ceann Loch Shiophoirt, and a wild narrow road it is, running first along the shores of Loch Sgiobacleit, then cutting through the moor until it drops into the little bay where the present Eishken Lodge stands. The last time I was there, the Lodge ponies had been grazing outside the gate. My wife,

121. Isgein Ponies

122. Isgein Lodge

Chris, who was driving, rolled down her window to get a photograph of the ponies – and soon found a whole horse's head inside the car, snuffling for titbits!

Isgein was a part of MacNeill's farm of Pairc, sublet to Roderick MacLennan of Tabost, but passed in 1776 to the tack of Cro Mor, held by Colin Crichton of Steornabhagh. In 1780 Isgein, with Stiomrabhagh and Orasaigh were let to 'John MacEiver, merchant in Stornoway', then passed in 1787 to 'John Ross, merchant in Stornoway'. Neither of these merchants would have lived in Isgein, but would have sub-let it, probably to fishermen, and the only clue we have to their identity is the Militia List of 1797, where John Nicolson and Donald MacFarlane are listed in Isgein.

Isgein becomes a township in its own right in 1807, with seven tenants. This gradually rose to 14 by 1835, but it was cleared in that year, and its people scattered across Lewis. Isgein then became the headquarters of the Pairc Farm and the later deer-forest.

Isgein remained a lodge in its own deer-forest, despite the raid. It is an attractive place, though hardly the Elysium Alasdair Alpin MacGregor describes in his *Searching the Hebrides with a Camera*:

> The site of the garden, and of the spacious dwelling to which it is attached, has been admirably chosen; and the floral extravagance of the former bears witness to the manner in which the hand of man can create an oasis of perfumed beauty in a wilderness of moor and rock, tarn and mountain stream.
>
> On three sides a number of dark green pines and a few deciduous trees – chiefly mountain-ash, plane-trees and beeches – protect this

spot from the havoc wrought by prevailing winds. A cluster of holly-bushes and several evergreen shrubs of the rhododendron or laurel order lend to the flower-beds additional security from the blighting winds that sweep our Hebrides at erratic intervals through the year.

You would love the warm, velvety flowers at Eishken in autumn-time, sheltered from moorland winds by dark pines and a sprinkling of beeches.

And, oh, God, the golden tipped bees at Eishken![180]

Lush the gardens may have been, but hardly as lush as Alasdair Alpin's prose!

Ceann Loch Shealg (Loch Shell Head)

It does not seem likely that there was ever a crofting community at Ceann Loch Shealg, but there was an inn, noted by Rev. Robert Finlayson in the New Statistical Account of Lewis in 1833 as one of the three stone houses in the parish of Lochs, and the only one to have a slated roof. He also notes that it was the only inn in the parish, and frequented by seafaring men only. Lord Teignmouth visited the inn in 1836, but according to his *Sketches of the Coasts and Islands of Scotland* was less than impressed:

> We landed at Loch Shiell in Lewis, and proceeded to the inn, a neat slated house. To our dismay, as we had consumed our original stock of provisions, we found, save a bowl of excessively sour milk, the negative catalogue complete. We were assured moreover that not even oat-cake could be procured in any of the cottages in the neighbourhood; and as to whisky, it was not to be found in the whole country. The latter statement was very questionable.[181]

There is no mention of the inn at Ceann Loch Shealg in the 1841 census, so it had presumably closed by then – hardly surprisingly if Teignmouth's account of their customer relations was the norm.

Buthainis, Ailtinis and Mol Chadhagearraidh (Bunish, Altenish & Molhagery)

Along the south shore of Loch Shealg from Isgein lay the township of Buthainis, and a mile or so beyond it Ailtinis.

Buthainis appears in late-eighteenth-century rentals, then disappears into the farm, to re-appear as a crofting township of seven crofts from 1820 to 1826. Before that date there was a MacKenzie presence in Buthainis, for there are many families in the Pairc who claim descent from Hector MacKenzie – Eachann Buthainis. According to the generations of his known descendants Eachainn would appear to have been born in about the 1740s.

Ailtinis also appears in rentals of the later 1700s, then disappears for a time into the Pairc farm, reappears again as a township of three crofts in 1820, but disappears again in 1827. The factor's note in 1820 mentions that:

> Roderick MacLean at Altinish is deep in arrears, a troublesome fellow. If he gets land it should be in the neighbourhood of Stornoway where he will be near the reach of the law.[182]

When Buthainis and Ailtinis were cleared in 1826, several of their tenants were removed to Tunga, including Malcolm Smith, of whom the factor's note states 'The Bownish Tennants are good kelp manufacturers, except Malcolm Smith, his character is but so-so!' Another two of the Buthainis tenants were the Campbell brothers, John and Colin, of whom we heard in the history of the church in Tunga.

The coastline south of Ailtinis turns southward towards Rubha Uisinis, where there is a small lighthouse. I passed it often in my days with the IDP (Integrated Development Programme for the Western Isles) in the 1980s – never by land or sea, but only by air, going down to Benbecula in the little Loganair planes of the day, usually flying so low that you felt you had to bend your knees to keep your feet out of the water!

It was in this way also that I have seen Mol Chadhaigearraidh, in its little bay facing into the Minch, between Usinis and Ailtinis. There were four crofts there for a time in the 1820s, three of them with tenants with the Hearach names of MacKay and MacInnes. Thereafter Mol

123. Mol Chadhaigearraidh

Chadhaigearraidh was the base for shepherds, among them a Norman MacDonald, a good example of how shepherds travelled around the area as work was available – and incidentally illustrating one of the problems of genealogical research!

Norman MacDonald was born in Harris in 1820, and was married to Isabella Thomson, daughter of Norman Thomson, shepherd at Bhalaidh in North Uibhist, but of Skye origin. In 1851 he was working at Losgaintir in Harris, but by 1861 he was in Mol Chadhaigearraidh. In the 1880s, when the Pairc became a deer-forest again, he moved to Creed Cove Cottage in the castle grounds at Steornabhagh as a river-watcher. Some of our readers may remember his great-grandson Duncan Robertson in Murdo MacLean's shop in Steornabhagh. The genealogical puzzle is his mother's name, which appears in the Register of Deaths for Steornabhagh as Catherine Jingles! His son Norman, who was born and brought up at Mol Chadhaigearraidh, was the informant to the registrar, so we cannot even blame a Hearach accent, so what was the name that the registrar interpreted as 'Jingles'?

Brolum (Brollum)

Turning west from Rubha Usinis we come to a coast deeply indented by fjords – Loch Brolum, Loch Claidh and Loch Siophoirt itself. Furthest east is Loch Brolum, with the little village of Brolum about one-third of the way up the loch. Although it is mentioned in rentals of the Pairc in 1733 and 1766, it later disappears, to re-emerge as a township of seven crofts in 1820, only to disappear again from 1826. The 1820 crofters include MacInneses, and MacLennans, names which are more associated with Harris than with Lewis, along with a Louis Nicolson – a quintessential Pairc name. When we look at the names of the tenants who were in the villages around the shore of the Pairc in the 1820s, we see that most of them are Harris names – those found in North Harris before it was first cleared in the early 1800s. So the tenants of the 1700s must have left and been replaced by Harris families. We cannot imagine the local families being evicted in order to make room for Hearaich, and in any case there seems to be a gap between the two settlements.

This idea is reinforced by a story from oral tradition: Donald MacInnes from Harris had a house in Brolum, but there was a large boulder on the hill above the house, and he was always worried in case the boulder fell on to the house. It did, eventually, but by that time he and his family had left Brolum to settle in Grabhair. But he would hardly have built the house himself in that position, if he was so worried about the boulder, so he must have moved into a house vacated by some earlier settler.

Na h-Eileanan Mora (Shiant Isles)

Although the English name of the islands is derived from the Gaelic *Sianta* – holy or enchanted – they are almost always referred to locally as na h-Eileanan Mora – the Big Islands. They lie about 7 miles to the east of Bhalamus, out in the Minch towards Skye. Geologically they really belong to Skye, but historically they were part of the Pairc Farm and worked from Bhalamus. Lord Leverhulme in the 1920s transferred them officially to Harris, and it was with Harris shepherds, mainly from Scalpaigh, that I used to visit the islands.

There are three main islands in the group – Eilean Mhuire (Mary's Isle) to the east, Eilean an Taighe (House Isle) to the south and Garbh Eilean (Rough Isle) to the west, with a chain of weirdly shaped rocks running west from the point of Garbh Eilean, known as na Galltaichean.

My first visit was with shepherds taking sheep to and from Eilean Mhuire, the eastmost of the three islands, and I can still remember my surprise, after a fairly stiff climb from the shore, to find a flat grass-land on the top of the island, with clear signs of cultivation and habitation.

On the east side of Eilean Mhuire is a bay named Bagh Chlann Neill, which could mean the Bay of Neil's family, or the MacNeil's Bay. I know of one or two places of that name in the islands, and they would all be hopeless anchorages, so I wonder whether the name means that only the MacNeils of Barra – famous for their seamanship – would anchor there! More prosaically, the name is probably a distortion into Gaelic of an older Norse name.

Dean Monro, in his description of the islands in 1549 mentions an arch at the east end of Garbh Eilean:

> On the eist side of this Ile their is ane Bow made like ane Volt, mair nor ane arrow shot of any man, in manner of ane Volt under the earth, throw the quhilk we useit to row or sail with aire boats, for fear of the horrible brak of seais that is on the outwart side of the point quhair that Bow is, but na great schippis may cum their.[183]

It was near na h-Eileanan Mora that a fishing boat from Scalpaigh trawled up a piece of bent wire, which proved on cleaning and further examination to be a gold torc from the Late Bronze Age.

Much has already been written about na h-Eileanan Mora, not least by Adam Nicolson in his *Sea-Room*, so I shall only quote here the notes from Rev. Simpson in the Statistical Account:

> Black-cattle are pastured on them all, and they are famous for fattening sheep. There is one family residing on the largest of the islands for the purpose of attending the cattle. The head of this family has been so unfortunate as to lose, at different times, his wife, a son,

124. Na h-Eileanan Mora

125. Na h-Eileanan Mora

126. Na h-Eileanan Mora

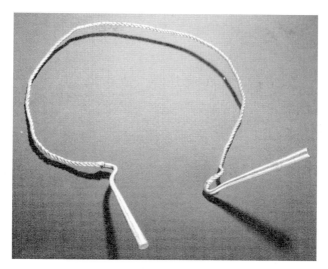

127. Gold Torc

and a daughter, by falling down great precipices; the mother and son met with this catastrophe in following sheep and the daughter by going in quest of wild-fowl eggs.[184]

Bhalamus (Valamus)

Bhalamus lies about midway between Lochs Brolum and Claidh. It was the centre of the Pairc Farm, with the farmhouse on a sheltered bay at the head of the loch and Bhalamus Bheag opposite, on the west side of the loch. The last time I was there was with Murray MacLeod of SeaTrek on a trip to na h-Eileanan Mora. It was a beautiful day, and on the way back we took a turn up Loch Bhalamus. As usual, the bay was full of seals, and many other seals sun-bathing on the rocks around the shore. The walls of the old sheep-pens and fanks showed clear behind the house, but it was disappointing to see how much further damage there had been to the roof of the house itself. Little is left to suggest the days when Bhalamus was the centre of the Pairc sheep-farm.

Rev. Robert Finlayson notes in the New Statistical Account of 1833 that Bhalamus, his own manse at Ceos, and the inn at Loch Sealg are the only dwelling-houses in the parish built of stone and clay, so it is a shame to see the old house at Bhalamus collapsing. There is the old problem: there is little point in restoring a building unless there is some use to be made of it, and it is hard to think what commercial use could be made of Bhalamus house today.

128. Na h-Eileanan Mora

Bagh Reumsabhagh (Bayremsevay)

Just before the mouth of Loch Siophoirt are the two lochs of Bagh
Ciarach and Bagh Reumsabhagh. These were for a time a part of John
MacLeod's tack of Seaforth, but by 1820, they are shown with six
tenants and two landless cottars. The factor's note at that time was that
'the Bayreamsavay tenants were not much in the habit of manufacturing
kelp, having no kelp in their lease'.[185] No doubt they, like the other
small tenants in the Pairc, were relocated elsewhere in Lewis, or went
to Cape Breton like those in Ath Linne. It is strange to me that in our
genealogical research at *Seallam!* we have been able to trace only one of
the Bagh Reumsabhagh tenants, but perhaps there is a reason for this:
Bagh Reumsabhagh had a bad name in Lewis tradition!

At one time, a boat-load of men from Mealasta in Uig had gone to
Gairloch on the mainland for a cargo of timber. On their way back
across the Minch, they hit a snow-storm so bad that they lost their way,
and found themselves at the Bagh Ciarach. There they were found by
the local men, who instead of giving them succour, as would have been
expected, killed them for the sake of their cargo. Of course, they kept
quiet about this, and no word of their men came back to their wives
in Mealasta. One night, many months afterwards, one of the Mealasta
widows saw her sweetheart in a dream, and he sang a song to her – *Muirt
Fir Mhealastadh* – the death of the Mealasta men –

'Se nighean mo ghaoil
An nighinn donn og

Nam bithinn ri taobh
Cha bhithinn fo leon.

Tha m' chuideachd am bliadhna
G a m' shireadh 's 'gam iarraidh,
'S a tha mis' am Bagh Ciarach
Aig iochdar an loin.

Tha fearaibh na Pairce
Air tomhadh na lamh-thuagh,
Ach 's e sinne bhi gun thabachd
Dh'fhag iadsan gun leon.

Bha Donnchadh 'g am fhaire,
Fear-siubhal nam beannaibh;
Tha saoghal ro-charach,
'S gur mealladh an t-or.

'S ann a' direadh na bruthaich
A chaill mi mo luths'
'S fo leacan an Rubha
Tha 'm Fear-Buidhe 'g a leon.[186]

We do have a translation of this poem by another poet, Donald S
Murray –

The girl of my love is the young brown-haired one.
I would not suffer harm if I were with her alone.
My people have been searching for me all year
While I lie in Bagh Ciarach, within a bog here.
The Park men set about us with axes and arms,
Yet all our exhaustion left them unharmed.
The mountain-man Duncan set his blade in my head;
The world is deceitful and led by men's greed.
While climbing this hillside, I lost strength and will.
By the crag of this headland, your lover was killed.

The Mealasta woman remembered every word of the song, and so the
fate of their men became known. But there was a sequel; much later this
girl was at the annual Drobh – cattle sales – in Steornabhagh, and saw
a man from Pairc wearing the *geansaidh* (sweater) he had stripped from
the body of her lover, and which she herself had knitted! Of course she
challenged the Pairc man, but tradition does not tell whether she was
successful in having the murderer brought to justice. Would a knitting
pattern have been acceptable as evidence?

Donald S Murray also wrote a series of poems on various aspects

of the story, under the title of *Speak to Us, Catriona*. Here is the first
section, entitled *The incident in Stornoway*:

> I knew it from the thread,
> Pattern, wool and weave,
> That his clothes came from the dead,
> From one who lived and breathed,
> Close to me, sewn tight
> Inside a bundling blanket
> Throughout long winter nights.
>
> And then the consternation,
> That moment when
> I imagined I was seeing
> The fairness of his face again.
> Later still, the realisation
> That it was not his ghost,
>
> But the figure of another man
> Kitted in his clothes,
> The instant when an accusation
> Sparked off my tongue.
> The cry of 'Stop! That man's a killer!'
> Echoing through town.
>
> And as my fingers grabbed his shoulder
> Wool was torn and ripped,
> The jersey I'd spent winter knitting
> Tugged apart by tightness of my grip.

The eleventh section takes the same incident from the point of view of
someone standing nearby, noting,

> And he ran – his jersey torn; that sudden dash
> That almost forces pause for thought,
> Making one consider what she said might be true,
> That her man may be murdered; that these words were not
> Delusions of the grieving, for there are times despair
> Can twist comfort out of falsehood.
> Causing heart and eye to mistake and mislead,
> Resurrecting men that sleep in bog or shoreline everywhere.[187]

Taobh Loch Shiophoirt (Loch Seaforth-side)

The south end of the shore of Loch Siophoirt consists of the wild cliffs
of Caiteashal, but northward, opposite Maraig in Harris, was Ceann

a' Mhuire, behind its hammerhead-shaped headland. There were four tenants there in 1820, but none in 1828. Later it became the house of a series of gamekeepers, mostly from the mainland, and the ruins of their house on its green patch of old cultivation can still be seen from across the road above Maraig. When the first detailed maps of Lewis were made by the Ordnance Survey in 1851, the census of that year records a party of the Sappers billeted on Roderick MacLean, the shepherd of the time. There is another entry for a Daniel Balfourd from Ireland with his wife and two children, with the note 'living in a canvas shelter' – they were a hardy lot, the first Ordnance Surveyors!

Further north lay Scealadal, and behind it, rises the hill of Muaitheabhal, soon to be the site of the first major windfarm in the Islands. Like all proposals for development in the Islands it has been vehemently opposed by many people and the conservation bodies, often in the most extravagant terms. There are definitely drawbacks to inappropriately sited developments, but there is a great danger that automatic objection to all development proposals can make other people approve them, not on their merits, but because of distrust of the opposition!

Almost at the narrows of Loch Siophoirt lay Sromos, on a most unusual site, as it was not on the coast, but inland, under the foothills. According to John MacLennan, in his evidence to the Deer Forest Commission in 1894:

> it is not adjacent to the shore, but it is the prettiest township in the whole place. It cannot be seen from the sea, not until it is reached. The hill is more suitable for stock than any place that I know occupied by crofters in the parish of Lochs. Then again, Loch Seaforth is a better loch for winter fishing than any loch in the Lews, and that fishing can be prosecuted there without doing any harm to the working of the croft.[188]

Ceann Shiophoirt (Seaforth Head)

On the north shore of Loch Siophoirt we come to the settlement of Ceann Shiophoirt. It was in this area that the Seaforth MacKenzies are said to have had the hunting lodge from which they later took their title. Dr MacDonald of Gisla mentions in his *Tales and Traditions of the Lews* that he

> read as a footnote to an old paper given to the Society of Antiquaries that the first Seaforth who settled in Lewis on a small farm on the North of Loch Seaforth, could not have been superstitious, for he had built three standing stones of a druid circle into the walls of his new castle.[189]

129. Ceann Shiophoirt

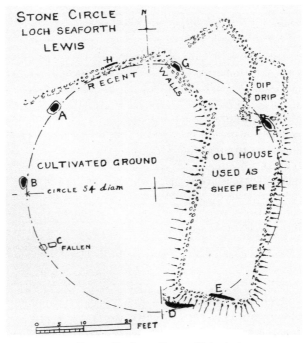

130. Stone Circle at Ceann Shiophoirt

He was also told locally that when Croft No 6 Seaforth Head was made in 1886 the daughter of the tenant had been told by old people that there had been a castle with a circular tower, and that standing stones had been built into the walls of the building.

I have not tracked down MacDonald's original reference, but the *Proceedings of the Society of Antiquaries of Scotland*, Vol 70, include an illustrated note by Wallace Thorneycroft of a stone circle on the site, with at least seven stones then visible.[190]

Though Ceann Shiophoirt may have been a part of the sheep farm of Pairc for a time, from 1820 to 1826 it was let to ten tenants, among them an Alexander Stewart, an ancestor of Donald Stewart, for many years MP for the Western Isles.

Thereafter, Ceann Siophoirt reverted to the Pairc Farm until 1886, when it was resettled as a crofting township, along with Sildinis at the head of Loch Eireasort. Oddly enough the two settlements were treated as a single unit, so that Croft Nos 1–3 Seaforth Head are in Sildinis, and Crofts Nos 4–6 are a few miles away by road at Ceann Shiopoirt, although their grazings are back to back.

Airidh a' Bhruthaich (Arivruach)

There is something very strange about the very existence of Airidh a' Bhruthaich! It was settled as a new crofting township in about 1845, at a time when the main aim of the landlords was to replace crofting townships with farms – and the first six of the new tenants came from Harris, from the Isle of Tarasaigh! One of them, Alexander MacAskill, had been a shepherd/keeper at Ceann Tharabhaigh and perhaps he was the link that brought the Tarasaich there. By 1851 there were 13 crofts in the township, some of the new ones for sons of the original settlers and others for cottars from Baile Ailein and elsewhere in Sgire nan Loch. There is another difference in Airidh a' Bhruthaich also – the crofts there are much bigger than in the other townships of the area.

John MacLennan of Baile Ailein, himself a native of Airidh a' Bhruthaich and of Tarasach stock, gave evidence to the Deer Forest Commission in 1894 that

Airidh Bhruthaich is a recent crofting township, built on the pasture of Balallan, and that the people who came there first said that it was a most unlikely place to be tilled – much more so than any place on either side of Loch Seaforth; and I heard my father and grandfather, who were the first to go there, say that they were put there as a crew to ferry people across, there being no road at that time. This was done by Mr John Scobie as factor for Sir James Matheson.[191]

The far shore of Loch Siophoirt was then a sheep-farm, and I doubt that a ferry would have been made for the shepherds' benefit, but perhaps what was meant was a ferry down the loch to Ath Linne and the Lodge there.

From my younger days of walking from Steornabhagh to Harris, I have fond memories of the Halfway House, at the boundary with Ceann Tarabhaigh, where Mrs Montgomery had a tweed shop with a tearoom upstairs – a welcome retreat and rest, especially on a wet day; not like the story of the man walking to Harris, who stopped for shelter from the rain in a house by the roadside, where the *cailleach* was leaning over the fire in the middle of the floor, stirring a pot of porridge hanging from the *slabhraidh*. She had a cold, and he could not help noticing that a drip was gathering at the end of her nose. 'Will you stay for porridge?' she asked. '*A reir mar a thuiteas a' bhoinneag*,' was his answer – depending how the drop falls – which could have referred to the rain, but I don't think he stayed!

It is said that at one time the river at Ceann Tarabhaigh was the boundary of Harris, and it has to be said that this would be a much more understandable boundary, running up Loch Siophoirt to the shoals at Ceann Tarabhaigh, then west through the geological fault valley to Os Fid on Loch Langabhat and through to Loch Reusort.

At the other end of Airidh a' Bhruthaich there is a monument, representing, I understand, a tear-drop. It is beautifully crafted from stone, and is to commemorate the arrival of Prince Charles Edward, on his abortive attempt to obtain a boat in Steornabhagh to take him back to France in 1746, after the Battle of Culloden. He had been staying with Donald Campbell on the Isle of Scalpaigh in Harris, as told in my *Harris in History and Legend*.[192]

Ned Burke, who was with the Prince tells:

> In Scalpa we stayed about three days, sending from thence our barge to Stornoway to hire a vessel. By a letter from Donald MacLeod we came to Loch Seaforth, and coming there by a false guide, we travelled seven hours, if not more, under cloud of night, having gone six or eight miles out of our way.[193]

They were heading for MacKenzie of Kildun's house at Airinis as we have seen already, but meantime we can note the memorial in Airidh a' Bhruthaich to one of the most romantic and ill-conceived episodes in Scottish history.

Aird an t-Sroim

Loch Siophoirt forms a T-shape, with the stem of the T running from its mouth to the shoals, with a short cross-piece running west to Ceann Tarabhaigh and a longer one east to Ceann Shiophoirt. At the join of the T and the cross are the shoals which are believed to have given its name to the Loch in the Old Norse form of *sjar-fjord* – the pent-up or held-back fjord. As the tide drops these shoals form falls in the loch, but at a high tide the flow reverses, allowing small boats into the upper loch. According to Rev. Robert Finlayson in the New Statistical Account of 1833 'the tide runs at the rate of eight miles an hour, and makes a noise with spring tides that can be heard in calm weather at many miles distance'.[194]

'Sixty-One' records one occasion when bottle-nosed whales had appeared in Loch Siophoirt opposite Ath Linne:

The whales passed round the island without hesitation, and pursued their way upwards, our boats following slowly. There was little delay or stoppage till we came to the Narrows. There the whales paused, and did not much seem to relish the idea of putting their noses to the stream. Towards dawn, it was low water then, and it was quite clear that the whales were waiting for water before proceeding higher – once past the Narrows, they were ours.

A reinforcement joined our fleet, and a curious and, as it turned out, most unfortunate one; it was in the shape of the one of the dirtiest, crankiest tubs of a boat. The crew consisted of three of the ugliest, noisiest, most ill-conditioned-looking viragoes of women I ever looked upon. There they were, perched up in their boat, like so many witches, barring their broomsticks. One of them sat upon a turf creel in the bows, knitting for her bare life. What Hebridean female, be she witch or not, does not under every circumstance and every occupation knit as if her bare life depended upon that exertion?

The tide was now making fast. The rocks over which the rapids had been foaming were disappearing. We could see the leaders of the band of bottle-noses moving about, and gradually feeling their way as to taking the Narrows. Half an hour's patience now, and this band, like the last that had visited Loch Seaforth a few years before, would be ours; when just at this critical moment, this triumvirate of demons, with an indescribable yell, broke loose, and being on the outside, but nearest, flank to the whales, rushed their boat at the Narrows with the incoming tide. In a second the whales turned, and the game was up. The moment the whales turned it was all over, unless they could be met and turned again at Seaforth Island. Ahead of us the loch seemed to seethe like boiling milk, and for some seconds – I do not know how long – our boat stood on whales; but it soon passed, and to our infinite delight, we found our boat floating again. But it was touch and go. One crack of one whale's tail would have smashed our boat, and landing on the whales would not have been very pleasant.[195]

The shore south of Airidh a' Bhruthaich goes by the name of Aird an t-Sroim, after the Strom or tidal falls. In the 1820s there were six tenants in this area, in the townships of Grigaspol, and Pol Dubh, rather incongruously translated as Blackpool. The Forestry Commission planted large experimental blocks of conifers on the Aird, but these, like a similar plantation near Loch a' Ghainmhich in Uig, did not prove commercially viable. Then, a number of years ago, an unusually mild winter allowed the spread of Pine Beauty Moth, whose caterpillars caused an amazing amount of destruction on the part of the forest between the main road and Loch Seaforth. The forest changed from green to a depressing purple-gray haze of dead tree-trunks, as huge swathes of the forest succumbed to the jaws of the caterpillars.

Parts of the forest have recovered to some extent, and much of the area has now been taken over by Aline Community Woodland, a Community Trust who obtained finance to clean out the dead trees, construct a series of board-way walks and generally convert the forest into a recreation area, though financial problems have meant that progress has been much slower than was originally anticipated.

Ath Linne (Aline)

John MacDonald of Urgha in 1805 tells:

> That Patrick McStalker, alias McDonald, who was Donald McLeod of Berneray's servant, told him That, on one occasion when his master and he were returning from Stornoway, they passed Athalinne when Angus Laidir was erecting the first house at Athalinne, and that Berneray took hold of the only couple set up, and laid it on the ground, warning the man that the next person who found it re-erected, when sent to pull it down, might not do it so civilly; That the other asked Berneray where he wished him to build, Berneray directed him to rebuild his house at the distance of three musket shots to the north, and to this Angus Laidir complied. Duncan MacKay of Ardvoorlich (Aird a' Mhulaidh) adds that Aonghas Laidir (the by-name means Strong Angus) was alias Mac Thiunlaidh-chaird (presumably Mac Fhionnlaidh Cheaird – son of the Finlay the smith) and that this might have happened about sixty or seventy years ago.[196]

Aonghas Laidir appear to have been followed at Ath Linne by Archie MacArthur, then aged 76, who deponed in 1805:

That he was born in the Parish of Uig, and has been tenant at Athalinne for these thirty-two years back; That Mr Gillanders, the chamberlain of Lewis, sent the deponent to Athalinne on purpose to defend the line of the march deponed from the encroachments of the Harris people.[197]

Eventually a complete township was settled at Ath Linne, along the shore from the boundary north, where the ruins of houses are still to be seen. This was in the heyday of the kelp industry, and there were many disputes with the Harris people over the kelp on the shores of Eilean Mulag, now Seaforth Island, which belonged equally to Lewis and Harris.

In 1814 Ath Linne was divided into eight crofts, two of which remained in MacArthur hands, and by the 1820s there were a further three houses, but by this time the kelp industry had failed, and the Seaforth Estate was looking at clearing much of Lochs Parish to make sheep-farms. In an undated document, but from internal evidence from the 1820s, the factor was reporting on what the tenants of various townships would do if removed, and for 'Achlinn' his note is 'The most of the Achlinn Tenants will go to America if removed; they are very decent obedient tenants and good kelp manufacturers.'[198]

'Go to America' is just what they did! From our records, we can trace all of them in the St Anns area of Cape Breton. William Buchanan, known as Red William, and his son-in-law John Smith took up land at Eel Cove, on the west shore of St Anns Bay, opposite the town of Englishtown. Another tenant at Ath Linne was Arthur MacArthur, probably a grandson of Archie MacArthur of 1805, and he also settled at Englishtown, but he and his descendants appear there under the name Campbell. The same change of name occurred in Carloway area also, and probably derives from the historical links of the Campbells and MacArthurs in their original traditional homeland of Argyll.

There is no doubt that the Ath Linne tenants were forced to remove by the Seaforth Estate, but it looks as though the tenants made their own decision to emigrate, rather than be relocated elsewhere in Lewis, like the tenants of most of the other townships of South Lochs.

After the tenants left, Ath Linne became a shooting lodge. By 1850, the tenant was Rev. George Hely Hutchinson, author of *Reminiscences of the Lews* under the pseudonym of 'Sixty One'.

The Lodge of the Aline shooting stands over Loch Seaforth, looking down towards the Minch, and on a soft summer's evening, on a

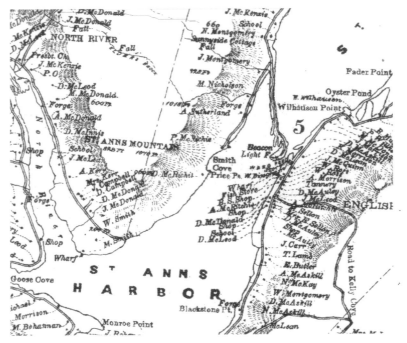

131. Church's Map of St Anns Harbour, Cape Breton, c.1870

fairer or more lovely spot never did the eye of man rest. The sea-loch, without a ripple, at your feet; Glen Scaladale's dark side, falling down upon its shores; and Cleisham towering into the evening mist, with the peaks of Langan Glen and the other Harris hills clustering round, form a scene that often and often have I passed hour after hour looking on, and thanking God for such a sight and the power of enjoying it.[199]

Could an adopted Hearach be so crass as to note that the view he liked so much was from Ath Linne looking towards Harris?

Hely-Hutchinson was at Ath Linne at the time of the settlement of the boundary dispute, and he played host to the visiting legal dignitaries and to Captain Burnaby and the sappers of the Royal Engineers, who had been involved in making the first Ordnance Survey Maps of Lewis. He notes:

That the boundary would have been given in favour of Harris, but for too much proving; an old patriarch swore to some cinders placed years ago by his ancestors as a landmark, but which turned out be

132. Loch Siophoirt

the remains of a fire lighted there by the sappers some four months back. This was, as you can conceive, damaging.[200]

Aline Lodge still stands a little to the north of the boundary, and a footpath runs along the hillside just above Allt a' Mhuill, leading to a magnificent view into the deep gully of Loch Langabhat. It is good to see a notice at the end of the track welcoming walkers, though it would be useful if there was some place where walkers could park the vehicles that brought them there.

And speaking of notices, how long will it be before Comhairle nan Eilean Siar can be persuaded to change the misspelt notice at the boundary, welcoming visitors to 'Eilean na Hearradh' instead of the correct 'Eilean na Hearadh'? When one thinks of the cost of such road-signs, surely someone should be checking and insisting that they are spelt correctly?

There was never any serious dispute that the boundary on the shore was at the mouth of a little stream called Abhainn a' Mhuil, which runs into the stony beach known as Mol na Hearadh – the stone beach of Harris – the main area of dispute was in the hill-ground behind the shores of the loch.

We told the story of the boundary dispute in Part 1 of *Lewis in History and Legend*, and now we have returned to the same spot, where we left Donald Matheson nursing his sore back after being whipped to make sure that he would remember the boundary. Surely it will have healed by now?

PART 5 – STEORNABHAGH

And so we come to the town of Steornabhagh itself – Steornabhagh mor a' Chaisteil:

Steornabhagh 's e Steornabhagh
Am baile 's boidhche leam fo 'n ghrein
Steornabhagh 's e Steornabhagh.

Tha Steornabhagh aluinn nan sraidean 's nam buth
'S Gearraidh Chruaidh nan allt 'is na coilltean tha dluth
'S an caisteal as boidhche 'se prois an Taobh Tuath
Anns an eilean laigheas aluinn 's a' chearnaidh mu Thuath
Leodhas mo ghraidh.[201]

Lovely Steornabhagh, with its streets and shops, the Gearraidh Chruaidh of the streams and woods close by, the lovely castle, pride of the north, in the gentle isle that lies in the north. My beloved Leodhas.

So much has been written about the history of Steornabhagh by writers from W C MacKenzie to Jim Shaw Grant, from Sandy Matheson to Catherine MacKay, from Fred Silver to Frank Thompson, that it would seem rather pointless, and superfluous, to repeat what they have already dealt with so excellently. So I have taken a rather different approach, selecting some individual events which I have found interesting, and for which sources are less readily available.

Little is known of the church in Lewis during the days of the old MacLeod chiefs – and indeed the character of many of them was such that we would not expect religious matters to have troubled them overmuch. W C MacKenzie, in the *Book of the Lews*, tells us:

The credit for restoring Christian rites in Lewis belongs to Mr Farquhar MacRae, Vicar of Gairloch, then a young man of thirty, whom Lord Kintail brought to Lewis in 1610. The condition of religion in the island may be gauged by the fact that he found it necessary to baptise all under forty years of age, and to re-introduce, practically, the institution of marriage.[202]

This perhaps should not be taken too literally – there are plenty examples in later times of reformers who claimed that there was no religion, when they really meant that there was none of their own form of religion!

The same source tells that the first Earl of Seaforth, a pious and religious man, built a church in Stornoway, St Lennan's, the pre-Reformation church having probably fallen into a state of disrepair. According to Rev. Murdo MacAulay:

> It stood on North Beach Street where the National Bank and the Sailors' Home now stand. The bell of St Lennan's, which reputedly had been used by the Cromwell garrison at Stornoway, was removed when the ruins of the church were demolished in the first half of the 19th century. During the Matheson period it was hung at the Manor Farm, and in the agrarian disturbances of 1887–88 it was rung to summon the Royal Scots on parade, as they were quartered on the farm. Later it found its way to Mr John Morrison of Galson Farm, and finally ended up in St Peter's Episcopal Church.[203]

Captain Dymes, in his *Description of Lewis* in 1630 has this to say of Steornabhagh and its church:

> As for ye situation of ye towne, first for the benefit of a good ayre wch is chiefly to be considered. It is vpon a drye peece of level ground wch doth enjoy the benefit of the sonne from ye morning vntil the evening, wch is not easily found againe in the Ile because of the huills and boggs. Then for those two elemts of fire and water they are there most conveniently at hand. Moreover this place lyeth near the midst of the Countrey for the more conveniency of all the inhabitants wch must resort thereunto. It beinge alsoe the place wch hath bene always most frequented both of the inhabitants and strangers, where there are already some fewe buildings with a pious worke of the Earle of Seafort, who doth build a church there wch is a good foundacion for the rest of the worke.[204]

He adds a phrase which will raise a few hackles: 'As for the inhabitants theire languadge is a kind of bade Irish'!

Unfortunately the church in Lewis was not free of the superstitions which pervaded the church of the day, even to the acceptance of the belief in witchcraft. There had been an earlier witch-hunting panic in the 1590s, but it had died down quickly. Now in the 1630s it had reared its ugly head again, and even far Lewis did not escape the infection:

> Christian Riache in Stornoway, long tyme bygane suspect and delate guiltie of the detestable cryme of withcraft, sorcerie, inchantments and uthers devilish practices offensive to God, scandalous to the trew religioun and hurtfull to diverse our good subjects as her confessions and depositions showne to our privie counsell beir upon quhom necessar it is that justice be ministrat conforme to the lawes of our

133. South Beach, showing the Old Castle

realme for quhilk purpose we have made and constitute Andro
Mackenzie of Milbois baillie of the Lews, Murdo Mackenzie of
Shader, Alexander Mackenzie, John Mackenzie of Holmekill and
Lorne Mackenzie of Brace or any three of them, our justices in that
part to the effect under writtin, givand the courts and sutes and in
the saids courts the said Christiane to call be ditty to accuse and
her to the knowledge of ane assise to putt and as she shall be found
culpable or innocent of the said cryme of witchecraft to cause justice
to be ministrat upon her conforme to the lawes of our realme. Given
under our signet at Halyrudhos, the 20 day of Januarie and of our
raigne the sext yeere 1631.

There is no direct record of what eventually happened to Christiane,
but later the same year, there is a record of another trial: 'Marie
McGillimichell, sister to umquhill Christiane Reiache burnt for
witchcraft'.[205]

The actual burning was probably carried out at Dingwall, the county
town, but the new tacksmen appointed by the MacKenzies were at least
complicit in the crimes. The fact that the two accused were sisters could
suggest that some family feud was being played out. It could be claimed
that this happened during a period of at least nominal Episcopalianism,
but the Presbyterian church was infected with the same poison, for
in 1649 the Synod appointed persons in their parishes 'to take trial of
all witches, sorcerers, charmers, palmisters, jugglers, second-sighted
diviners, soothsayers, necromancers, consulters with spirits and such
like'. We have no later records of witchcraft trials in Lewis, and can only
hope that the lack of records means a lack of cases to report.

Captain Dymes also reports on the fishing:

But the great and rich commoditie wch might bee made of this land
is the Fishinge whereof the inhabitants doe make but small benefit
besides theire owne food, their beinge in the Island not above a
dozen boates wch doe kill anie fish for sale. But the Dutch wch have

fished there theis last two yeares past have found that great and
extraordinary gaine therof, whoe only with 4 busses wth 16 men
and 25 netts in a Busse have within the space of three monethes
killd three hundred last of Herrings wch Herrings by theire factors
and owne confession vnto mee was sold the last year at Danske for
400 gilders. The master of one of these Busses wch transported me
from the Island into the mayne continent did protest vnto mee that
the fish was in such abundance yt they were sometimes constrained
to cast it into the sea againe they haveing more in halfe theire netts
then they were able to save, and he was of the opinion that if there
had bene a thousand Busses more there was fish enough for them all.
As for the Cod and Ling the Dutch doth kill none of it themselves,
but buyeth it at easie rates of the Inhabitants; wch are alsoe so far
from having the true industry of killinge that fish, that one boate
with our Newfoundland men will kill more in a daie then they doe
with one of theire boates in a yeare.[206]

Charles I reckoned that he could get in on the act with the Dutch,
and so did Seaforth, but while they were fighting about it, the Civil
War intervened – and so did Cromwell, as the castle remembered only
too well.

John Morisone, indweller, writing in 1680, remembers also:

Of anie famous battle in the Countrie I cannot say much but manie
and assiduous skirmishes hes been of old betwixt the inhabitants.
The fights and skirmishes betwixt the Countire men and the Lairds
of Fyff are to be found in Spotswood his Ecclesiasticall historie, to
which I refer the reader; Onlie the late Earl of Seaforth coming with
a fleing armie fought with the English garrisone under Cromuall,
killed many of ther men but being destitute of artilrie, could not
storm the garisone, notwithstanding that he assaulted the trenches;
neither would they be drawne out to the fields to encounter.

The Loch of Stornuway being a verie good and ordinarie harbour
within, but in the entrie hath twa rocks invisible with high water, one
on each syde of the entrie; that on the Northsyde and the outmost
of the two is called the beasts of Holm and that on the Southsyde
and innermost is called the Roof of Arinish. Within these two there
is no danger of rocks.[207]

One could wish that that had been remembered almost 240 years
later.
    Although the Seaforth of the time was involved in the Jacobite
rebellions of 1715 and 1719, Steornabhagh itself was not much affected,
and managed to maintain this lack of involvement even when another

famous visitor called in 1746, looking for a ship. My friend John MacLeod suggested that the reason he was unsuccessful was that it was a Wednesday afternoon, and everything in Steornabhagh was shut, but Donald MacLeod of Gualtragill gives a more detailed explanation:

> May 1st: Donald MacLeod was dispatched by the Prince to Stornway in the Isle of Lewis in order to hire a vessel under a pretence of sailing to the Orkneys to take in meal for the Isle of Sky, as Donald used to deal in that way formerly. Donald got another boat from Mr Campbell in Scalpay in which he sailed for Stornway, where he remained some time without making out the design on which he was sent. But at last he succeeded, and then dispatched an express to the Prince in Scalpay.
>
> May 5th Donald was sent back to Stornway to get things in readiness. But when he came there, to his great surprize, he found no less than two or three hundred men in arms. Donald could not understand at all what was the matter that occasioned such a sudden rising of men, and therefore, without fear or dread, he went directly into the room where the gentlemen were that had taken upon themselves the rank of officers, and asked them what was the matter. Every one of them immediately cursed him bitterly, and gave him very abusive language, affirming that he had brought this plague upon them; for that they were well assured that the Prince was already upon the Lewis, and not far from Stornway, with 500 men. This they said exposed them to the hazard of losing both their cattle and their lives, as they heard the Prince was come with a full resolution to force a vessel from Stornway. Donald very gravely asked, How sorrow such a notion could ever enter into their heads? 'Where, I pray you' said he 'could the Prince in his present condition gett 500 or one hundred men together? I believe the men are mad. Has the devil possessed you altogether?' They replied that Mr John MacAulay, Presbyterian preacher in South Uist, had writ these accounts to his father in the Harris, and that the said father had transmitted the same to Mr Colin MacKenzie, Presbyterian teacher in the Lewis. Donald saned these informers, very heartily, and spared not to give them their proper epithets in strong terms. 'Well then' said Donald 'since you know already that the Prince is upon your island, I acknowledge the truth of it; but then he is so far from having any number of men with him that he has only but two companions with him, and when I am there I make the third. And yet let me tell you farther, gentlemen, if Seaforth himself were here, by G . . . he durst not put a hand to the Prince's breast.'

Here Donald desired me to remark particularly for the honour of the honest MacKenzies in the Lewis (notwithstanding the vile

abusive language they had given him) that they declared they had
no intention to do the Prince the smallest hurt, or to meddle with
him at present in any shape. But then they were mighty desirous he
might leave them and go to the continent, or anywhere else he should
think convenient . . . The wind being quite fair for the continent
Donald desired they would give him a pilot, but they absolutely
refused to give him one. Donald offered any money for one, but said
he believed he would not have got one though he should have offered
£500 sterling, such was the terror and dread the people were struck
with. Donald then returned to the Prince and gave him an honest
account how matters stood, which made them all at a loss to know
what course to take, all choices having but a bad aspect.[208]

Charlie headed south, but, as we have seen, had to take shelter on
Eilean Iubhard at Leumrabhagh.

The Government sent a detachment of the Regiment of the Buffs
under Captain Barlow to check on the Islands in June 1753:

> On the 8th we set sail again with a favourable wind and anchored
> safely the same evening in the Harbour of Stornway and put the
> party ashore The next day I put my own Party ashore likewise, in
> order to refresh them, and that they might clean their Arms, which
> were but in a bad condition. I halted there two days and waited upon
> Mr McKenzie who is Factor to my Lord Fortrose where I observed
> three pieces of Brass Cannon, the largest carrying a Ball of about
> Four Pounds, the second about a Pound shot, and the smallest half
> a pound. I spoke to Captain Fergussone about them, and he told me
> they belonged to my Lord Fortrose, and that General Campbell saw
> them in the year 1745 when he was in the Country, and as he took
> no notice of them I had better not, till I had acquainted you, and
> received your Directions. If therefore you think it necessary I shall
> take them away and send them to Fort William.[209]

Does any one know what happened to them eventually?

> This country belongs to Lord Fortrose; the inhabitants are Protestants,
> and in number about Six Thousand. They live mostly on the Western
> Coast which is tolerably fertile and capable of great improvements,
> but they support themselves chiefly by their Fisheries, so that their
> lands are much neglected.
> Stornway is the Chieff Town and contains about One Hundred
> Houses or Huts, miserably built, and the only covering is loose straw
> or Heather shook upon them which is bound down with ropes made
> of the same materials to prevent the winds blowing it away. They
> carry on a considerable trade with Norway, France and Holland,

134. In the Harbour

having a very safe commodious Harbour, and about Thirty vessels great and small belonging to the Town. There is the remains of an Old Fort built by Oliver Cromwell, which was demolished by the English garrison when they were withdrawn from that country in the Reign of King Charles 2nd. Several of the Merchants of Stornway are in good Circumstances and the place might thrive mightily, were it not, that the Inhabitants labour under great tyranny and oppression from the unbounded Authority of his Lordship's Factor, who is a Sheriff Substitute, but never held a Court nor took cognisance of any one Crime punishable by Law. I have been lately informed that he is dead; if so it will be a great relief to those poor people, unless another of the same Mercenary Disposition should be appointed in his room.[210]

Fifty years later, Rev. Colin Mackenzie was raising a warning about over-reliance on fishing:

Stornoway is furnished with an excellent and well-frequented harbour, where vessels of every description may anchor with safety. The attention and industry of its principal inhabitants are chiefly directed to fishing of herrings, of which, in successful years, they take some thousand barrels, and have about thirty-five vessels from 20 to 80 tons burden, annually fitted for the bounty at great expence, and by the profits arising from them they are chiefly supported. In some late years notwithstanding their utmost endeavours have been almost wholly frustated by the failure of the fishing.[211]

John Walker in his *Report on the Hebrides* in 1764 praised the herring industry:

The People of Stornoway made Trial last Year of the Buss fishing with one Vessel. She sailed from Stornoway for the rendezvous at Campbelton about the middle of August, and at Loch Tarbert in the Isle of Harris very near completed a cargo of Herrings, which She carried to Campbelton, and sailed from thence upon the Bounty in the middle of September. This one experiment points out Stornoway as the Place most advantageously situate of any in Scotland for carrying on the Buss fishing. By Law, the Herring busses are oblidged to rendevouze at Campbelton on or before the 15th of Septemeber, when they proceed to the Winter fishery. In the Voyage to this Rendevouze, a Vessel from Stornoway may be pretty certain of making a compleat cargo of herrings, provided She is ready to leave that Port at the Proper time, that is, upon the first Information of their Appearance in the Minch, which is always about the middle of July. While She follows them in their Progress Southwards, She is continuing her Voyage, and had a fair chance of arriving at Campbelton fully loaded, where she can dispose of her Cargo to advantage, and be furnished with a Fresh supply of Salt and Casks. She may by this means have the opportunity of making two Cargoes, during one Fishing, while the Busses from the South can only have the opportunity of obtaining one, and the only Inconvenience or additional expence she need incur for this great advantage is that of leaving the Port of Stornoway a Month or Six Weeks sooner than she would otherwise do.[212]

Frank Bigwood has carried out a fascinating research into herring busses from Steornabhagh and their crews. So we learn that the *William* of Stornoway was built at Carron Water in 1763 and was owned by William Crichton, merchant in Stornoway, and that she sailed on the bounty from 1767 to 1776. She had seven of a crew, including a Rory MacKenzie, 35 years of age, 5' 5" in height, with brown hair! We also have such details as that she caught 222 barrels of herring in 1773, when Norman Crichton was commanding her.[213]

Despite the fishing there was great destitution in Lewis and in July 1773 no less than 840 people sailed for America.

Alarmed with this, Lord Fortrose, their master, came down from London about five weeks ago to treat with the remainder of his tenants. What are the terms they asked him, think you? The land at the old rents, the augmentation paid for three years backward to be refunded, and his factor to be immediately dismissed.[214]

In the following year, the *Friendship* and the *Peace and Plenty* sailed for America, the main reason for emigration being stated as poverty.

At the same time, in 1777, the old village of Cnoc nan Gobhair –
Goathill – was cleared when a list of 22 named persons:

> All inhabitants of Knocknagour & Stornoway being complained upon
> by many of their neighbours for lodging and sheltering Strangers and
> Straglers and people of bad fame in their houses in manifest violation
> of the articles of last set & the regulation & good order of the town
> in so much that the honest industrious inhabitants looses their peats,
> kail, potatoes & every other thing that those vagabonds can get hold
> of & as this trespass upon conviction is declared a breach of the lease
> the whole above named people being convicted of the same here
> this day, the Baily finds they have forfeitied any lands last sett and
> Declares their houses &, possessions Void against Whitsunday next
> and ordains the Baron officer to intimate this sentence to every one
> of the above persons.[215]

Changed days in Goathill!
The development of the American colonies also created a demand for
ministers – both Gaelic- and English-speaking – like Colin MacIver:

> To Thomas Chalmers
> From Fayetteville NC 2 Oct 1843
>
> I must give you a brief account of myself, inasmuch as there is no-one
> here, having the pleasure of a personal acquaintance with you, who
> can furnish me with a letter of introduction.
>   I am a native of the Island of Lewis, in Ross-shire, North Britain,
> and I spent the first nineteen years of my life in the town of Stornoway
> in that island. About forty years ago, I came to the United States of
> America; and for something more than the last thirty years I have
> laboured in this country in the Ministry of the Presbyterian Church.
> For the greater part of my Ministerial life I have been labouring
> among the Scottish Highlanders and their descendants residing in
> the neighbourhood of this place, and that I preach regularly to them
> in the Gaelic language as well as in English.[216]

> Ann an eaglais Galatia bha a' searmon-achadh an comhnuidh an
> Gaidhlig an t-Urramach Colin McIver, agus na dheidh lean Mhgr
> J. Sinclair. Chithear clo-bhualadh coig leabhraichean Mhaois an
> Gaidhlig anns a' Charolina Room de'n Oilthigh North Carolina,
> agus aig ceann an leabhair sgriobhar an t' ainm Colin McIver,
> agus ri taobh tha na litreachan JS ris an t-am, ainmichte mar
> June 30, 1852.[217]

135. Barbecue Church, North Carolina

In the Galatia Church the Harvest service was always held in Gaelic by Reverend Colin MacIver, and after him by Mr J Sinclair. A print of the five books of Moses in Gaelic is in the Carolina Room in the University of North Carolina, and at the beginning is written the name Colin MacIver, and beside it are the letters JS beside the date, and dated June 30th 1852.

Rev. Colin MacIver had links with the Barbecue Church at Sanford, which Chris and I visited on a lecture tour of North Carolina in 2003. Like all the churches there it was timber-built, with ornate doors which, on principle, are never closed. Apparently at some time in the past they used to be locked, but one morning, after a bitterly cold night, an Englishman was found, frozen to death, lying up against the door, which he had been trying unsuccessfully to open to get shelter in the church. So it was determined that that would never happen again. When we asked our guides how they knew it was an Englishman, one pointed out that a Scot would have picked the lock, while the other reckoned that a Scot would have had enough alcohol in his bloodstream not to freeze!

It is clear that many of those leaving for America were businessmen, taking capital with them to set up businesses in New York in particular, and the consequent drain of capital was a great worry to the Seaforth Estate, who saw themselves in danger of being left without a proper mercantile class in Steornabhagh.

Luckily for them, the declaration of war against France in 1793 resulted in a great demand for the minerals produced in kelp-burning,

136. At the Battery c.1901

creating an industry which would not only employ the existing redundant population, but would actually create a demand for an increased population, which led to the creation of the crofting system in the rural areas. The destination to which most of the kelp-slag was shipped was Liverpool, and many Lewis businessmen set up links with that area, like the MacIvers, who were later to set up the Cunard Shipping line.

Steornabhagh was visited by Robert Heron in 1799:

> The only town in Lewis is Stornaway. Though not of any considerable extent, yet, by the attention of the noble proprietor Lord Seaforth it is become a flourishing town and is daily increasing. A considerable number of fishing busses belongs to it; and it has the advantage of a custom-house and a post-office. The trade is largely in fish, kelp, oil, feathers and skins. In front of it, there is a large bay and a commodious harbour.[218]

The suburb of Einacleit or New-town dates from about this time:

> On the north side of the town there is a great number of miserable thatched huts, occupied by sailors, fishers and other people, with their families. The poor inhabitants of those huts have built more commodious thatched houses along the shore of the bay, east of the town; and Mr MacKenzie of Seaforth gives every head of a family one guinea to encourage them to remove and to help defray the expenses incurred on the occasion. He gives those poor people 20 years lease of their dwelling-places, to each of which a small garden is joined, and they pay three Scotch merks yearly for every such house and garden.[219]

At about the same time, the Hudson's Bay Company and its rivals the North-West Company began recruiting in Steornabhagh, and though many of their recruits were for boatmen and trappers, there were opportunities too for clerks and businessmen, as we saw in Cro Beag. The town of Steornabhagh continued to develop, as James Hogg, the Ettrick Shepherd, found in 1803:

> I was indeed greatly surprised at meeting with such a large and populous town in such a remote and distant country. There is one full half of the town composed of as elegant houses, with even more genteel inhabitants, than are generally to be met with in the towns of North Britain which depend solely on the fishing and trade. The principal and modern part of the town stands on a small point of land stretching into the harbour in the form of a T and as you advance back from the shore the houses grow gradually worse. The poor people have a part by themselves, on a rising ground to the north-east of the town, and though all composed of the meanest huts, it is laid out in streets and rows as regularly as a camp.[220]

James MacDonald visited the town in 1811:

> The town of Stornoway, with its neat slated houses, straight streets and public spirited, independent and active population, yields a striking contrast to the rest of the Island. It was gratifying to find a thriving town in this remote land, in possession of a brisk trade and fishery, and its principal merchants connected by regular correspondence and commercial intercourse with all parts of Britain and Ireland. There are two excellent schools regularly taught in the town; there were attended in 1808 by 219 scholars of either sex, who owe much to the kind and laudible inspection of the Rev. Mr MacKenzie, the minister of the parish. This gentleman did ample justice to the benevolence of the noble proprietor, Lord Seaforth and of his amiable lady, who contribute handsomely to the support of the public education of boys and girls upon their vast estate. But notwithstanding all their efforts, such is the degraded state of the great mass of the population that they will not put their children to school or afford them the means of ever bettering their present hapless condition. When reproached on this head they answer 'If we give them education, they will leave us.'[221]

Shipbuilding prospered too, as shown in the *Inverness Courier* of 27 May, 1813:

> On Friday the 30th last month there was launched at Stornoway, witnessed by a great concourse of people, a fine new brig, of about 200 tons burthen, the largest vessel ever built in the Hebrides. She went into the water in the finest style and immediately on her

starting was with the usual ceremonies honoured with the name of Lord MacDonald.[222]

The town prospered, but the end of the French Wars in 1815 meant that the kelp trade gradually declined, and the population of the rural areas found once again that their labour was no longer required by the estate.

William Daniell, the artist, was impressed by the situation of the town, and of Seaforth Lodge, as we saw in the Prologue:

> The harbour is excellent, and is much frequented as a place of shelter by Baltic traders, either homeward or outward bound. One hundred and thirty vessels, and among them many large ships, have been seen at anchor at the same time in Stornoway; a considerable number usually winter here. The pier, which is a very convenient one, was built a few years ago. The chief pursuit of the people is the herring fishery, for which about fifty vessels are annually fitted out. A more than ordinary bustle seemed to prevail in the town, in consequence of the annual fair or market, which is held on the second Wednesday in June.[223]

He was less impressed by some other aspects of the town:

> At the period of this visit the town was incommoded by an intolerably noisome odour. On inquiry into the cause, it was stated, that a short time previous a shoal of about two hundred whales had been driven ashore. After the blubber had been extracted, the carcases being turned adrift, were thrown on the land through the effect of a strong wind; they were again towed out to sea, but to no purpose, for the breeze continuing, they were stranded once more; and as the islanders could not, on account of the rocky nature of the ground, adopt the expedient of burying them, they were suffered to putrify in the heat of a summer sun. As the natives shared from this adventure a profit amounting to about one thousand pounds, they might find no difficulty in reconciling themselves to such a contingency, but to a stranger it was absolutely insufferable.[224]

Thomas Headrick in 1800 was more worried about the defence of the town:

> Government should erect a battery here for the defence of the town and shipping; I know of no place that might more easily be defended against the greatest force. They should also have a sloop-of-war or stout gun-boat stationed at Stornoway, to cruise occasionally between the Butt of Lewis and the Orkneys. Since convoys were appointed, privateers commonly nestle about the Faro Isles, and run

137. In the Harbour

down between the Butt and Cape Wrath, where they find the trade defenceless, as the convoy commonly leaves it at the east entrance of the Pentland Frith. The people of Stornoway have suffered much by such captures during this war, and last summer one of their vessels was taken almost in sight of the harbour. Two insignificant privateers had even the impudence to threaten the town, and the shipping which had taken shelter in the bay, and paraded in the Minch almost a whole fortnight without being called to account. The property which passes through this sea is immense, and a single armed vessel stationed as above would render it perfectly secure.[225]

Another visitor to Steornabhagh at this period was Lord Teignmouth in 1827:

The landlord at Pol-ewe produced wheaten bread, and informed me that it is brought from Stornaway; the bakers of Glasgow having thus their rivals in the most north-western island of the Hebrides. The packet sails once in the week from Pol-ewe to Stornaway. It is an ill-found vessel, its tackling ill-suited to bad weather, and its crew insufficient, being in summer only three; a fourth is added in winter. The cabin was such that none of the passengers would venture into it; the hold affording far preferable accommodation. Warning should be taken from the fate of its predecessor which foundered in the gale on November 1824. The accident was owing to the unfortunate determination of the minister of Stornoway, who insisted on the skipper sailing, against his better judgment. We landed in the harbour amid the ruins of an old castle.[226]

It is singular that, notwithstanding the importance of the harbour of Stornaway, and its being the resort of the vessels engaged in the Baltic trade, there is no light-house at its entrance. A light-house in the port of Stornoway would be rendered particularly useful, by the liability to mistake the head-lands to the northward of the harbour. A merchant vessel of Stornoway in which I had engaged my passage to Thurso, was, happily, prevented from sailing on the day at first proposed, by the increasing symptoms of a gale which raged violently during the following Sunday. The harbour, which had been for some time receiving a continual accession of vessels, became now completely choked up; and several brigs and sloops, the latter principally laden with fish, were aground opposite the houses of the town. Such an assemblage of vessels, chiefly involved in the Baltic trade, several of them Russian and Norwegian, afforded a display of bustle and opulence, strangely contrasting with the generally desolate appearance of the Hebrides.[227]

The reference to the packet to Poolewe leads me to the Petition in the Seaforth Papers for:

Alexander MacKay, Lochganvich, who asks for help to pay his fare home from Poolewe to Stornoway. He had been sent by kind Stornowegians to the waters at Fodderty. Although destitute of money he could not have come home but for a drover from Beauly put him on his own horse, and so got to the packet at Poolewe.[228]

This refers properly to the Spa at Strathpeffer, in the Parish of Fodderty, and readers may remember that the habit of taking the waters there was referred to in the story of Seonaid Alasdair.

By the mid-1820s much of the marine traffic leaving Steornabhagh was that of ships taking emigrants from the islands to the New World. As yet most of the emigration was still voluntary, if reluctant, but this was soon to change.

In 1832 it was reported that:

the Hudson's Bay squadron has been in this bay from the last four days. They have taken on board forty young men and sailed last evening. Besides this advantage they have taken beef, pork, poultry etc. Alex Stewart sent a present aboard from Hon. Mrs Stewart of a small supply of vegetables from the Lodge Garden for which they were very thankful. He gave them every attention as they are to call here next year and will probably continue to do so. They have not called here since 1810.[229]

Rev. John Cameron in 1833 reported on the expansion of the town:

Stornoway contains a population of 1000 souls. Bayhead, Guirshadir and Laxdale adjoining contain nearly 900. Inaclite, Sandwich and Holm, quite contiguous, contain as many; Steinish, Culnagrien and Cross Sreet contain a population of 130, which makes total of almost 3000 in the immediate vicinity of the town, at no greater distance from the burgh than one mile.

The modern buildings are Seaforth Lodge, the church, St John's Lodge or Masons' Hall, neat and spacious; a female school jointly endowed by Mrs S MacKenzie and Miss Mary MacKenzie Carn, who gave £300 sterling; three mills, one for grinding corn, with a saw-mill and excellent kiln appended to it – the other for carding wool; all built by the proprietors at a considerable expense, and perfectly complete in their kind. There is also a distillery on a grand scale, with coppers of large diameter, furnaces, vats, coolers, flake-stands under a running stream, also a very large malt-barn and mill. No expense had been spared by the spirited proprietor to make it complete; but it is not yet in operation. A light-house is being built on the point of Arnish, that will enable vessels to make the harbour at night – which attempt, hitherto, was not considered advisable but by those well acquainted with the ground. The site had been chosen and fixed upon by the proprietor and Captain Benjamin Oliver of his Majesty's Revenue Cutter *Prince of Wales*.

In Stornoway there are 18 houses regularly licensed for the vending of spirituous liquors. The number comprises four respectable inns, namely the Royal Oak, Crown, Star and New Inn; seven are shops, and the remaining seven miscellaneous, but which perhaps would be better distinguished under the appellation of petty public-houses, the pest of the morals of the people.

The present church was built in 1794. Three years ago, the people of the parish became alarmed about the insufficiency of the front wall and the weight of the roof – when partial repair was given to it; but this did not remove the alarm, the front wall was still off the plumb-line several inches; the wall receded from the seats in the gallery and no consideration would make the people enter to attend divine service. The repairs are now on the eve of being finished. When these are completed, the church will not be surpassed by any in the Western or Northern Hebrides.[230]

James Wilson was in Steornabhagh in 1841 on his tour of the Highlands and Islands:

We re-entered Stornoway by what is probably regarded as the main street, as it consisted of two-storey houses, many of them excellent, all of them tidy and brightly whitewashed, and the street itself, as were indeed the others, extremely nice and clean. Respectable looking shops were obvious here and there, and no want of inns and other places of refreshment. Turning into another street, we visited the Masons' Hall, in which there is a ball-room and reading room, the former hung with brass chandeliers, the latter with maps. We also met a dancing–master (whom we detected by his walk), and proceeding onwards returned towards our place of embarkation by a street leading along the harbour, which is quite within the town, very snug, with a soft bottom and a good quay. Towards the upper end where a streamlet enters, there is a distillery erected and for sometime worked by Mr Stewart Mackenzie, whose residence (or his lady's) of Seaforth Lodge is partially seen on rising ground upon the opposite side. Near it, and in a little dell descending from it, we observed some thriving trees. The house seemed old-fashioned, with a centre and pair of wings, and by the water side there was a convenient slip for landing from the harbour.[231]

We know from the census returns that the dancing master was a Robert Goldie – and the fact that he was recognised by his walk could provoke some rather ribald comments!

For a time there had been a private school in the Masonic Lodge, to which the young Evander MacIver of Griais was sent in about 1815:

The first school to which I was sent was taught by a man named Pollock. The better classes in Stornoway were not satisfied with the parish school, attended as it was by children from whom infectious complaints were caught, and many of whom could not speak English. The parents of the upper classes in Stornoway united and became bound to pay a yearly salary to a good teacher, and they had the use of a large room in the Masonic Lodge of the town as a school.

[In Edinburgh] I was laughed at for my Stornoway intonation and pronunciation, and soon got rid of part of it, but when excited or in a hurry it broke out unknown to me for months after my arrival, which was really painful to me on several occasions.[232]

The *Imperial Gazetteer* of 1868 gives a description of Steornabhagh then:

A stranger, on arriving at it by any route, or from any quarter, is surprised to see so large and flourishing a place in so remote a corner. Its capacious bay, its well-appointed piers, its occasional crowd of shipping, its market place and shops, its stir of trade, its streets and public buildings, and the vicinity to it of the princely pile of Stornoway castle, all render it a very striking object in so rude and sequestered a region as the Outer Hebrides. The parish church, the

138. Airinis Lighthouse

Free church, the Episcopalian chapel, the female seminary, and an edifice which is variously disposed in news-room, public library, masonic lodge, and assembly room, are all interesting structures.

The port of Stornoway has a customs-house, with a collector, a comptroller, and a tide-waiter. Its own harbour accommodations are good and ample. A lighthouse and a beacon stand on Arnish point, at the south side of the entrance of Loch Stornoway. The lighthouse shows a revolving bright white light every half minute, in two arcs, the one facing the entrance to Loch Stornoway, the other facing up the harbour. The harbour has a Morton's patent slip, worked by steam, and suitable for a ship of 800 tons. The fishery district of Stornoway, in the year 1855, employed 468 boats of aggregately 4333 tons, with 2063 fishermen and fisherboys, 62 coopers, 1207 gutters and packers, 3280 net-makers, and 41 fish-curers The number of cod and ling fish taken in that year (1855) within the district was 443,547; the number of barrels of herring cured was 36,221; the number of barrels of herring caught but not cured was 5,005, and the value of the boats, nets and lines employed was £19,401.[233]

But like the kelp before it, the herring bubble burst.

The Stornoway catch in 1907 was upwards of 219,000 cwt., in 1911 it was but 65,320. The once famous fishing carried on from Stornoway in May and June has dwindled to a mere shadow of its former self. In 1898, 469,000 cwt were landed during these months in Stornoway; in the same period in 1911, only 35,000 cwt.[234]

Even if the peak of the fishing was past, it could still make its presence felt, as A R B Haldane found out in August 1921:

The Minch was not in a tranquil mood, and the position was not improved by the presence on board of a large number of girls just back from the herring packing at Grimsby, full of laughter and cheerfulness, but bringing with them pungent proof of their recent occupation. I can hear now the popular and sentimental song they sang so repeatedly, their voices rising against the background of the sound of the wind in the rigging and the break of the waves, as they huddled in a pool of light from a lamp near the stern of the ship. These things acquire in retrospect a beauty which at the time one was little able to appreciate, and by the time we reached Stornoway we wanted never again to see the inside of the *Sheila*.[235]

Louis MacNeice, of course, in 1938, was not impressed – was he ever?

My hotel was in Cromwell Street and looked across the narrow tongue of harbour to the wooded grounds of Stornoway Castle which are now known as Lady Lever Park. The trees in the park are almost the only trees on Lewis. In Stornoway Castle, a huge castellated building in the Scotch Baronial style, Lord Leverhulme, I was told, used to sleep in a room in the tower with a bath alongside his bed and no roof above him. When he left Lewis because the people were unsympathetic towards his plans, he gave the Parish of Stornoway to the people. The castle has proved an encumbrance. In the summer they attempt to lease it to English grandees. The alternative plan which some have suggested is to take off the roof. Stornoway in April was quiet. I passed a church which had been turned into a tweed depot and the Town Council Chambers, a repellent turreted building of heather-purple stone with brown facings to the windows.

But he did at least have a different explanation for the decrease in the herring-curing industry:

Stornoway was badly affected by Prohibition in America. The Stornoway herring is exceptionally large and tasty and the Americans, being connoisseurs in this matter, used to import large quantities of these herrings, salted, for use in their saloons – the salted Stornoway herring being a great thirst-maker.[236]

The old families of Steornabhagh and the houses where they lived have already been written up in many books, not least the publications of the Stornoway Historical Society, so I will restrict myself to a small selection of buildings whose history I have found particularly interesting, basing them on the town plan of Steornabhagh as surveyed by John Wood in 1821.

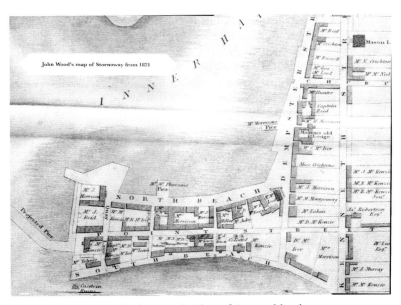

139. Detail of J Wood's Plan of Steornabhagh, 1821

We can begin on South Beach, at the corner of Quay Street. It is shown on Wood's plan as occupied by Captain Mackenzie. Details are added by a memorial inscription in Sanndabhaig cemetery, as recorded by Stornoway Historical Society in an excellent project, well worth emulation elsewhere:

> Captain John Mackenzie formerly of HM 73rd Foot one of HM Justices of the Peace for Rosshire who died the 8th day of August 1830 aged 67. He formed one of that gallant and immortal band of heroes who under Elliot defended Gibraltar against the combined forces of Spain and France, also of his beloved wife Agnes Murray Reid, who died the 15th day of March 1845 aged 68, the former was distinguished for honour integrity and wisdom and the latter for virtue and all the Christian graces.[237]

Also buried in the same plot are their son Daniel Lewis Mackenzie and his wife Helen Mylne Mackay. Helen had been born in Cawnpore in India, a daughter of Major Donald Angus Mackay of the Royal Horse Artillery, and had previously been married in Singapore.

In a Directory of Lewis in 1898, Mrs D L Mackenzie is still living at Tigh na Cloinne, South Beach Street, though part of the site was taken over by Duncan MacIver, who combined the businesses of fish-curer and coal merchant.

A little way along South Beach was the Carn House, its site now occupied by a rather forlorn looking garden. On Wood's plan it is shown as belonging to Colonel MacKenzie. Colonel Colin was the subject of a detailed biography by W C MacKenzie – *Colonel Colin MacKenzie, First Surveyor-General of India* detailing his subject's life, from his joining the East India Company in 1783 to his role not only in the acquisition of India, but also in the wars of the 1810s in Java, in the then Dutch East Indies.

This much distinguished officer and eminently scientific character died on the 8th May 1821 at Chowringhee near Calcutta aged 68 years, 40 of which were passed in the service of the East India Company and rendered useful to his employers and to science in general by the most active and indefatigable researches into the history and antiquities of India. The merits of Colonel Mackenzie and the devotion of his whole time and fortune to the advancement of science were rewarded a few years since by his honourable employers, when they united the Surveyor-Generalship of the three Presidencies into one office of all India and appointed him to fill it.[238]

Colonel MacKenzie had a sister Mary in Steornabhagh, who died in 1827. Her funeral at Aiginis was attended by Lord Teignmouth:

The funeral was attended by all the principal inhabitants of Stornoway. As soon as we reached the cemetery, the coffin was deposited in the grave with all possibly decency, and the whole body of mourners instantly adjourned to a tent pitched in the cemetery, within a few

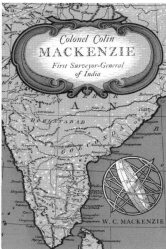

140. Colonel Colin Carn MacKenzie

141. In Front of Carn House

yards of the mausoleum, where we found the tables groaning beneath a plentiful repast. A few of the guests continued long carousing, and one of them was brought to Stornoway on the bier which conveyed the body to the grave.[239]

Part of the Carn site later became the Estate Office, the seat of power for many years of Donald Munro, the Estate Factor and holder of virtually every other administrative office in Lewis in his time. It has become the fashion recently to depict him as the Genghis Khan of Lewis – the epitome of evil – but that is to aggrandise the man away beyond his true status. He was clearly a little tin-pot tyrant, able to cause a lot of trouble in little pettifogging ways, forever insisting on the importance of his position – a man of little accomplishment of his own, relishing the power given to him by his position as factor.

But somehow the idea put about recently of the people of Lewis cringing in fear of the tyrant does not square with descriptions of the Lewismen of the time, or later. Donald Munro could harass individuals, but as soon as he threatened a community, in Bearnaraidh, they took him on and defeated him, as told in Volume 1.

The story of Donald Munro was told by James Shaw Grant in his *A Shilling for Your Scowl*, recently repeated by John Macleod in his *None Dare Oppose* – certainly a more entertaining book to read, with his demonisation of the main characters, though I personally prefer Grant's more restrained factual approach.

The later Town Hall was built on part of the Carn site, at one time the civic pride of Steornabhagh but today, like so many of its important buildings, under scaffolding in an attempt to remedy the neglect of more recent years.

142. The Town Hall

Across the end of Cromwell Street is the Waverley Building, in which, as we will see, I have a certain personal interest. The 1820 plan shows the corner site of South Beach and Cromwell Street as occupied by Dr MacIver. This was Dr Alexander MacIver, a son of John MacIver, tacksman of Tolastadh. He contributed a section on climate to the New Statistical Account of Steornabhagh in 1833:

> The climate of Lewis is chiefly remarkable for its extreme humidity, and for the change which, within the last twenty years, had taken place in it, in regard to mildness. Even in winter, excessive snow is now unknown – it being a rare occurrence for snow to remain three successive days on the ground.[240]

According to his tombstone in Sanndabhaig Cemetery:

> He was a good husband, tender parent, and ever the friend of the poor, with a capacious mind and an energetic will he manfully struggled against the difficulties of his position, and when he left the busy scene in which he was one of the foremost, few there have been more truly and universally lamented.[241]

By 1861 we find on the site – but no doubt in a new building – a James Fraser, baker, from Portree and his wife Jane Ann Ross, a daughter of Allan Ross of Cro Beag. James had come to Steornabhagh to live with his uncle John Fraser, from Culloden, who also had a bakery a few doors along Cromwell Street. After James's death, his widow moved to Francis Street, and the building passed to Matthew Russell.

Matthew Russell was from Glassford in Lanarkshire, but had

married Georgina Gerrie, daughter of William Gerrie of Goathill and later Stoneyfield Farm. Their son William G took over the business, and advertised in a directory of 1911:

> If you wish to buy at the keenest price
> IT IS IMPERATIVE
> that you visit the
> WAVERLEY BUILDINGS
> South Beach Street.
> WILLIAM G. RUSSELL'S principle is to do a LARGE
> BUSINESS on the SMALLEST
> POSSIBLE PROFIT. NO OLD GOODS at the WAVERLEY
> BUILDINGS.
> Any goods soiled or otherwise out of condition are cleared out
> regardless of cost
> at the ANNUAL STOCK-TAKING SALE IN SPRING. FRESH
> ARRIVALS of NEW GOODS every week,
> and everything up-to-date

When he went to live at Mount Pleasant in Matheson Road, the upper floors became the Waverley Hotel, occupied by the Misses Margaret and Normanna MacKenzie, daughters of Alexander MacKenzie of Cro Beag – great-grand-daughters of Mairi Laghach. Was it the MacKenzies who put the busts of Sir Walter Scott on the roof when they called it the Waverley, or did it get that name because the busts were there already? I have often wondered. For a time the rest of the lower building was occupied by 'The Lewis Polytechnic' run by Alexander MacFarlane from Sgiogarstaigh in Nis, another grandchild of Mairi Laghach of Cro Beag, and his brother-in-law Neil MacCallum from Argyll – some of our readers may remember his grand-daughter Moira MacKay in Kenneth Street. Another shop in the block was occupied for a time by the Cabrelli brothers from Italy.

When I remember the corner shop, it was occupied by Burton the Tailors. I have no idea how they obtained it, no doubt at the height of the Harris Tweed industry, but I am almost sure that I was responsible for closing it! I was working at the time with a Glasgow firm of surveyors, and we got a phone call from Burton's headquarters in Yorkshire to run up to their shop in Steornabhagh to look at a problem and report the next day. When I pointed out that travel made that impossible, they wanted to know why, so I told them to look at a map, and see where their branch was. When they eventually found a map which showed the islands, and realised where their shop was, they closed it!

Further along South Beach, but still on the original Dr MacIver site, was the Imperial Hotel, and beside it Louis Bittiner's Baltic Boot

143. South Beach Street

and Shoe Shop, both names well known in later years in Steornabhagh, though not on this site.

Then across Kenneth Street and we have Mr Wylie, Collector of Customs, whose daughter we met in Marbhaig, and Dr John Millar, father of Dr Roderick Millar, and contributor to the New Statistical Account of Lewis. Detouring slightly along Kenneth Street to the corner of James Street (Point Street on Wood's plan) is a site marked only 'McLeod Esq'. This, the later site of Martin's Memorial Church, is remembered as the birthplace of Alexander MacKenzie, the Canadian explorer. MacKenzie is best remembered for his pioneer crossing of the Rockies to establish a land route across the whole width of Canada, though the route itself was too difficult to be economically viable. A previous attempt to find a passage had proved a failure when the MacKenzie River (which he called the Disappointment River!) proved to flow north to the Arctic rather than west as had been hoped. My wife Chris is fascinated by the thought that MacKenzie's reaction was to come back to Britain to take a course in navigation, then go back to Canada to try again. My own preferred picture is the one MacKenzie describes himself of camping at the shore of yet another lake in the desolate, fog-bound Arctic, only to find that his tent was getting wet, and realising that it was the incoming tide, and he had reached the Arctic Ocean after all!

W Kaye Lamb sums up his achievements in his *The Journals and Letters of Sir Alexander MacKenzie:*

> The starting point of both journeys was in Fort Chipewyan, a trading post of the North-West Company on Lake Athabasca, in what is

144. Sir Alexander MacKenzie

now Northern Alberta. On the first expedition he discovered and explored the MacKenzie River and followed it to the Arctic Ocean. On the second, he crossed the Rocky Mountains, discovered the Fraser River, and became the first white man to cross the full width of North America. Literally and figuratively he added new dimensions to the knowledge of two vast areas of the continent.[242]

Two Lewis-born MacKenzies – Colin of India and Alexander of Canada – famous all over the world, but celebrated in Steornabhagh only by little plaques which, unless you knew where to look, would escape notice completely!

Turning back down Francis Street, where Hugh Matheson had a baker's shop

---

The bread for Quality and Purity
Sweet as a nut, made from the Highest Grade
Flour and by up-to-date machinery
HUGH MATHESON
Baker, Confectioner, Grocer
And Provision Merchant
Families waited on daily
Sole Agent for Bermaline Bread, Melrose's and Invitation Teas,
Bettafed Bacon, Kunzle Cakes & Chocolates.
4 AND 6 FRANCIS STREET

145. Gladstone House, Cromwell Street

If we turn along Cromwell Street (Dempster Street on Wood's plan), we find sites feued to Mr Loban, the architect; the Misses Crichton – daughters of Colin Crichton, the fishcurer and merchant who was drowned off Ranais; Colin MacIver, the shipowner, and his wife Mary Ann Morrison, born in Jamaica of a branch of the Morrisons of Nis; William Morrison, shipowner, whose daughter Isabella was married to Donald Lees, of a family which claimed, with whatever justification, to be the only island descendants of the Fife Adventurers. Then, on the corner of Church Street, Charles Hunter, clothier, and his wife Ann Gilzean from Elgin.

A new building was built on this site in 1886, according to Mary Miers' *The Western Seaboard,* a fascinating book on architecture on the west coast of Scotland. One of the original tenants was John Harrold from Wick, steamboat agent, but later it was shared between George Morrison and Donald MacLennan. George Morrison was from am Bac, and he and his brothers had been among the emigrants to the Canadian Prairies in 1888; but George returned, and set up his business in Cromwell Street, where he was succeeded by his son Donald Duncan. Donald MacLennan was from Circeabost in Bearnaraigh, and his shop passed to Lipton's, the first multiple grocer to come to the island, and then to Loch Erisort Woollens.

Further along Cromwell Street was Ardanmhor, which claimed to be the oldest feu in Steornabhagh. The house, which was recently demolished, stood high above Cromwell Street, and at right angles to the line of the street – no doubt another consequence of its age.

146. Smith family at Ardanmhor

The sequence of houses along the streets in the old census returns is rather chaotic, but it appears as though the occupier in the mid to late 1800s was a Donald MacIver, who at the time of his marriage in 1831 was a shipowner, though later he appears as an innkeeper. In the census of 1871 his son John appears as a 'gold-digger' – there must surely be another story behind that!

The MacIvers moved to Plantation Street in the 1890s, and Ardanmhor passed then to Malcolm MacLean, whose family had come from Skye to Manor Farm. They set up a number of retail businesses about the town, including the Stag Bakery, which now has a country-wide sale for its products, under the sales banner of *from the Hebridean Isle of Lewis* – illustrated by a picture of the MacLeod Stone at Horgabost – which just happens to be in Harris!

From the MacLeans, the house passed to Donald Smith, a shoemaker who had his business, like many others of his trade, in North Beach Street. His sons kept on the business around Ardanmhor until a year or so ago, but I have a feeling that the building will be remembered not so much for the shoemaker's business as for the 'chat-room' in the back shop, where the local worthies used to gather to put the world to rights.

Moving out to Bayhead, there is an interesting old building at No 20. This at one time belonged to the MacFarquhar family, who appear to have come originally from the Redcastle area of Easter Ross. Robert MacFarquhar, who was born in about 1760, seems to have been the

147. 20 Bayhead Street

first of this branch of the family, with sons Alexander, a cartwright, and John, a blacksmith. John's son Donald lived here along with his aunt Grace, then married Catherine Hunter of Barvas Inn. Donald appears in an 1895 directory as a blacksmith, but by 1935 there are entries for his sons Donald – wholesale fruit and vegetable merchant – and James – Central Depot for Hay, Grain and Artificial Manures.

Now it is the base for the veterinary surgeon's business, but the low doors and ceilings are still there as evidence of the age of the building.

One further shop in Bayhead – that of Allan Craig. His father George Craig had come to Garrabost at the time of the brickworks there, and later moved into Steornabhagh. Allan was married to Isabella MacNeil, whose father Donald had a saddler's business on the Perceval Square side of Cromwell Street in Newton. I do not know what Allan Craig sold – probably everything! – but I do know that his shop was a jumble of all sorts of things thrown together haphazard, for it was a by-word for anything in a complete muddle – *mar buth Ailein Craig*!

I liked the description of Buth Ailein Craig in an article by Deirdre MacDonald in the Stornoway Historical Society's Journal of January 2011:

Alan Craig's was the most fascinating of all. It was tiny and crammed full of every conceivable kind of object. While the others were mainly grocery shops, Alan Craig sold everything from a needle to an anchor. I must admit that I never saw an anchor in his shop but that's not to say there wasn't one somewhere!

Alan Craig himself was a small man, slightly stooping, with a bald head fringed with white hair. He was kind and gentle and very fond of children. Most of my Grannie's shopping was done in Maggie Grant's but occasionally I would be sent to Alan Craig's for a message. I was always pleased when this happened because there was always a bonus in the form of a little poke twisted by Alan from a wee scrap of paper and filled with mixtures.

It was quite usual to have to wait to be served, but in Alan Craig's that was no hardship as there was plenty to look at. Outside the counter, which was at right angles to the door, stood the bags of grain, and above them were shelves, which held an incredible number of dishes, pans, and cooking utensils of all sorts. Every inch of ceiling had something dangling from it - brushes, girdles (for pancake-making), spades, garden tools, zinc and enamel pails and basins of all sizes, shovels, frying-pans, all in a welter of confusion. The goodies were laid out in the front window, which they shared with a large grey cat, and in the summer-time, several wasps. I suppose we all developed antibodies and survived!

At noon every day, Alan would come out from behind the counter, take a handful of corn from a sack and scatter it on the pavement outside, and out of the sky would materialise a couple of dozen pigeons of all colours, mainly grey with iridescent, rainbow feathers along their backs, but some dusty pink with white markings and pink feet and, very rarely, a bird that was pure white. They were quite tame, and would peck at the grain while we watched them.[243]

We could go on and on with more and more notes on buildings and families, but a halt has to be called somewhere if this book is to be of a publishable size. So just one last house, in which I had an interest myself – 82 Keith Street.

This was built in the 1880s for James Mason 'merchant and carriage hirer' and his half-brother William MacAulay. They were children of Isabella MacRae, daughter of Alasdair Ruadh, tacksman of Scaliscro and later Riof, and had been living until then further down Keith Street. They had a business at 22 Francis Street.

Neither of them was married, and after them the house passed to William MacLean – Uilleam Fhearchair – from Barabhas Iarach, who had a cooper's business in Inacleit, and his son J S MacLean. From them it passed to Millar's garage – and then to me, for the period I was in charge of the Integrated Development Programme for the Western Isles, a five-year, partly European funded, development programme from 1980 to 1985. Now it belongs to a grand-daughter of Dr Donald Murray, the first MP for the Western Isles.

148. 82 Keith Street

I remember my first contact with my new neighbours. Even then, I had an extensive library, and from one of my Paisley neighbours, who had a licensed grocery, I had got a lot of heavy cardboard whisky boxes, to carry the books in. When my removal arrived in Keith Street it of course aroused great interest among the neighbours, one of whom came across the road, looked at the boxes with a big smile on his face, and said 'I don't know who you are, but I hope you'll be inviting me to the party!'

EPILOGUE

So we come to the end of another volume in the 'In History and Legend' series. There is only so much ground which can be covered in a volume of this size, and I have selected items which struck me as interesting, and of necessity ignored much more. Where I felt that a topic was adequately covered in the previous volume, I have not repeated that coverage – after all, the publishers and I want you to purchase both volumes! Despite this, I am sure that there are many loose ends hanging from both Lewis volumes, but perhaps I will have encouraged you to start knitting them together for yourselves.

This book is no doubt a bit of a Buth Ailein Craig, but as my neighbour in Keith Street would have said – it was my party, and I hope you enjoyed it.

149. Cromwell Street from Castle Grounds

REFERENCES

1 *The Book of the Dean of Lismore*, Edinburgh, 1862, p146
2 *Acts of the Lords of the Isles*, Scottish History Society, 1986, p235
3 John Elder, *The Royal Fisheries Companies*, 1912, p3 & 6/7
4 James Fraser of Wardlaw, *Polychronicon*, 1699, p41
5 James Fraser of Wardlaw, *Polychronicon*, 1699, p239
6 W C MacKenzie, *The Book of the Lews*, Paisley, pp87–8
7 *The Jacobite Attempt of 1719*, Scottish History Society Vol. XIX, 1895, p276
8 Statistical Account of Scotland, Parish of Stornoway, 1796, p19
9 William Daniell, *Scotland,* Vol 1, Edinburgh, 2006, p198–9
10 Catriona MacIver, *On Foot in the Western Isles*, Edinburgh, 1933, pp72–3
11 Statistical Account of Scotland, Parish of Stornoway, 1796, pp30–1
12 Emily MacDonald, *Twenty Years of Hebridean Memories*, pp42–3
13 William Daniell, *Scotland*, Vol 1, p203
14 George C Atkinson, *Expeditions to the Hebrides,* Maclean Press, Skye, 2001, p125
15 George C Atkinson, *Expeditions to the Hebrides*, Maclean Press, Skye, 2001, p144
16 Donald MacDonald, *Tales and Traditions of the Lews*, Paisley, 1927, pp260–1
17 SRO Seaforth Estate Papers GD46/13/55
18 A A MacGregor, *The Haunted Isles*, London, 1933
19 RCHAMS, Outer Hebrides, 1928, p14
20 George Morrison, in *Bardachd a Leodhas,* Glasgow, 1969
21 Forfeited Estate Papers, 1718

22 Judicial Rental, 1754, GD427/2/1
23 John Munro MacKenzie, *Diary 1851,* Stornoway, pp125–6
24 Donald MacDonald, *The Tolsta Townships,* Stornoway, 1984, pp106–7
25 *An t-Eilean mu Thuath,* Glasgow, 1972, p23
26 T S Muir, *Ecclesiological Notes on the Islands of Scotland,* Edinburgh, 1885, p44
27 SRO Seaforth Estate Papers, GD 46/17,
28 SRO Seaforth Estate Papers, GD 46/1/ 158
29 Evander MacIver, *Memoirs of a Highland Gentleman*, Edinburgh 1905, pp1–2
30 Evander MacIver, *Memoirs of a Highland Gentleman*, Edinburgh, 1905, pp 164–5
31 W Anderson Smith, *Lewsiana*, London, 1875, pp114–15
32 New Statistical Account of Scotland Parish of Stornoway, 1833, pp116–17
33 RCHAMS, Outer Hebrides 1928, p16
34 RCHAMS, Outer Hebrides 1928, p17
35 Daniel MacKinlay, *The Isle of Lewis and its Crofter-Fishermen*, 1878
36 John Bickerdyke, *Days in Thule*, Westminster, 1894, p102
37 John Bickerdyke, *Days in Thule*, Westminster, 1894, pp144–5
38 John Bickerdyke, *Days in Thule*, Westminster 1894, p52
39 New Statistical Account, of Scotland, Parish of Stornoway, 1833, p122
40 W Anderson Smith, *Lewsiana*, London, 1875, pp222–3
41 Napier Commission, pp1033–4
42 Mairi Nic a' Ghobhainn, *Sheòl mi'n Uiridh*, Clàr, 2009, p108

43 SRO Seaforth Estate Papers, GD 46/17/11
44 John Knox, *A View of the Highlands*, London, 1784, p7
45 SRO GD 427/264/1
46 SRO GD/427/264/1
47 Public Record Office, 47/12
48 Crofter Colonisation Report, 1889, p15
49 Crofter Colonisation Report, 1889, p18
50 Colin MacDonald, *Highland Journey*, Edinburgh, 1943, pp157–8
51 Napier Commission, 1884, p1036
52 SRO Seaforth Estate Papers, GD 46/17
53 Rev. N C MacFarlane, 'The "Men" of the Lews', pp33–4
54 *Tong – the Story of a Lewis Village*, Stornoway, 1984, pp126–9
55 Donald MacDonald, *Lewis, A History of the Island*, Edinburgh, 1978, p113
56 New Statistical Account of Scotland, Parish of Stornoway, 1833, p129–30
57 W Anderson Smith, *Lewsiana*, London, pp114–15
58 Highland Relief Board, Report on the Outer Hebrides, 1849
59 John Munro MacKenzie, *Diary 1851*, Stornoway, p21
60 Prof. Donald Macleod, *The Living Past,* Stornoway, 2006, pp11–12
61 RCAHMS, Outer Hebrides, 1928, p16
62 Calum Smith, *Around the Peatfire*, Edinburgh, 2001, p75
63 Statistical Account of Scotland, Parish of Stornoway, 1796, p29
64 New Statistical Account of Scotland, Parish of Stornoway, 1833, p140
65 Murdo MacFarlane, *An Toinneamh Diomhair*, Stornoway, p16
66 Scottish History Society, 1978, p182–
67 Scottish History Society, 1978, p212–
68 From *Malin, Hebrides, Minches*, poems, Ian Stephen, photographs, Sam Maynard, Dangaroo Press, Denmark, 1983
69 Eilean Fraoich, Stornoway, p169
70 Peter Clarke, *The Timeless Way*, Stornoway, 2006, pp41–3
71 Peter Cunningham, *The Castles of the Lews*, p104
72 Judith H Beattie, *Undelivered Letters to Hudson's Bay Company Men*, 2003, pp323–3
73 J MacGregor, *Luinneagan Luaineach*, London, 1897, p121
74 J MacGregor, *Luinneagan Luaineach*, London, 1897, p93
75 A A MacGregor, *The Western Isles*, pp207–8
76 Taped interview with Mrs Chris Lawson
77 Mairi nic a' Ghobhainn, *Sheol mi 'n Uiridh*, Clar, 2009, p66
78 New Statistical Account of Scotland, Parish of Stornoway, 1833, p123 & p133
79 Bill Lawson, *Croft History of Lewis Vol. 9 – Mealabost and Braigh na h-Uidhe*
80 Peter Cunningham, *The Castles of the Lews*, p103–4
81 Bill Lawson, *Croft History of Lewis Vol. 9 – Mealabost and Braigh na h-Uidhe*
82 Murdo MacFarlane, *An Toinneamh Diomhair*, Stornoway, p11
83 Murdo MacFarlane, *An Toinneamh Diomhair*, Stornoway, p25
84 Murdo MacFarlane, *An Toinneamh Diomhair*, Stornoway, p53
85 Murdo MacFarlane, *An Toinneamh Diomhair*, Stornoway, p38
86 Malcolm MacLeod, *Settlement of the Lake Megantic District*, New York, 1931
87 Lord Teignmouth, *Sketches of the Coasts and Islands of Scotland*, London, 1836, p183
88 Bill Lawson, *St Columba's Church at Aignish*, 1991
89 W Anderson Smith, *Lewsiana*, London, 1875, pp112–23 & p183
90 Donald MacDonald, *Lewis – A History of the Island*, p109
91 Quoted by Michael Robson in *Cornelius Con*, Ness, 2002, p6

92 Napier Commission, 1884, p1045
93 Napier Commission, 1884, p3141–2
94 Trial of Aignish Rioters, AD 14/88/224
95 Trial of Aignish Rioters, AD 14/88/224
96 RCAHMS, Outer Hebrides, 1928, p14
97 SRO Seaforth Estate Papers, GD 46/1/58
98 James Shaw Grant, *The Gaelic Vikings*, Edinburgh, 1984, pp52–8
99 Evander MacIver, *Memoirs of a Highland Gentleman*, Edinburgh, 1905, pp16–17
100 Gillanders of Highfield Papers, SRO, GD/427/7/1
101 New Statistical Account of Scotland, Parish of Stornoway, 1833, p126
102 Mary Miers, *The Western Seaboard*, Edinburgh, 2008, p282
103 HBC Archive
104 Bill Lawson, *St Columba's Church at Aignish*, pp33–4
105 Ewing, *Annals of the Free Church of Scotland*, Vol 1, p224
106 James A MacKay, *Islands Postal History 3 – Lewis*, 1978, pp36–42
107 SRO, Judicial Rental 1754, GD 427/2/1
108 Napier Commission, 1884, p1051
109 Iain Crichton Smith, *The Long River*, Edinburgh 1955, p10
110 Derek Thomson, *Creachadh na Clàrsaich*, Edinburgh 1982, p42
111 Derek Thomson, *Smeur an Dochais*, Edinburgh, 1991, pp98–9
112 Ann Frater, in Ian Stephen, *Siud an t-Eilean*, Stornoway, 1993, p154
113 Lord Cockburn, *Circuit Journeys*, Hawick, 1983, pp8–9
114 Lord Cockburn, *Circuit Journeys*, Hawick, 1983, p8
115 Laurie Robinson, *Sea-Fishing in Scotland*, London, 1970, p125
116 Sheriff Court Papers, SC 33/17/20
117 W MacKenzie, *Cnoc Chusbaig*, Glasgow, 1936, pp11–12
118 W MacKenzie, *Cnoc Chusbaig*, Glasgow, 1936, pp20–1
119 Ian Armit, *The Archaeology of Skye and the Western Isles*, Edinburgh, 1996, p102
120 Report of Board for Congested Districts, 1902
121 Poem and translation from CD *Sguab is dloth*, by Donnie Murdo MacLeod, 2000
122 Donald MacKay, *Cnoc a' Charnain*
123 Bill Lawson, *St Columba's Church at Aignish*, pp21–2
124 Eilean Fraoich, Stornoway, 1982, p202
125 Ann MacKenzie, *Amhran Anna Sheumais*, p15
126 RCAHMS, Outer Hebrides, 1928, p15
127 Calum Ferguson, *Children of the Black House*, 2003, pp153–4
128 Brian Wilson, *Blazing Paddles*, Oxford, 1988, p128
129 Donald MacLeod of Gualtragill in Bishop Forbes *The Lyon in Mourning*, pp68–9
130 Bill Lawson, *Croft History of Lewis Vol 7*, p24
131 PSAS Vol 106, p172
132 PSAS Vol 106, p176–7
133 Laurie Robinson, *Sea-Fishing in Scotland*, London, 1970, p125
134 *Stornoway Gazette*, 1955
135 *Stornoway Gazette*, 1955
136 Bill Lawson, *Croft History of Lewis, Vol 6 – Ranais*, p17
137 Bill Lawson, *Croft History of Lewis, Vol 6 – Ranais*, p17
138 Bill Lawson, *Croft History of Lewis Vol 4 – Crosbost*, p22
139 Bill Lawson, *Croft History of Lewis Vol 4 – Crosbost*, p20
140 James A MacKay – *Islands, Postal History – Lewis*, p38
141 Eilean Fraoich, Comann Gaidhealach Leodhais, 1982, pp3–4
142 Elliott Merrick, *Northern Nurse*, 1942, Canada, pp279–81
143 *Stornoway Gazette* 1956
144 *Stornoway Gazette*, 1956
145 Bill Lawson, *Croft History of Lewis Vol 18 – Achmore and Lochganvich*, pp35–6
146 Greta MacKenzie, *Why Patagonia?*, Stornoway, 1995

147 Garbhan MacAoidh in *Gairm* Vol 94, 1976
148 'Sixty-One', *Reminiscences of the Lews,* London, 1875
149 New Statistical Account of Scotland, Parish of Lochs, 1833, p164
150 New Statistical Account of Scotland, Parish of Lochs, 1833, p167
151 SRO Seaforth Estate Papers, GD46/17/80
152 New Statistical Account of Scotland, Parish of Lochs, 1833, pp159–61
153 Eilean Fraoich, Stornoway, 1982 p205
154 Bill Lawson, *Lewis Families & How to Trace Them – Lochs*
155 Napier Commission, p1133–5
156 Napier Commission, p1138–9
157 Dean Monro, *Description of Western Isles of Scotland,* repr 2002, p335
158 New Statistical Account of Scotland, Parish of Lochs, 1833, p163
159 J Sands, *Out of this world or Life in St Kilda,* Edinburgh, 1878, pp68–9
160 J Logan, *Sar Obair nam Bard,* p369
161 M Chenoweth, *New Light on Canada's 19th Century Climate*
162 RCHAMS, Outer Hebrides, 1928, p11–12
163 From LP *The Lochies*
164 MacBain, *Place Names of the Highlands and Islands,* Stirling, 1922, p96
165 Eilean Fraoich, Stornoway, 1982, p189–90
166 SRO, Rental 1780, 46/1/212
167 *Stornoway Gazette,* 1952
168 HBC Archive
169 HBC Archive
170 Dean Monro *Description of Western Isles of Scotland,* repr 2002, p335
171 SHS, *Lyon in Mourning,* Vol 1, pp169–72
172 Angus Macleod Archive, Ravenspoint, Cearsiadar
173 SRO Seaforth Estate Papers, GD 46/1/539
174 Bill Lawson, *Croft History of Lewis, Vol, 14 – am Pairc,* p18
175 Dean Monro, *Description of Western Isles of Scotland,* repr 2002, p337
176 Iona Club, *Collectanea de Rebus Albanicis,* Edinburgh, 1839, p192
177 Martin Martin, *A Description of the Western Islands of Scotland,* London, 1703, p
178 SRO Gillanders of Highfield Papers, GD 427/49/1
179 I M M MacPhail, *The Crofters' War,* Stornoway, 1889, pp204–5
180 A A MacGregor, *Searching the Hebrides with a Camera*
181 Lord Teignmouth, *Sketches of the Coasts and Islands of Scotland,* p173
182 SRO Seaforth Estate Papers GD46/17/80
183 Dean Monro, *Description of Western Isles of Scotland,* repr 2002, p
184 Statistical Account of Scotland, Parish of Lochs, 1796, p14
185 Notes on Lochs tenants in Seaforth Papers GD 46/17/80
186 D S Murray, *Speak to me Catriona,* Port of Ness, 2007, p39
187 D S Murray, *Speak to me, Catriona,* Port of Ness, 2007, p41
188 Royal Commission (Highlands and Islands), 1892, p1071
189 Donald MacDonald, *Tales and Traditions of the Lews,* Stornoway, 1967, p93
190 PSAS, Vol LXX, 1936, p12
191 Royal Commission (Highlands and Islands), 1892, p1071
192 Bill Lawson, *Harris in History and Legend,* Edinburgh, 2002, p175
193 Bishop Forbes, *The Lyon in Mourning,* Edinburgh, 1895, p191
194 New Statistical Account of Scotland, Parish of Lochs, 1833, p159
195 'Sixty-One', *Reminiscences of the Lews,* London, 1875, pp76–9
196 Lewis Harris Boundary Dispute, SO GD/274/37/19
197 Lewis-Harris Boundary Dispute, SO GD/274/37/19

198 Notes on Lochs tenants in
     Seaforth Papers, GD 46/17/80
199 'Sixty-One', *Reminiscences of the
     Lews,* London, 1875, p13
200 'Sixty-One', *Reminiscences of the
     Lews,* London, 1875, p27
201 Eilean Fraoich, Stornoway, 1982,
     pp31–2
202 W C, MacKenzie, *The Book of the
     Lews,* Paisley, 1919, p146
203 Rev. Murdo MacAulay, *Aspects of
     the Religious History of Lewis,* p19
204 W C MacKenzie, *History of the
     Outer Hebrides,* Paisley, 1903, p594
205 Louise A Yeoman in *Witchcraft
     Cases 1630–1642,* in Scottish His-
     tory Society, Fifth Series, Vol 14
206 In W C MacKenzie, *History of the
     Outer Hebrides,* p593
207 *MacFarlane's* Geographical
     Collection, Vol 2, SHS, Vol 52,
     p210
208 Donald MacLeod to Bishop
     Forbes, *Lyon in Mourning,* Vol 1,
     pp166–7
209 In W C MacKenzie, *History of the
     Outer Hebrides,* p599
210 In W C MacKenzie, *History of the
     Outer Hebrides,* p604
211 Statistical Account of Scotland,
     Parish of Stornoway, 1796, p13
212 Margaret MacKay, *Walker's
     Report on the Hebrides,* 1764,
     Edinburgh, 1980, pp44–5
213 Frank Bigwood, *Vessels Claiming
     the Bounty from Stornoway,* 2002
214 Edinburgh Evening Courant,
     29th September 1773
215 SRO, GD 427/47/1
216 From papers of Donald
     MacDonald, Tolastadh
217 Prof. U Holmes, quoted in Rev.
     Douglas Kelly, *Carolina Scots,*
     1998, p132
218 R Heron, *Scotland Delineated,*
     1799, p39
219 Statistical Account of Scotland,
     Parish of Stornoway, 1796, p35
220 James Hogg, *Highland Tours 1803,*
     Hawick, 1981, p108
221 James MacDonald, *General View
     of the Agriculture of the Hebrides,*
     Edinburgh, 1811, p812

222 *Inverness Courier,* 1813
223 William Daniell, *Scotland,*
     Edinburgh, 2006, Vol 1, p200
224 William Daniell, *Scotland,*
     Edinburgh, 2006, Vol 1, p200
225 Headrick, *Report on the Island of
     Lewis,* Edinburgh, 1800, pp43–4
226 Lord Teignmouth, *Sketches of
     the Coasts and Islands of Scotland,*
     London, 1836, p160
227 Lord Teignmouth, *Sketches of
     the Coasts and Islands of Scotland,*
     London, 1836, p228
228 SRO Seaforth Estate Papers, GD
     46/13/180
229 From papers of Donald
     MacDonald, Tolastadh
230 New Statistical Account, Parish
     of Stornoway, 1796, pp137–140
231 James Wilson, *Voyage round the
     Coasts of Scotland and the Isles,*
     Edinburgh, 1842, pp371–2
232 Evander MacIver, *Memoir of a
     Highland Gentleman,* Edinburgh,
     1905, pp9–13
233 J M Wilson, *Imperial Gazetteer of
     Scotland,* pp758–9
234 J P S Day, *Public Administration,
     in the Highland and Islands,*
     London, 1918, p15
235 A R B Haldane, *By many waters,*
     London, 1940, p31–2
236 Louis MacNeice, *I Crossed the
     Minch,* London, 1938, pp38–42
237 Memorial Inscriptions in Old
     Sandwick Cemetery, Stornoway
     Historical Society, 1997, p23
238 W C MacKenzie, *Colonel Colin
     MacKenzie,* Edinburgh, 1952,
     pp196–7
239 Lord Teignmouth, *Sketches of
     the Coasts and Islands of Scotland,*
     London, 1836, p186
240 New Statistical Account of
     Scotland, Parish of Stornoway,
     1833, p119
241 Memorial Inscriptions in Old
     Sandwick Cemetery, Stornoway
     Historical Society, 1997, p13
242 W Kaye Lamb, *The Journals and
     Letters of Sir Alexander MacKenzie*
243 Deirdre MacDonald, in Storno-
     way Historical Society, 2011

PICTURE CREDITS

The illustrations in this book are sourced partly from photographs collected by the author and his wife and partly from the collection of old postcards gathered and published by the late Bob Charnley. Details of these and other illustrations and their sources are shown below:

1 The MacLeod Castle
John Keltie in *History of the Scottish Highlands etc*
2 Steornabhagh *c*.1880
Bob Charnley in *The Western Isles – a Postcard Tour*
3 The MacLeod Chiefs at *Seallam!*
Chris Lawson
4 Steornabhagh 1819
W Daniell
5 Lews Castle
Stornoway – Lewis (Guide Leaflet)
6 MV *Loch Seaforth*
Bill Lawson
7 Loch a' Tuath
Bill Lawson
8 Sron an t-Seileir
Bill Lawson
9 Near Dibeadal
Bill Lawson
10 Dun Othail
Bill Lawson
11 Bridge to Nowhere
C E Tholastaidh bho Thuath
12 Caisteal a' Mhorair
Bill Lawson
13 Traigh Mhor Tholastaidh
Bill Lawson
14 Hudson's Bay Contract
HBC Archive
15 Bucheron Tholastaidh
L Matheson
16 Launching *The Brothers' Delight*
C E Tholastaidh bho Tuath
17 Griais Church
C Burgess in *Ancient Lewis and Harris*

18 Shooting Pigeons near Griais
J Bickerdyke in *Days in Thule*
19 Griais Lodge *c*.1875
Mary Miers in *The Western Seaboard*
20 Lac MacKenzie
Bill Lawson
21 Seal Cave at Griais
A A MacGregor *The Haunted Isles*
22 Griais Farm
A A MacGregor in *Searching the Hebrides with a Camera*
23 Murdo
J Bickerdyke in *Days in Thule*
24 On the Moor
J Bickerdyke in *Days in Thule*
25 Kennie
J Bickerdyke in *Days in Thule*
26 George Stewart and Margaret MacDonald at C.E. a' Bhac
Chris Lawson
27 Clann-nighean an Sgadain
Gairm Vol 81, 1972
28 Fradhlaic
Alex Martin, B.E a' Bhac in *Croft History of Lewis* Vol 17
29 Passenger List of *Friendship* of Philadelphia
PRO 47/12
30 Murdo Stewart
L Klaasen
31 Tunga Local History Society
In *Tong – the Story of a Lewis Village*
32 Upper Fort Garry
From HBC website
33 Detail from Map of Hudson's Bay Territories
P Newman in *Empire of the Bay*

MAPS

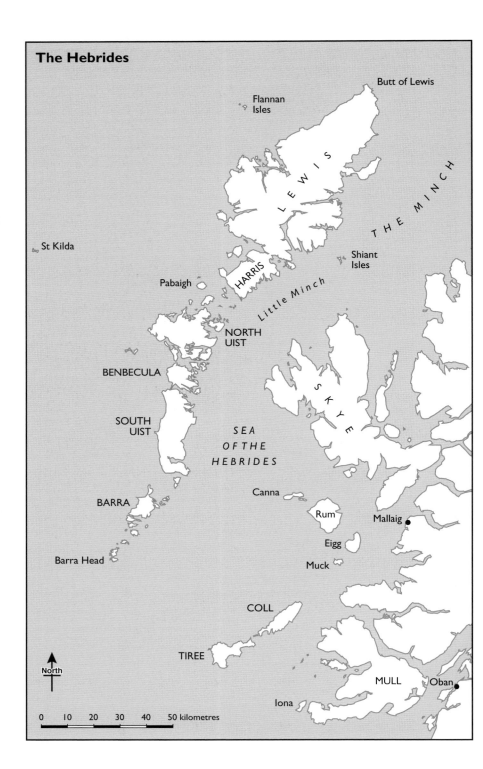

The Hebrides

Butt of Lewis

Flannan
Isles

LEWIS

THE MINCH

St Kilda

Shiant
Isles

Pabaigh

HARRIS

Little Minch

NORTH
UIST

BENBECULA

SKYE

SOUTH
UIST

SEA
OF THE
HEBRIDES

BARRA

Canna

Rum

Mallaig

Eigg

Barra Head

Muck

COLL

TIREE

North

MULL

Oban

0   10   20   30   40   50 kilometres

Iona

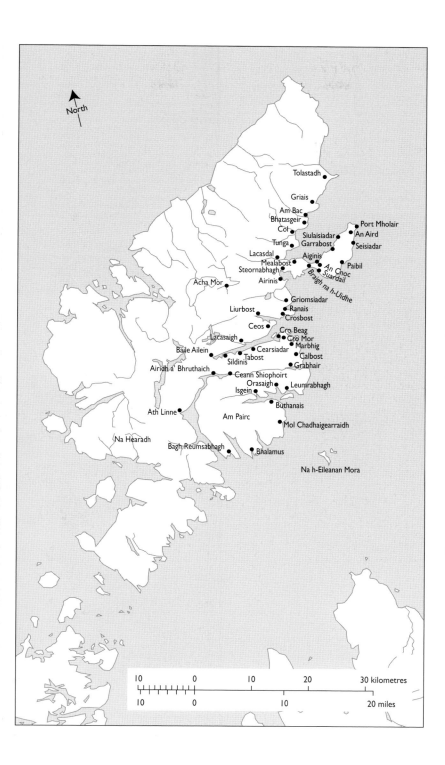

North

Tolastadh

Griais

Am Bac
Bhatasgeir
Cot
Siulaisiadar
Garrabost
Tunga
Lacasdal
Aiginis
Mealabost
Steornabhagh
An Choc
Airinis
Suardail
Acha Mor
Bragh na h-Uidhe

Port Mholair
An Aird
Seisiadar
Paibil

Griomsiadar
Liurbost
Ranais
Crosbost
Ceos
Cro Beag
Lacasaigh
Cro Mor
Baile Ailein
Marbhig
Cearsiadar
Calbost
Sildinis
Tabost
Grabhair
Airidh a' Bhruthaich
Ceann Shiophoirt
Orasaigh
Leumrabhagh
Isgein
Ath Linne
Buthanais
Am Pairc
Mol Chadhaigearraidh
Na Hearadh
Bagh Reumsabhagh
Bhalamus

Na h-Eileanan Mora

| 10 | 0 | 10 | 20 | 30 kilometres |

| 10 | 0 | 10 | 20 miles |

INDEX OF PERSONS

INDEX OF MAIN TOPICS

INDEX OF PLACES